STREETS
OF
TEARS

STREETS
OF
TEARS

LARRY J. HILTON

For information about this title or to order other books and/or electronic media, contact the publisher:

Newport Publishing
P.O. Box 7395
Chandler, AZ 85224

ISBNs:
978-0-9967861-3-3 (hardcover)
978-0-9967861-4-0 (softcover)
978-0-9967861-5-7 (eBook)

Printed in the United States of America

Cover and Interior design: 1106 Design

For Patty, who began as my wife fifty-four years ago and became my friend.

Contents

Foreword

The Streets of Tears is fiction and all the characters and adventures of the Baur family are developed in the author's mind. However the events, from the horrors of trench warfare of World War I, to the collapse of the Austrian government and the Anschluss with Nazi Germany, are accurate. The words of the great personages in the story, such as Voltaire, Marcus Aurelius and Friedrich Hayek, are derived from their writings. No work of this size can be free of error, but it is hoped that the readers will see the events that led to the Holocaust as the shame of mankind.

1

Elke Baur

1945

Frederic C. Tubach wrote the following in his book, German
Voices: *"The military reports from the various fronts were mas-
terpieces of creative imagination, what we call today spin. This
positive spin was kept up until the German army had withdrawn
to the German borders, at which point the Nazis spread a rumor
about a miracle weapon that would end the war in Germany's
favor. As the war progressed, a noticeable split grew within the
German population. On the one side were the Nazi fanatics, who
believed up until the last weeks of the war that a German victory
would come, the rest of the Germans remained circumspect in
expressing their views about the war prospects ... Increasingly,
German soldiers simply went AWOL, fleeing their fighting units
and undertaking long treks through the forests and back roads
of Europe to return to their homes and families ... Armored SS
units sometimes made final sweeps through towns to hunt down
any deserters from the retreating German army."*

In the dense woods south of Munich, Germany, two young women were searching for shelter for the night. It was late April 1945; the war in Europe was rapidly drawing to a close. The women had left Vienna almost a week earlier and managed to survive, thus far, by scavenging food wherever they could find it. Occasionally they encountered a train headed in their direction, and they could usually find an empty freight car to make the trip faster while getting some much needed sleep.

As members of the BdM (Bund Deutsches Mädel; in English, The Union of German Girls), the girls' section of the Hitler Youth, they had to be careful not to attract attention. While Gretchen Müeller, of medium height with long blond hair, was a secretary with the organization, her fellow traveler, Elke Baur, despite being just twenty-six, was a high-ranking official in the BdM. Elke was eagerly being sought by the Austrian Resistance, a small group of fierce fighters looking for revenge against those they felt had betrayed Austria.

The forest was still wet from a recent rain. As the late afternoon sun began to set, the western sky gave off an eerie glow against thin clouds behind dense green spruce trees. The women were looking for a small hut deep in the thick forest. Gretchen was familiar with this alpine area of southern Germany and northern Austria, for in the years before the war, she had been a novice in the BdM. The group had hiked and camped in this area many times. Unlike on Gretchen's earlier outings with the BdM, tonight there was little food and no compass to help navigate the formidable woods.

Elke was not what one would expect a Nazi to look like, that is, an athletic blue-eyed blonde. She was a tall brunette with long, straight hair, brown eyes and an attractive figure. She had been raised in an upper middle-class family and it showed in the commanding presence of someone who cared about her appearance and the people who worked for her. Her father, Viktor, was a banker. Her mother, Else, was a caring woman and a meticulous housekeeper of their apartment in the northern suburbs of Vienna. She had a brother, Fritz. However, he was four years older. When they were children, he'd never seemed to have much time for the silly younger sister. Fritz had joined the SS in 1937. She'd not heard from him since the battle of Stalingrad in early 1943 and presumed he had been killed. They had never discussed politics and really had little in common.

The women could sense they were approaching the American lines when they heard the faint but distinct sound of a motor vehicle. At that moment, Gretchen spotted the hut. "There it is!" she whispered. They ran to the small wooden structure like children at a birthday party running toward a cake.

"This isn't much, but it looks like it will protect us if it rains tonight," said Elke, looking over the interior. It had likely been used by hunters before the war as a sporting hut. Although devoid of comfort, it did have a couple of well-used chairs and a small table, probably for playing cards. For these two exhausted young women, it was fine. Even the straw-strewn floor looked like a feather bed to them.

"Do you think we can make the American lines tomorrow?" Gretchen said with undisguised fear as she put down her small kit bag and collapsed in the nearest chair.

"I don't know, but I believe we are headed in the right direction," Elke replied, with a hint of weariness; Gretchen had asked the same question a hundred times. "The sound of that car was encouraging. What do we have to eat?"

"Just apples and turnips."

"I hope the Americans will feed us better."

Exhausted from their two hundred mile trek, they lay down to get some sleep. For Elke, however, sleep, did not come immediately. It seemed like only a day earlier they'd been trying to help hold the Office of Propaganda together as part of the BdM in Vienna. The office didn't look much like an office. With bombs falling from American planes and shells from the large Russian guns, the entire local area was a shambles. As the Russian army was nearing the suburbs, rumors were rampant of what the sex-starved, vengeful Russian soldiers would do to the first female they met, regardless of age or attractiveness. Yet the girls had been undecided about whether to leave and head west, to the American army.

Elke, a no-nonsense leader, had remained steadfast in her belief in Hitler, the entire system of National Socialism (Nazism), and the Nazi leadership. Hitler was her idol, and Germany must be victorious, even when every sign pointed to its defeat. She ardently believed, even as the war was ending, in the Nazi "scorched earth" policy of leaving nothing of value standing. She had gone into the war prepared to die, but the human instinct for self-preservation became more important.

Their ultimate superior in the propaganda office was *Herr* Joseph Goebbels. He had said often if the Russians invaded, they would try to kill everyone; anyone who survived would be sent to the mines of Siberia. He said every form of civilized life would come to an end—as the Russians would destroy all civilization—and the women believed him.

Whether or not to leave Vienna was quickly answered when Inga Haschmann stumbled into the office, hysterical. She had been sent to the wine-making suburb of Grinzing to gather a story on the heroic German soldiers who were holding off the Russian hoard. Inga was Elke's assistant and a good reporter, about five or six years older than Elke. She was dedicated to her job and to the Führer and also believed in final victory. Now she was lying on the floor, bleeding and uncontrollably sobbing, her once-modest dress torn and muddy, her light-brown hair in disarray.

"Inga, for God's sake, what happened?" Elke exclaimed.

"Oh! It was awful! I thought I would never get back here."

Elke and Gretchen began to remove Inga's dress, revealing cuts and abrasions all over her body. Gretchen poured Inga a glass of schnapps. They let her rest until she was composed enough to tell her story.

"When I got to the wine country I came across a revolting sight," she said. "German soldiers were hanging from trees with a rope around their throats. Some were barefoot. Almost all had signs pinned to their jackets that said, 'I am a traitor.' Many had military decorations on their jackets."

"Why were they called traitors?" Gretchen said.

"They had probably deserted their regiments," Elke said, dismissively. "They deserved what they got."

"I think they are just fed-up with war and wanted to go home to their families," said Gretchen, with a hint of sorrow.

Inga continued in a low voice, "The streets of Grinzing were strewn with German corpses. I had to pick my way around the bodies." She began to sob again. "It was like walking through Hell itself. Oh, what have we and Hitler brought upon ourselves?"

Inga collected herself. "It became dark, and I found a small, empty house to try and sleep for the night," she said. "I chose a dark room to lie down in. Oh why! Why did I not come back here? It was impossible to rest with a low human wailing sound all around me. It was like a soft screaming that seemed to come from the sky. And all night long I could hear drunk Russian soldiers talking. I was lucky. Twice a soldier opened the door to my room. It was so dark, I guess he assumed it was a closet."

Gretchen broke in, "Inga, you *were* lucky."

Inga looked at Gretchen as if she were a small child. "No, my nightmare had only begun. When daylight came, I left my hiding place. I thought I was safe using side streets. The sound of women being raped by soldiers in the back alleys will be with me forever. I made a wrong turn, and a Mongolian Russian soldier saw me. Oh

God! How will I ever get this out of my mind? He had a pockmarked face and a scar down his left cheek . . . and wristwatches on both arms up to his elbow. He grabbed my wrist. I tried to get away but it was futile, so I started screaming with all my might. The last thing I remember was his hand slamming against my face. I woke up in an old barn with several other women. I heard a gunshot as a woman tried to run away. I was raped . . . I have no idea how many times. I wanted to die. Finally, the soldiers left. I knew it would be safe here with you, but I have no idea how I got here."

Elke said, "We can't stay here, but where do we go?"

Gretchen said, "We have to get to the American lines near Munich. I know that area well. We will be safe there."

Inga, who was now sitting in a chair wrapped in a blanket, stared out the window at the smoldering shells of buildings. Her eyes were ringed with purplish bruises. Her nose was caked with dried blood. Her weeping seemed to have ended. Inga said sadly, in a soft voice, "I am not going anywhere. Vienna is my home and I will live or die right here. I have had enough of war and our Führer who promised us so much and has given us nothing but death and sorrow."

"Let's get you to the hospital," Gretchen said.

*   *   *

"Gretchen, wake up," Elke said, shaking her companion. "It is almost dawn and we need to keep moving. I am sure the Resistance men are not far behind."

A sleepy Gretchen mumbled, "It is dark, cold, and the forest scares me. Do we have to go this early?"

"I remember reading in school the Roman soldiers feared the forest as well. They believed there were evil creatures lurking. If these Resistance fellows catch up to us we will know what those soldiers meant. Let's go, grab your kit bag."

It had not rained during the night, and the morning sun in the eastern sky was a welcome sight. Although they feared every sound their feet made, whether stepping on fallen tree branches, brushing through dense brambles, or being startled by curious forest creatures, their fear of the Austrian Resistance men kept their tired muscles in constant motion. The Americans were an unknown. Rumors abounded that they treated prisoners with courtesy, but it had been a long, cruel war and people were often overcome with a need for vengeance.

About two hours later they came across a small gravel road they hoped would take them close to Munich. After another hour they saw a car approaching. Should they run into the woods? The thought was discarded; it was too late and best to leave things to fate. Fate brought them a 1930s-era black Ford driven by two American soldiers. The big car with overlarge fenders seemed out of place in this war-torn world, but obviously the soldiers considered it a "prize of war." Their wide grins showed they were enjoying the ride. The driver spotted the women and brought the car to a quick stop on the gravel.

"*Fräuleins*, what are you doing out here?" he called in German. The two soldiers were curt and all business as they carefully inspected the dirty, tired women. In friendly voices, they asked their names, where they had come from, and where they intended to go. The women, exhausted from hours of walking with little food, relished the chance to ride. After the brief interrogation, the taller soldier called in their information on their hand-held radio. He turned to his partner, the driver, "We're to bring them onto the base."

The soldiers held open the backseat doors, and the women got in gratefully. "We will take you to safety," yelled the driver over the noise of the engine and the tires on the gravel. "Have you heard Hitler is dead? Yeah, killed himself in a bunker in Berlin. The war will be over soon now."

Strangely, the news of the death of Hitler, Elke's idol, produced no reaction. Despite the jolting car and the noise, the women were soon asleep.

"You need to wake up now," murmured the driver as they pulled up to a busy American military post. A Negro sentry approached the car, and sudden fear gripped the women. Most Germans were unfamiliar with black people and found Negros intimidating. The driver said something unintelligible to the soldier, who waved them through.

As the car drove up to an official-looking building, they were greeted in a business-like manner by an American officer. Seeing his intense gaze, Elke got a feeling he suspected she and Gretchen might be important.

"*Fräuleins, Bitte*," said the officer in German, with a pronounced American accent. They followed him into the building, which abutted a hospital, and up a flight of stairs. The stark structure was made of concrete, probably, Elke thought, designed to withstand the Allied bombing. They were joined by an NCO (noncommissioned officer) who motioned for Gretchen to have a seat outside a small office.

Elke and the officer entered the office, a tiny, sparse room with blank walls, a metal desk, and two chairs. The officer was short and a little overweight, with a receding hairline, which Elke saw when he removed his military cap. However, he was pleasant and courteous, obviously trying to put her at ease. He began with small talk, asked her name, and commented on the cold, wet weather. He mentioned what a beautiful city Munich must have been prior to the war.

"Where was *your* village, *Fräulein* Baur?"

"I was born and raised in the city of Vienna; it is not a village," she replied testily.

"Ah, another lovely city. I have never been there, but I hear wonderful things."

"It was lovely before you bombed it," she said with a touch of venom.

The officer countered, "Well, these things happen in war; however, I think I remember your air force was bombing London long before we could bomb your cities."

Elke almost leaped across the table in rage. She screamed at the man: "We were only bombing military targets in England; your Jewish pirates were bombing unarmed civilians in their homes who were of no threat to you whatsoever."

The officer looked at her through narrowed eyes. "Well, we have other things to discuss here, *Fräulein*. What did you do during the war?"

"I was merely a Labor Service Leader, mostly in Silesia helping with farmers' children, planting potatoes, anything to help the farmers in the area."

"Were you ever a member of the Nazi Party?"

"I was only a worker helping the farmers in Silesia, like I said before," Elke snapped.

"Now *Fräulein*, how does a young woman from the city end up showing Silesian farmers how to plant and harvest potatoes? So, I will ask you again, were you or were you not, a member of NSDAP?"

Elke paused. "I remember a willingness to join the party at one time or another, but I don't know if they accepted me," she said.

"Were you given a membership number?"

"I don't recall that I was."

"Did you ever fill out a *Fragebogen?*" [A military government questionnaire]

"We were always getting those to complete."

The officer dropped his polite tone. "*Fräulein* Baur, I am tired of your lying. You will begin telling me the truth or I will see to it that you stay in this prison for many years. I know you were in the BdM and rather high in authority in Vienna; I want to know what your duties were."

"I was a labor Service Leader, mostly in Silesia helping with farmers' children, planting potatoes, helping the farmers in the area," she repeated, almost word for word.

"Damn it, bitch! You will talk to me or I will make your life here unbearable." The officer opened a file on his desk. It contained a military questionnaire, signed by Elke Baur and showing the exact date of her membership in the Nazi Party: 10 March, 1938.

"What is your date of birth, *Fraülein*?"

"11 November, 1918."

"Interesting date, the end of the war. So, you were only nineteen when you joined the Party. You must have been quite committed?"

"I joined only in the enthusiasm of the moment of the Anschluss, but I swear to you I was never an active member of the party."

The American zeroed in: "Then how," he said, reaching into the folder, "do you explain this photograph taken with yourself and the head of the BdM?" he said with a smirk, having caught her in an obvious lie.

Elke was stunned. The photograph was real, taken in happier times when she was being honored for her work with the BdM. The officer continued, "We know your standing in the BdM, so there is no need to lie anymore. You will be a prisoner here until your case is heard. It may be weeks, or it may be years. Your treatment will be in response to your conduct and behavior. Cooperate and you will be treated with courtesy."

Elke felt she had taken the American's best shot and hadn't wavered. The officer called in an Army NCO. "Take her away!" he barked. She was led into the next room, where Gretchen still waited. The soldier motioned to a chair near Gretchen and put a finger to his lips; she was not to talk. Then he left the room.

Gretchen leaned over and softly said, "What was it like? How were you treated?"

Elke replied just as softly, "They're vile."

At that moment the NCO burst into the room and slapped Elke's face hard, twice. She fell back in her chair, but instead of crying, Elke laughed in his face. She would show this American pig how a Nazi woman reacted to brute force.

She and Gretchen stood and hugged; they realized they might never see each other again. Gretchen was then led into the office for her interrogation.

She sat in the chair Elke had just vacated with extreme trepidation. The officer began with the usual questions: Where did she come from? Where was she educated? What was her job during the war? She gave short answers with a coy expression. She thought his German was so good he must be related to the Jews who had been forced to emigrate; now they were getting their revenge on German soldiers and workers like herself.

"Tell me, *Fräulein* Müeller, what was your main job during the war, and where did you work and live?"

"I was merely a secretary for the Wehrmacht," she replied, her expression dry.

"And where were you stationed?"

"I was assigned to the Lviv area in southern Poland. I was there until 1944 as the Russians were pushing the front back toward Germany and Austria. I managed to get to Vienna late that year."

The officer pushed back from his desk. "Why would you leave the relative comfort of Germany to move closer to the fighting?"

"It was an opportunity for a poor Austrian farm girl to have a good-paying job, see some new country, and meet important people," she said, tightlipped.

"*Fräulein* Müeller, did you have Jewish friends in school? Were there Jewish merchants in the neighborhood where you grew up?"

"I didn't pay much attention."

"Were there Jewish families in your neighborhood?"

"I remember a family down the street, but they moved away after the war began."

"You mean they were taken away?"

"I don't know. It probably had something to do with the whole 'Jewish thing.' After all, they couldn't stay in Germany after the war began."

"Why not? Weren't they Germans?"

"Well, it was obvious Germans and Jews couldn't coexist; they were the enemies of the Reich, the scum of society, they were the very people we were fighting, the very people trying to destroy our beloved Germany. These subhumans had become 'bolshevized'; they had to be moved out of Germany," she said, moving to the edge of her chair.

"You said you worked in the Lviv area of Poland. Were you helping to resettle German families in the area? Also, what happened to the former residents of Lviv? Were they the Jews of the 'Jewish thing' you mentioned?"

"Oh, I had nothing to do with that. It was before I got there. My job as secretary was to be an organizer."

"You mean you 'organized' who would be sent to the gas chambers and 'organized' the train schedules?" he said.

"I was just doing my duty."

"Even if that duty meant people would be killed?"

"I was doing what I was told to do in order to keep my job."

The officer stood up. "The war is over *Fräulein* Müeller, your Führer is dead, your country is in shambles. I suggest you get on with your life as best you can." He escorted Gretchen to the door, and into a difficult, unknown world.

Gretchen followed the NCO toward a cell and her residence for God only knew how long. She grew frightened, knowing she had disclosed too much to the American. She vowed never to talk with anyone again regarding what she had seen and done while stationed in the East.

*   *   *

Almost an hour later, Elke was led to a large truck and ordered to the back with other female prisoners. The truck drove to Augsburg, west of Munich. The prison there was terribly overcrowded and divided with one section for women and another for men. On the women's side, four women occupied a cell intended for one. In that section most inmates were political prisoners, petty criminals, or prostitutes.

Elke was led to the men's side and placed in a small cell by herself. The cell was about eight feet square; a barred window provided the only air or light. There was no running water and a bucket served as the toilet. Elke was alone, safe in a locked cell, but surrounded by men. She felt isolated and frightened during the long moonless night, alone with her thoughts. Her Führer was gone but she knew the Wehrmacht and the SS were still fighting. She also knew the Austrians were among the most determined of all.

The last six months of the war had been appalling, with the sight of disfigured corpses and smoking ruins a daily horror. She had encountered desperate people everywhere, whose minds were disturbed and whose souls were numb with pain. She could only resist succumbing to despair as long as she could believe her suffering had a point and would lead to victory.

She thought of the Third Reich and about the millions of Germans who had sacrificed their lives, their health, and their property to the war. Everything she had believed and fought so hard for since Hitler entered Vienna in triumph in 1938 was gone. All had burst before her eyes like a bomb going off in front of her. She lay face down on the floor and wept until there were no tears left.

By dawn, she felt a bit better. She decided she had two choices: She could yield to her despair and likely kill herself, or, at best, finish her days in an asylum. Or, she could resist this misery with all her strength and hopefully survive the collapse of her world, in which she had been so happy. But to do so, she had to keep her thoughts and feelings under control.

Elke remained in that isolated cell for one night. She thought perhaps it had been her penalty for lying to the officer. Early the next morning, a female guard moved her to the women's section. Her new accommodation was like a dormitory room, small, with two beds. There was no running water and no light except for a barred window high on the wall. For several days she remained alone. Then one morning, a female warden came to see her. She was rather cheerful and somewhat overweight. Her floral print dress seemed out of place.

"Well, *Fräulein* Baur, how is our young Nazi this morning?"

Elke remained silent.

"With your attitude I should leave you in solitude, but with the overcrowding, I have no choice. You are getting a cellmate," the warden said. "Her name is Erika. However, the bad news is she is prone to being a little crazy. She needs to be carefully watched because she can have attacks of frenzy. I was told she rammed her head against a wall and then smashed to pieces everything in the room. However, I know about your work with the BdM. I think you can handle her. Let us know if you need anything." The warden abruptly turned and left.

Erika, when she arrived, seemed merely lackluster. Her stringy blond hair desperately needed a washing, and her worn clothes hung on her thin frame. Only her eyes had a strange intensity, which made Elke feel uncomfortable. Erika talked incessantly, even claiming to have been a Nazi agent in Spain. Elke was upset to have lost her now-vanished period of solitude. She offered an occasional, "um" or a "*Ja*" to Erika's comments or to questions she hadn't clearly heard.

One warm May day, after finishing her exercise time in the yard, Elke found her cellmate sitting on the sloping, barred windowsill, completely naked. Somehow, she had used their (empty) toilet bucket to stand on, reach the window bars, and hoist herself up. She was comfortably chatting in German with a Negro soldier who stood guard outside. She spoke no English and asked Elke: "How do you say in English, 'I love you and give me a cigarette?'"

Erika was soon moved to another location. No one seemed to know where, although after this incident she was the talk of the prison. Elke didn't care; she was just glad to be rid of her.

Life in prison went on with a dreary routine—same food, brief exercise, and little conversation with any one. Due to the overcrowding another cellmate soon appeared, much to the disappointment of Elke. Ingrid from Berlin was a woman in her early fifties with well-kept blond hair done up in curls. Elke assumed she was imprisoned for prostitution but wasn't interested enough to ask.

Ingrid was charming and a joy to talk with. At first, they liked each other because Elke, who didn't smoke, gave her cigarette rations to Ingrid. They had no place to sit except on their beds with the window giving the only light during the day. Ingrid surprised Elke—she liked to talk politics while lying in bed at night. They discussed the war, Hitler, and the Allied bombing of German cities.

One moonlit night, Elke, seeing the glow of Ingrid's cigarette, asked, "What is Berlin like now?"

"It is terrible, the women are constantly abused by the Russians. When I was there a month ago there were corpses lying in the street: Germans, Russians, and horses, with no one to remove them. Entire blocks were burned out with nothing but the walls standing. I had a small flat on a street near *Kurfürstendamm*. Fortunately, on a day when the bombing began, I was out. When I got home virtually everything was gone. The staircase leading to my apartment was still intact and the radiator hung on the only standing wall. The rest was rubble and ashes. But by this time the bombing was so routine I felt indifferent, even when it was my own apartment."

"Where did you go then?"

"Mostly from shelter to shelter. Then I got lucky, I met a man that offered to put me up in his place in an area that wasn't being bombed regularly. Of course, he wanted sex but he wasn't violent and he took care of me and fed me. Then one day the bombs found our secluded area of Berlin. Fortunately for me I was out and found a bomb shelter; my friend wasn't so lucky."

Elke thought about this. "I have been in the Hitler Youth since I was nineteen," she said. "I believed firmly in National Socialism. Compared with socialism and democracy, I believe National Socialism is the best form of government for the German people. I was sure it would help Austria's socially underprivileged. I have always believed in the Führer. I would have given my life for him."

"Well, I don't want to burst your bubble, but I was in Berlin on Hitler's birthday on April twentieth. The people who would yell *Heil* in years past now hate him; they suffer misery and death because of him. But they had neither the strength nor the courage to free themselves from his power. Just before I left Berlin, someone had put up a large banner, roughly painted, on a ruined building in Lützowplatz. It read, 'For this we thank the Führer!'"

Elke recognized the words; they had been used countless times by Dr. Goebbels, but they were not intended as an epitaph for Germany's ruins.

She replied thoughtfully, "I was only in school, but I read about the destruction of the Austrian kronen, the catastrophic unemployment and depression. The chaos in Vienna, no food or jobs, was unbelievable, so when I first heard Hitler speak I felt he might have the answer to the disorder. The democratic Austrian government was unable to solve the country's problems, again, no food or jobs. People were starving. Hitler's words sounded a call to my friends for the need for major changes in the government. Social unrest could only be quelled by a man and a party with new solutions, a strong leader who advocated for law and order. I wanted to restore the honor and tradition of Germany, the Germanic way of life. But our government had only brought us Bolshevism and the subhuman Jews."

Elke didn't have much to say after that. For some reason, she began thinking of the paintings of the old masters like Correggio during the Baroque era. She remembered the fall of the damned, of those falling human bodies, distorted faces and knotted arms and hands reaching out to each other for support, but serving only to drag one another into the depths, like something from Dante's *Inferno,* truly godforsaken people.

*   *   *

Most of the female prisoners hated the idleness of prison, but for Elke it was a precious gift. She had worked hard to rise through the ranks of the BdM. She had done this for herself, of course, but also, and maybe even more so, for the Fatherland. She firmly believed the Nazi propaganda that a war of civilization was coming—and only Hitler could defend Europe against "Asiatic pestilence and Bolshevism," the political left (particularly the communists and socialists), but especially the Jews.

Even though she had grown up in an upper-middle-class home in a pleasant area of Vienna, she could remember beggars, almost daily, coming to their apartment building asking for work, food, or any handout. *"Meister, hast du keine Arbeit?"* (Boss, don't you have any work?) These scenes still echoed in Elke's mind. Hitler had shown in

Germany how he could revive the economy; she'd been sure he could do the same for Austria.

She remembered the bright red collection boxes for small change to which all members of society, rich or poor, well fed or hungry, contributed. They helped foster a sense of solidarity among all residents. Those boxes had the purpose of collecting money, but more important, to make it apparent to all that the Nazi state cared for everyone. The younger generation, like Elke, did not fail to notice this apparent altruism, which bred a sense of loyalty to the regime.

*　*　*

As the days turned into weeks and weeks became months, the severe restrictions on the women were gradually eased. The doors to each cell were now left unlocked, which allowed prisoners to visit each other and develop friendships. They could now learn news of someone's hometown or of a friend or relative. For Elke, this small bit of freedom was both good and bad; she longed to be able to walk again in the woods and be alone with her thoughts. She enjoyed the political talk, but realized most prisoners wanted to forget National Socialism, go back to their families, and get on with their lives.

2

Captain
Grant Edwards

1945

In his book, The German War, Citizens and Soldiers, *Nicholas Stargardt wrote: "Interviewers found that the 'Jewish war' still provided the key explanation for American actions against Germany and German defeat seemed only to have confirmed the 'power of world Jewry.' Hardly anybody thought that the German people as a whole were responsible for the suffering of the Jews, although 64% agreed that the persecution of the Jews had been decisive in making Germany lose the war. Still 37% . . . were prepared to endorse the view that 'the extermination of the Jews and the Poles and other non-Aryans had been necessary for the 'security of the Germans.' It was clear that most Germans still believed they had fought a legitimate war of national defense. This was not what any of the victorious allies had intended. The Americans had pursued the most ambitious re-education and denazification policy in 1945 and 1946, forcing Germans to visit the liberated concentration camps or sometimes, to view film footage from Buchenwald and Dachau before receiving ration cards. Many turned their faces away, unwilling or unable to look. Others began to disparage the films and photographs as propaganda staged by the Allies."*

D espite the bombed-out ruins of southern Germany in September 1945, young military officers, especially those educated in American colleges, could always find a semi-comfortable facility to drink beer with their comrades. The war in Europe had ended four months earlier; most Americans in the military wanted to just do their jobs and get home to anxious families.

Many American soldiers felt resentful; they had seen the Germans as a violent people that had started the war and kept it going when all was lost, leading to destruction of countless irreplaceable historic treasures. Many college men felt that they'd merely delayed the start of their careers.

Fortunately, not all felt this way. Twenty-five-year-old Capt. Grant Edwards was a graduate of the University of California and commissioned an army officer upon graduation. He was of medium height, with sun-bleached brown hair, and looked every inch a Californian. He'd seen combat in France and Germany after D-Day. His current assignment was to interview prisoners and decide if they posed a threat to society. Grant had volunteered for this assignment; he hoped one day to write a book about the Nazis and what made them believe so ardently in Hitler and National Socialism. He had a writer's curiosity about people who would follow their leaders blindly into such enormous death and destruction.

Then there was 1st Lt. Phil Goodman, a southern boy who had attended the University of North Carolina. Phil had one interest: getting back to his parents' farm near Asheboro, North Carolina. A true southerner of twenty-four years, he had dark brown hair and a stomach that was beginning to show his other love: beer. He'd been in the U.S. Army since graduating from ROTC and had trained in Jump School to be a paratrooper. Having been injured during a routine jump in England prior to D-Day, Phil spent his time in a hospital outside Oxford, listening to the news of the invasion. He and Grant developed a close relationship during their assignment interviewing Nazis, but the project didn't interest Phil as much as it did Grant. Phil made it plain he was unhappy having to stay in Europe with the war over and having to clean up the mess the Germans had created.

The third officer was 1st Lt. Karl Rosen, also twenty-four and single. A Jewish kid from the Bronx in New York City, Karl stood only about five foot six. His occasional aggressive nature seemed to counterbalance his lack of height. He'd been a German history major at the City College of New York, with hopes of becoming a lawyer after the war. Karl, however, had no idea how he would be able to pay for law school. His father owned a small tailor shop in the Garment District of Manhattan and was unable to help financially. Karl had never been out of the city before being commissioned a second lieutenant at City College and then boarding a troop ship to England. He was then off to war-torn Europe, which was an eye-opening experience.

Karl spoke fluent German and had been interrogating German officers for the War Crimes Commission; his stoic side had helped him through these interrogations. He was just now learning about the treatment of the Jews for the first time. He was unwilling to show any emotion during these hearings; afterward he would go to his room and cry. He had to hold back his urge to kill every German he came in contact with. Fortunately, he met Grant and Phil, and their sense of humor was just what Karl needed.

The three men had developed a strong bond during this assignment, as will happen in war. Though they had little in common, they were brothers in arms. Something they did share was a love of beer; and German beer tasted a lot better than the beer they were accustomed to in America. At four o'clock each afternoon most officers gathered at their home away from home, a place familiar to every young junior officer in the Army or Navy—the officer's club. The Munich club was unlike those in Washington, D.C., or San Francisco: It was basically a shack with whatever mismatched furniture the Army had "requisitioned." But the beer was good and they were sheltered from the destruction that had both surrounded and overwhelmed them since arriving in Europe.

"*Guten Tag*, guys!" said the voluptuous blond barkeep. Kristl had become a favorite of the young officers at the camp—and not just because of her physical attributes. The G.I.s loved that she was trying harder to learn American slang than they were trying to learn German. Kristl especially liked Grant, much to the consternation of Phil and Karl. On this day, she greeted them with three large steins of their favorite beer.

"Ah! Kristl," said Phil, "you are looking more than lovely today." Ignoring Phil, she turned to Karl. "Karl, you are not going to be my sour puss, Jew-friend today, are you?" To no one's surprise the anti-Semitic greeting only made Karl smile broadly.

"No, I'm here to drink with my friends and then take you to bed."

"Maybe someday I will take you up on that," she teased as she walked back to the bar.

Phil said to the others, "Ah! Another day done. How many 'wake-ups' do we have left?"

"Too many to count, and besides, with your southern education, you can't count that far anyway," Grant said with a grin.

"Ha! Very funny! I used to know how to count, but I forgot living in Europe with you two assholes."

Grant turned serious. "I've been thinking you two could help me. I can offer you work that may make the time go by a bit faster."

"Is this for your book?" Karl said.

"Yes, I want to write about where this hatred of Jews came from. Why did Nazis believe Jews were not human beings? I mean, these Europeans aren't uncivilized, at least they didn't used to be. Let's not forget, they produced Mozart and Beethoven."

Karl chimed in, "I like the idea. You know, hatred is like a fire. You've got to put it out. I'm Jewish and my parents are safe in the Bronx. But don't think for a minute I'm not bitter against the Krauts. If we can prove they are guilty of atrocities, then shoot them and get it over with, but for God's sake let's get on with it. Brutality is more contagious than typhus and a hell of a lot more difficult to stamp out." He paused and remained silent for some time.

Grant noticed Karl's solemn expression. Karl was deadly serious about this.

Phil broke the silence. "Of course, I will want a percent of the profits."

"Good luck with that," Grant said. "I want to go to graduate school when I get home, and this could be my thesis. Anyway, I'd like to start with Elke Baur. She gave everyone a very hard time at her first interviews. She really is an unrepentant Nazi, even after the destruction of the war."

"It's going to be tough to get anything but '*Heil Hitler*' out of that bitch," said Phil.

"I agree, I just can't understand where this attitude came from, and that's what I want to explore," Grant said.

"Don't forget the inflation and the depression that brought down their economies," said Karl.

"Hell, we've all seen depression; my folks almost lost the farm in '31," said Phil, lighting a cigarette and taking a long pull.

Karl interjected, "I'd like to know more about the BDM. What was their training, their activities, and were they forced to join?"

"Yes," said Grant, "but I really want to learn her mind about the concentration camps. What did she know about them? Did she see any of these places?"

"Also," Karl put in, "what about when the Jews were taken from their homes in Vienna? What did she think was going on? Does she really believe those photos we showed her are merely an Allied plot to smear Germany?" He said this with more emotion than he usually displayed.

"I would just like a simple answer to the simple question: 'Why do you hate the Jews so much?' None of this makes any sense. We left our homes and families and came all the way over here to beat the shit out of a lot of people just like her, who basically destroyed a civilization that took two thousand years to build."

Grant smiled. "Phil, I didn't know you cared that much."

"I don't; I just want to go home to my family and good North Carolina cooking."

"Here is how I would like to proceed with this," Grant said. "We will never get her to open up if we try to overpower her. I want to sit down with her alone, in a non-threatening environment, to see if she'll talk honestly. I want to know about her parents, her childhood, her schooling, her friends and neighbors."

"You may have to promise her freedom if she cooperates," said Karl.

"What do you want us to do?" asked Phil.

"Well, mostly to help me make sense of it all. Keep me on the right track. Am I asking the right questions? What do you think of her answers? I may need you later, Karl. Elke speaks pretty good English, but your German is good. I don't think she will open up to you at first because you're Jewish, but if I can break down some barriers, you could be valuable."

"Let's do this. Maybe we can help this bastard do some important work when he gets back to California," said Karl. He signaled to Kristl. "But now I need another beer."

* * *

The tall brunette came into the meeting with Capt. Edwards expecting harsh treatment, but felt she could handle anything the American might do to try to intimidate her. To her surprise, she was escorted to a private room with two comfortable leather chairs.

Grant noticed Elke holding her arms across her chest; he wanted to put her at ease. "*Fräulein* Baur, please have a seat. Would you like something to drink?" She asked for a Coca-Cola.

As Grant handed her the cold coke, he said to her in a friendly manner, "I want you to know I appreciate your consenting to his interview. Let me assure you it is strictly for my academic research. No one else will know of anything we say here. If you decline to answer any of my questions that's fine. Your English is quite good, but if there is anything you don't understand, say so. If you are comfortable with this, I'd like to begin."

He got a nod from Elke, while taking out a notebook and pen and began, "Tell me about your youth in Vienna, and your parents."

Elke looked nervously about the room, cleared her throat, and said, "I grew up in a stately apartment building on Daringergasse in the 19th district of Vienna. It is an upper-middle-class neighborhood surrounded by trees on a cobblestone street. Our apartment was on the top floor— the third floor. The building was heavily Jewish, but our parents were friendly only with the gentile neighbors across the landing—a young man who was a banker like my father, his sister, a teacher, and their elderly mother. My brother Fritz and I liked them very much. They would bring us small treats occasionally when we were children. They were more political than our parents. I remember, when I was in early gymnasium, they called the Jews "foreigners," and said this with scorn.

"How did your parents feel about their Jewish neighbors?" Grant asked.

"The only Jews my parents had contact with were the Levys from the second floor. For many years we shared a telephone line with them.

Herr Levy was friendly, an old man with a full beard. They were the only Orthodox Jews in the building. This seemed more acceptable to our parents, probably because they were not of the 'new rich' Jews, or the hated *Ostjuden* who had come from eastern Europe after the first war. But we only exchanged greetings with the Levys when passing in the stairway.

"My father was an economist with the LänderBank. He was only mildly political but a great reader of newspapers. He would talk of political news beginning at breakfast, continuing through dinner, and after our homework was complete. He talked about the squabbling in the Austrian Parliament; when things become heated during the 1920s there were many splintered parties.

"One story has stuck with me; it was an example of the terrible unemployment in Vienna during those years. The son of some people we knew couldn't find work. When he received his government dole money, he would drink until he fell asleep in the backyard. One day, his mother was heard screaming as if she had lost her mind. He had opened an artery with a kitchen knife. She found him dead in their back yard. I had seen him a few hours before on the street, walking barefoot in a tattered army greatcoat with a little dog in his arms.

"I'm convinced that being unemployed killed him. I believed the National Socialists when they promised to do away with unemployment and the poverty of six million Austrians. I believed them when they said they would reunite the German nation. Our parents were of the conservative party and felt the economy would improve, given time. When I turned nineteen, I believed Hitler when he said he would bring greatness, fortune, and prosperity to Austria and see that everyone had work and bread, that every Austrian would become free, happy, and independent. I believed him. The downfall of Germany in the Great War was because of the Jews."

"Why did you believe that, Ms. Baur?"

Elke glowered at Grant. "The eastern Jews who wouldn't work were bleeding our country dry, and so were the rich Jew industrialists."

"Was your father in the first war?"

"*Ja*, but he never talked about it much. He lost his best friend on the last day of the war—the same day I was born. I like to think I helped fill a gap in his life. He did say that he couldn't understand how we lost that war. He said France had been destroyed—cities, towns, farms; but he saw untouched farms and villages in Germany and Austria when he returned from the front by train."

"Sounds like your father came back to a shattered economy. He was lucky to have a job."

"*Ja*, he managed to delay joining the army in order to finish his degree in economics. He always wanted to work for a bank."

"What was your mother like?"

"Oh! I adored my mother. She seemed to always know when I needed a hug or help at school. She was kind of the balance between my father and my brother, who would argue over politics a lot."

"What about your brother, Fritz? Where is he now?"

"My brother was in the Hitler youth as was I, but he joined the Austrian SS about a year or so before the *Anschluss*. When the war began, he was sent to the Russian front. He spent most of his time in Poland and Russia. I have heard nothing of him since Stalingrad."

"Why did he want to be in the SS?"

"I think he liked their uniforms," she answered, with a bit of a laugh. "My brother and I were not close. He was four years older and we did not stay in touch during the war."

"Why did you join the B.D.M?"

"I secretly joined the Hitler Youth when I was eighteen. I say secretly because my parents would not allow me to join, but I wanted to escape from my childish, narrow life and attach myself to something great and fundamental."

"Where are your parents now?"

This question struck the first cord of emotion in Elke. She looked at him with hatred, then started to tear up. "They were killed by your bombers. They were in a civilian area of Dresden, miles from any industrial or military complex. Your pilots were trying to kill as many people as possible."

To distract her, Grant turned the questioning in another direction. "*Fräulein*, you have told me you wanted to take a different road from your parents, but surely you understand now where that road led. Millions have died, thousands of cities have been destroyed. You talk of classes living together like brother and sister; what about the millions of innocent people who died only because their religion was different from those 'brothers and sisters'? You said the last time we talked, if Hitler had known what was happening to the Jews, he would have stopped it. You don't really believe that, do you?"

Elke cleared her throat. She said, "I learned from my parents' example that one could have anti-Semitic opinions without interfering in one's personal relations with individual Jews. In preaching that all the misery of the nations was due to the Jews, or the Jewish spirit was seditious, and Jewish blood was corrupting, I was not thinking of someone like *Herr* Levy. I only thought of the bogeyman, 'the Jews.' And when I heard the Jews were being driven from their professions and their homes and imprisoned in ghettos, my mind would not allow me to think such a fate could overtake old *Herr* Levi."

Grant paused. "What can you tell me about *Kristallnacht*?"

"I believed the Jews were the enemies of the new Germany. *Kristallnacht* was a warning to them if they continued to sow hatred against us all over the world, they must know what the repercussions would be. Hitler did not come to power because of anti-Semitism. His rise was based on a wave of nationalism and the miserable economy. What attracted all of us to National Socialism was the positive appeal to family, community, and the German homeland."

"*Fräulein*," Grant said, "I keep hearing Austrians say they were the first victims of Hitler. When Hitler entered Vienna on March 14, 1938, what was the reception like? I assume you were there?"

"Oh *Ja*, I was there. I was about to turn twenty and in my last year at gymnasium. The *Führer* had come to Austria to see the graves of his parents in Linz. The next day his motorcade drove 120 miles to Vienna. I was in the *Heldenplatz* (Heroes' Square) on that great day. The crowd was so large newspapers said the square could not hold any more people. The newsreels showed the crowds along the road and people hanging out of windows and standing on rooftops. Church bells peeled, and hundreds offered flowers for Hitler. He stayed that first night at the Hotel Imperial near the Opera. Newspapers the next day said he had been offered to stay at the Habsburg palace but declined, because as a youth in Vienna he had been employed by the Hotel Imperial shoveling snow in winter while the aristocracy was inside eating a gala dinner. But it was his speech I will never forget. He made me feel as though a great future lay in store for us."

"Our time is up. I promised I wouldn't keep you too long. Maybe we can do this again, because this is fascinating. *Fräulein* Baur, thank you for this. When you are released from here, I hope you find the future is not as dark as you think."

Elke returned to her cell and Grant to his office to write down in more detail what he had learned. He was convinced the economy had played a major role in the route Germany followed to National Socialism. However, he also saw that anti-Semitism was strong in Germany, and especially Austria, prior to Hitler's ascent. Maybe Hitler had simply seen an easy horse to ride to power.

*   *   *

The three young officers sat in Grant's office to discuss what he had learned. Grant said, "I'm convinced that the Austrians calling themselves 'Hitler's first victim' is merely to cover up their guilt over the Jews."

"Grant, I have been doing some research on this," Karl said. "Most Austrians were eager to join Germany going back as far as 1919, after the first war. Several plebiscites were held in Austria after the *Anschluss*, and an average of 95 percent of Austrians voted for *Anschluss* with Germany. It was an absolutely free vote, with a secret ballot and no outside influence."

"Yes Karl, I've read that," Grant replied. "But the Peace Treaty of St. Germain in 1919 forbid union with Germany. However, I'm sure the idea lived on in people's minds. It was strengthened when unemployment spiked and the economy crashed. Unification with the newly flourishing German Reich looked like the only way Austria could be saved.

"There's a wonderful Jewish writer living in Vienna I'd like to talk with. His name is Dr. Alfred Altschul. He wrote a famous book in the mid-1930s encouraging Jews to leave Austria before it was too late. It's called *My Austria of Yesterday*. I'd like to go to Vienna to interview him."

"Grant, you know Col. Barnett well. Would he let us do that?" asked Phil.

"I doubt it, we are needed here, but he might send one of us." Grant looked directly at Karl, who jumped up, out of his seat. "I'm not going to that anti-Semitic city. I hear it's in even worse shape than Munich. Besides, I'm not the history expert; you are, Grant."

"We don't need a historian to find out what we need to know. We need someone to conduct an interview with a Jewish writer. And you, 1st Lt. Karl Rosen, are perfect. You are Jewish, you have a better grasp of German than I do, and you have the temperament to get him to open up."

"Do you think the colonel will approve of this hair-brained trip?" said Phil.

"If I can get Dr. Altschul to agree to an interview, I'm sure he will. The army doesn't need the three of us to interrogate German prisoners of war here in Munich. Besides, it would be a feather in Barnett's cap to learn more about this."

3

Dr. Altschul

1945

By the end of 1945, Vienna was divided into four occupation zones. The American district was the most desirable; it was the safest and included the vineyard district of Grinzing. The Russians occupied the most territory, including the old Jewish districts on the other side of the Danube Canal and the Danube River. The French controlled shopping areas such as Mariahilferstrasse, and the British oversaw the airport at Semmering. The central city, bordered by the Ringstrasse (the grand boulevard serving as a ring road around Vienna's historic Innere Stadt district), was split; each occupying power was in control for one month at a time. This led to the ludicrous result of "four men in a jeep"; that is, the MPs of each occupier, in charge of security. The city was alive with Cold War espionage and a flourishing black market.

I t was a cold December afternoon when the military transport plane touched down at Vienna's Aspern airfield. First Lt. Karl Rosen fought a biting north wind as he strode to the single taxi waiting at the lone administration building. Karl settled into the back seat and directed the driver to the famous Hotel Sacher. Since the December sun set early, it was soon quite dark. Snow began to sputter against the car's windshield. Through his window, Karl saw a dark, gloomy city of bombed buildings and rubble-strewn streets. Over the Danube Canal, wooden planks were placed over partially destroyed bridges.

During much of the war Vienna had been spared by the Allied bombers—because the city was too far from England's air bases. Rumors abounded that Churchill had struck a deal with Hitler or that the Allies wished to preserve Vienna's beautiful buildings. These turned out to be bitter hopes. After D-Day, the Allies were able to build air bases in northern France and could then easily reach Vienna.

As the taxi turned onto the *Kärntnerstrasse*, once Vienna's Fifth Avenue, Karl was greeted by more scenes of debris and destroyed buildings. The city's most famous building, St. Stephen's Cathedral, was still standing, but the roof had been wrecked. They drove past the Vienna Opera House. Karl thought he'd never seen a more beautiful building even though the back portion had burned down. Unlike Berlin, Vienna was still recognizable under all the dust and rubble. Karl thought the city looked like an aging movie star dying in a poorhouse, one who could still shape her cracked lips into the confident smile of a woman whom many men had loved over the years.

The driver turned the corner to the Hotel Sacher, which had suffered only minor damage. Although open again, it was not the elegant resort it had been before the war, a time when it was preferred by Europe's rich and famous. It was also known for its dessert, the Sacher Torte, a decadent chocolate cake with rum and apricot preserves. The hotel, however, was still one of the nicest in Vienna and convenient to the University of Vienna, where Karl would meet Dr. Altschul the next day.

By the time he had checked into the Sacher, the sky had turned even darker. Karl was tired and hungry. A dinner of frankfurter,

sauerkraut, and a beer was all he wanted before retiring. He wanted
to be well rested before the next day's interview at ten o'clock. While
waiting for sleep, his mind kept turning over what life must have been
like in Vienna years earlier. He knew the Viennese people faced an
uncertain future. It was far removed from what it had been during the
nineteenth century—a vibrant city filled with the music of Strauss,
Mozart, and Beethoven.

*   *   *

Karl was up early the next morning. He walked to the University in
order to see the city better in the daylight. It was a cold, grey morning.
The sights he saw were not any brighter. Major landmarks were destroyed,
people were gaunt and dressed in torn, dirty clothes, and the soldiers
of the Red army brooded over the city like vultures. Women walked
down the burned-out *Kärntnerstrasse*, looking vacantly into gutted
store windows. It was hard to imagine that before the war this had been
one of the most fashionable shopping streets in Europe. It was now no
taller than eye level, as Allied bombs had leveled most second floors.

Food was the most pressing problem. Although the Germans
had kept food distribution intact, most people complained about the
monotony of what was provided. Yet they didn't starve. Ration cards
were supposed to assure the population of 1,500 calories a day, but
seldom did. Over the next nine months, beginning with the end of the
war in May, even that fell to a low of 800 calories, which led residents
to frequent the flourishing black market. Food could also be bought
from folks who tended little gardens on the outskirts of the city. But to
get there, people risked encountering the authorities, as well as other
starving Viennese, or worse, other black marketeers. They also risked
running into marauding Russians while getting back to their homes.

The smell of decaying garbage in the streets was overwhelming.
The city had no sanitation vehicles, and ex-Nazi Party members, who

were given the task of cleanup, merely dumped the messes at collection points on the main streets.

The university—one large building in the neo-Renaissance style, sat on the Ringstrasse. Its front was dominated by large, impressive arches that seemed to overpower the rest of the building, which was quite plain. It seemed to have borne little or no bomb damage, at least from what Karl could see from the street.

He entered and approached the main desk, where a young woman directed him to Dr. Altschul's office, on the second floor to the right. He found the professor surrounded by books, just as he had expected. The professor looked the part, with white hair, a small white goatee, a slightly rumpled tweed jacket, and a warm smile when he saw the young American officer approach.

"You must be Lt. Rosen?"

"And you must be Dr. Altschul? It is a pleasure to meet you, sir. I am sorry that I haven't finished *My Austria of Yesterday*. I had a difficult time obtaining the book, but the Army was of great help."

"Yes, I am sure it wasn't available in Austria or Germany," the professor said with a chuckle. "Now, young man, I gather the U.S. Army would like to learn how to deal with numerous intransigent Nazis, many of them women, who are unrepentant anti-Semites," the professor continued.

"They blame the U.S. for entering the war and upsetting the comfortable life they'd anticipated in the new, German, Europe."

"Yes, as long as everyone looks like everyone else." He smiled while taking up his pen and notepad, "And according to your book, this hatred in the Austrian people has been building for decades. We feel you can give us a little better understanding of those years. Oh, I might add, we've been surprised at how young these Nazis are."

"Ah, *ja*, like those youngsters who participated in the classes required by the Christian Church and the Jewish religion. National

Socialism's most important element is instruction for the children, to get them indoctrinated early. The Nazis recognized the most efficient way to bind youngsters to the Nazi state was to provide them with the kind of experience that would guarantee loyalty. For this reason, they arranged celebrations, marches, sporting events, and in general, a life full of exciting diversions. The party was able to shape a generation into conformists, and in the end, people who would follow orders willingly, no matter what."

"Professor, you saw the threat to the Jews in Austria before most Jews recognized it. What enabled you to see this and to act long before others did?"

"Well, it was not any great intellectual insight on my part; more like a slap in the face. It was 1934. I had been working late in my apartment in Vienna. I slept in the next morning, well past my normal hour of rising. My servant roused me with a worried look. He said there were policemen downstairs to see me. I was surprised, but I put on my dressing gown and went down. There stood four Austrian police, with orders to search the house and seize immediately any arms hidden there.

You Americans are fortunate. Your Constitution gives you the right to bear arms, and protects you from search and seizure. Here in Europe we have no such rights. At first, I was too dumbfounded to reply; it was absurd that I would even think of having guns in my home. I had never belonged to any party and never bothered with politics. I answered coolly, 'Please look around.'

"The men went through the house, opened a few chests, and tapped on a few walls. It was apparent from their sluggish manner that none of them seriously believed there were guns to be found. After half an hour they left. What a farce! I realized Europe had forgotten the sacredness of personal rights and civil liberties. Since 1933, searches, arbitrary arrests, expropriation of property, expulsion from home and country, deportation, and all other imaginable forms of humiliation had become almost matter-of-course occurrences. I had hardly any European friends who had not experienced something of the sort. But in 1934, a home search in Austria was still a tremendous affront to someone like me—that I, who had stood completely aloof from politics and for years had not even voted, should be searched.

"The Chief of Police in Vienna had been forced to take these measures because of the violence created by National Socialists who terrorized the populace night after night with bombs and explosives. Every day the authorities received letters threatening reprisals if 'they' kept on 'persecuting' the National Socialists. Therefore, it seemed a good idea to search my house to make a conspicuous example that no one was exempt from such measures. This episode showed me how serious the situation had become in Austria, and how overpowering was the pressure from Germany.

"That same evening, I started to pack my most important papers, determined to live abroad permanently. This meant more than giving up my house and country, for my family clung to the house as their home, and they loved the land. For me, however, personal liberty was the most important thing on earth."

"Professor, did you feel physically threatened by the policemen?"

"No, more like being physically violated. My private world had been intruded upon and I resented it. Although now when I think about that night, I did feel their hatred of me as a Jew. I remember reading the eighteenth-century English writer Charles Caleb Colton, who wrote that 'We hate some persons because we do not know them, and we will not know them because we hate them.' I really think this sums up the Nazi, and more generally, the European philosophy regarding the Jews."

"Yes, it does, but where does this German hatred of the Jews originate? Has it all come from Hitler and the Nazis?"

The professor recrossed his legs and replied with a frown, "Oh my boy, this is not a German attitude but a European attitude. Have you forgotten the Dreyfus Affair in Paris in the late 1890s? There were rioters in the streets wanting the head of a career Jewish army officer—a loyal officer convicted of treason on evidence that had been forged and presented illegally. Meanwhile, a French Army major, who was the real guilty party, was whitewashed by a military court. A colonel who had confessed to faking evidence against the Jewish captain killed himself rather than face the consequences and was hailed as a martyr to truth. A French journalist, Paul Brulat, asked: 'Where were the honest men of France?' The reply was: 'They are frightened.'

"But let's go back to what Colton said about hate. Hate can transform ordinary people into ruthless killers. Killing is a unique characteristic of humans. Why, your own Mark Twain said, 'The joy of killing! The joy of seeing killing done—these are the traits of the human race.' Guilt-free mass murder is a subject we must study if we hope to survive as a civilization. I firmly believe religion and ideology are the most common reasons for the ability to kill without guilt. Advocating hatred of the Jews was valuable to various movements for practical reasons. Hate is a better recruitment tool than love."

"Christians have always been angry with Jews for killing Christ, at least this is what I've always believed."

The professor replied, "Hatred, unlike anger, is not a reaction to the behavior of others, but a displacement of the repressed rage of those who hate. Those who incite acts of hate are seeking to rid themselves and the world around them of its unsettling, messy complexity. They see themselves as holders of greater truth, above reproach. The challenge is to imagine the feeling and thought of people who found killing the Jews both a moral necessity and a noble cause. Had we Jews of all Europe in the 1930s, empathized with Nazi Germany and grasped that the Germans perceived us as a threat to their survival, we would have realized the danger that lay ahead.

"Empathy is the ability to put oneself in the shoes of another person. Empathy results from an upbringing of moral socialization. If a child is taught the negative effects of one's actions on others, this increases empathy. If, on the other hand, one is disciplined, not through reasoning, but through harsh authoritarian power or assertive parenting that relies on punishment, then stereotypic thinking, submission to authority, and aggression against outsiders may result. Moral socialization is not developed and therefore there is little empathy. Fear hinders empathy. Empathy is essential to politicians, historians, writers, parents, and all others who wish to understand friends and enemies."

"Is it too late to convert someone like our Elke Baur into a tolerant human being?" Karl said. "After all, she is only twenty-seven. Yet I don't believe she possesses a conscience."

"Ah, conscience." Dr. Altschul brightened. "Conscience is the need to behave consistently with recognized ethical principles. Acting against conscience leads to feelings of guilt. Conscience, ethical values, a capacity for empathy, and the ability to love must be developed and nurtured in a child. The capacity to love and empathize come with development and maturation. Narcissism and rage are primal emotions. Parents, peers, and society create individuals and collective conscience.

"An institution, unlike an individual, does not have a conscience; it has a policy or a program. Societies that promote hate suffer the consequences of raising children who hate. Nazi Germany and especially the Austria of past writers like Georg von Schönerer and Burgomaster (mayor) Karl Lueger of Vienna taught children to hate.

"Adam Smith, known for his *Wealth of Nations,* also wrote *The Theory of Moral Sentiments.* In this he said that within each of us is the 'inner man' who acts like an 'impartial spectator' and passes judgement upon our behavior and that of others. The killing of the Jews did not violate the conscience of these people because they felt justified by religion and ideology to hate them."

Hearing this, Karl's face became drawn and he clenched his fists. He said, "Why was there not more resistance among the Jews? The Warsaw Ghetto uprising was the only armed resistance I know of."

With a knowing smile, the professor straightened up in his chair. He said, "Those Jews who resisted actually wanted to die. They wanted to die on their own terms but nevertheless wanted death—just not death in captivity. I feel that the opposite of Jewish passivity in German captivity was not armed resistance but the struggle for survival. Passivity and survival are incompatible. Survival was not a random event, but a contingent process. Indomitable courage, resourcefulness, and endurance in the face of brutal persecution were essential in order to survive."

The professor interrupted his monologue. "I think we can talk more freely over a whisky and soda at the Sacher bar," he said. "I love that place and am very glad the Allies didn't hit that building."

As the two men walked toward the hotel, a light snowfall dusted the streets. Karl had never been as cold as he was now, walking through wreckage and seeing desperation in the eyes of the people they passed. What's more, he keenly felt the absence of the constant roar of a city. He had been prepared for destruction, but not a city hushed to a whisper. Even the few Christmas decorations seemed to be displayed with little enthusiasm. Yet this Vienna was not a lifeless moonscape. It lived, even if in something of a zombie-like trance, as seen in the dazed looks of many of the people in the street, mostly old, bowed women.

The men found a quiet booth in the hotel bar. Each ordered a scotch and soda, then Karl asked what he had wanted to from the beginning: "Why didn't more Jews leave Vienna while they had a chance?"

"I had an opportunity to see the threat to Austria better than my friends in Vienna," Dr. Altschul said. "I had a small place in

Saltzburg located near the German border. Most Austrians regarded National Socialism as something happening 'over there' that could in no way affect Austria. Besides, the League of Nations of France and England were Austria's protectors. Not even the Jews worried; they acted as if canceling the rights of physicians, lawyers, scholars, and actors was happening in China instead of across the border three hours away in Germany, where their own language was spoken. They rested comfortably in their homes, rode about in their cars, and had a ready-made phrase: 'That Hitler cannot last long.' It was the self-deception we practice because of reluctance to abandon our accustomed life."

Karl said, "I look at the people and they seem distant. I'm sure hunger plays a large part in that. With the Russians in charge of the food supply, it looks like distribution has broken down. Is this due to Russian incompetence—or is it designed for vengeance?"

"I think a bit of both. Most Viennese are existing on worm-eaten peas and old potatoes. Sugar and meat can be bought only on the black market."

"Tell me about the black market, professor."

"The center of it is in a park at the *Karlskirche*, not far from here. There are virtually no police, thus it is possible to buy anything, literally anything: food, cigarettes. I have even heard of an airplane being bought. I would advise you not to go in uniform and to be careful if you go at all. You have to understand, people here are faced with an unsure future, but hopefully a future with Wiener Schnitzel. Most are interested only in the here and now. Only the old still love the city.

"My boy, you have a story here that needs to be told. I must say though, your young woman sounds typical of ninety percent of the people of Austria. They think they are innocent of the Jewish killings because they themselves killed no one. They believe they have no blood on their hands. But because they did nothing in the early stages of National Socialism, they do have blood on their hands, and it will never wash off."

The professor stood and extended his hand. "I must get back to my office. I need to get some work done today. Good luck to you and let me know if I can be of further help."

Talking with Dr Altschul had been a delight. Karl promised himself he would finish *My Austria of Yesterday*. But for the moment he sat contemplating his scotch and soda. It was still early afternoon, but he had little interest in exploring this depressing city. Their waitress appeared at his booth. There was a small tear in the sleeve of her blouse and her eyes looked tired, but at least she had a job in a respectable hotel. He'd heard that German women were prepared to have sex with American G.I.s for companionship and protection, or more likely, food, cigarettes, or stockings. A cigarette was worth four ounces of bread, so a pack of cigarettes was a huge bribe. She said, "Can I get you another scotch and soda?"

Karl noticed she had beautiful blue eyes. "Yes, thank you. I guess I am in no mood to go out in this weather. I sense so much loneliness in Vienna; as if it's a city with no future."

"I grew up here and have seen the beauty and now the ugly, but we will get through it," she said in a flat voice.

Karl was surprised at her command of English. "Did you go to University?" he said.

"Yes, I was studying English and literature at University when the war broke out, and I worked for an Austrian newspaper—you know, happy news for the home front. How well the boys were eating, things like that. What brings you to Vienna?"

Karl was in uniform so he couldn't pretend to be anything else. "I am part of a group researching the background of the civilian population that lead to hatred of the Jews. By the way, my name is Karl, Karl Rosen from New York."

"I am Inga." She didn't offer a last name. "Nice to meet you, Karl from New York. I am afraid I cannot be of much help. I never hated the Jews. I am a good Catholic who believed in helping my fellow man. I never believed the Jews would take over the world. I am afraid my hatred is for the Russians, but I don't want to talk about it." She said this quickly, turned and walked away.

Karl thought that even if some German women would do anything for food, none of that meant anything to Inga. He had the feeling she didn't want to talk with him, let alone sleep with him. He wished he could talk to her more, but his time was short.

The dawn brought heavy storm clouds and extreme cold, so returning to Munich by air was out of the question; he'd have to take the train. The Westbahnhof train station was alive with people. Many looked rumpled, as though they had spent the night here. He noticed a large wall with what looked like hundreds of notices pinned to display boards. Karl had to pick his way through the crowd to read the notices. Families had pinned photos or notes with addresses to the boards, hoping someone would bring news of missing loved ones.

The train to Munich was waiting on Track #1. He found a window seat, then stared blankly at the people who looked back at him from the platform. Munich might not be much better off, but at least there would be a lot more Americans there, he thought.

Karl was about to turn away from the window when he heard a small voice just below the window. It said, *"Bitte, G.I.!"* Karl looked down into the forlorn eyes of a seven- or eight-year-old girl. Her cupped hand was outstretched. She pleaded, *"Bitte, G.I., hunger G.I."* The train was beginning to move. Karl had just enough time to grab a Hershey's chocolate bar to toss to that small voice; the image of the girl stayed with him during the long trip to Munich.

4

Vienna

1947

In the Western Europe of 1947, it was generally believed that democratic solutions to postwar political problems could readily be found. For example, it was thought that the problems of Germany and Eastern European states such as Austria could be solved by free elections. Many in the United States even envisioned a world in which the use of force would no longer be necessary. There was no similar belief in Russia. Soviet leaders expected World War II to be followed by a wave of revolutionary movements like those that followed World War I, and they were eager to take advantage of the situation. It was the beginning of the Cold War and rising East-West tensions. As early as March 1946, Winston Churchill declared in an address in Fulton, Missouri, that "From Stettin in the Baltic to Trieste in the Adriatic, an iron curtain has descended across the Continent."

In February, Elke Baur was released and allowed to return to her home on Daringergasse in Vienna. The Americans had given her a one-way train ticket, plus some seed money to help make a start to a new life. She faced an uncertain future. When the train pulled away from the Munich station on a blustery day, dark clouds reflected her mood. She didn't know if her parents' apartment building had survived the bombers. She continued to mourn their deaths in the fire-bombing of Dresden, as well as to worry about her brother, Fritz.

The American soldiers, especially Capt. Edwards, had treated Elke politely, but it was obvious to her they were trying to relieve the guilt they felt over their bombing of civilian targets; bombing meant to injure and frighten the civilian population. They had also tried to infuse the German POWs with remorse and guilt over the Jews but had failed miserably. She continued to believe the Jews were the cause of Europe's troubles, from the hyper-inflation of the early '20s to the depression in the '30s. Although she had been too young to truly experience that era, she knew the stories well from her mother.

Else Baur had managed, God knows how, to keep the family together during those difficult years. Her father was a devoted employee of the Länderbank in Vienna, a well-run bank that had survived the depression of the 1930s. Elke could recall her father's stories over the dinner table of unethical business transactions by Jews. Yet, while growing up, she had always felt her father was too friendly with Jews, especially the ones in the apartment building. But she knew he was basically a kind man who had experienced firsthand the horrors of war. She knew he had lost his best friend in the Great War, and she was not sure he had ever gotten over the loss. She continued to believe that the Jews controlled the world, especially American Jews like President Roosevelt's Treasury Secretary, Henry Morgenthau. She thought that had America not entered the war against Germany, Europe would now be a quiet, unified continent, one where law and order prevailed and Christian culture finally outshone the heathen Jewish culture that had so dominated European art, theatre, and music during the last hundred years.

As the train rumbled through the Austrian countryside, she watched the snow-covered hills and mountains from the window. At another time she would have enjoyed the spectacular scenery, but now all she could think of was the cold. The unheated car was cold and damp. Her heavy wool sweater, worn wool coat, and tattered scarf barely kept her warm.

Sleep came sporadically as the old train chugged through the Austrian Alps. Elke worried about her future while trying to understand a past that had begun with bright hopes and ended so harshly for her beloved country and National Socialism. She believed Germany would have been the savior of Europe. The invasion of Russia in 1941 was probably a mistake, but necessary because the Aryan Germans needed more *Lebensraum* (living space) and the Jews needed to be removed from western Europe and relocated to the east so they could no longer contaminate the true Germans.

Elke didn't believe what the Americans told her about the millions of dead Jews. She was convinced the pictures they had shown her of dead bodies stacked on top of each other had been staged. She had even been taken to Dachau concentration camp near Munich but felt it had been built for Russian prisoners or Polish Resistance fighters; war can bring out the worst in all men. Soldiers fight for their lives and country in horrible conditions. There would always be a small element who are unable to control their base instincts. She was convinced if Hitler had known about these things, he would have stopped it. After all, he was a man who loved children, flowers, art, and music.

The train finally, slowly, chugged into the Westbahnhoff station as the thick overcast began to spit snow. A large crowd of people waited on the platform. Her eyes scanned each one with the faint hope of recognizing a familiar face. It had been several years since she had been to her hometown, and she tried to imagine her old classmates and how they might look now. Instead her gaze landed, not on a familiar face, but on an odd-looking old man. He was bizarrely dressed in a long, sable coat, and a large, eighteenth-century-type wig topped off by a red bonnet. He held a walking-stick with a handle in the shape of a crow. "What a strange person," she thought, then continued to scrutinize the crowd as the train ground to a stop.

Elke grabbed her small cloth satchel that held all her worldly belongings: a couple of changes of underwear, a second dress, toiletries, flannel pajamas, and a tube of an inexpensive red lipstick. She stepped off the train into a piercing wind, then walked through what was left of a neglected terminal to the street. She hoped to find a Strassenbahn running so she didn't have to walk across town all the way to the 19th District.

At the Ringstrasse she was pleased to see the streetcars were running, and a conductor said the Number 38 tram ran close to Daringergasse. The snow had stopped, but the wind was cold, and the streetcar windows were long gone. The people in the street and her fellow passengers on the trolly had unfocused, glassy looks. They seemed to have no more hope for the future than did she. After all, even though the Allies occupied three quarters of Vienna, it was now virtually a Russian city. Soldiers in U.S.-made jeeps were common, but always held four soldiers, one from each of the four powers: France, England, Russia, and the United States.

Elke remembered her last days in Vienna and the shock of seeing her employee, Inga Haschmann, after she had been beaten and raped by the Russians. Things were now better, especially since the Allies had partitioned off the city, but the influence of the Russians remained, and Josef Stalin was doing everything he could to force the Allies out of Vienna altogether.

The final stop on the Strassenbahn line was not too far from the apartment building where she had grown up. Turning the corner at

Daringergasse, she was surprised that the building seemed undam-
aged and was relieved to realize the Allied bombing had mainly been
confined to the industrial areas in the central city.

She needed no key to enter. If anyone lived there, they probably
didn't own enough to fear a thief. She was sure the Jewish families
who once lived there had been relocated to the East and wondered if
they would move back. But Elke's main concern was to get into her
parents' apartment, see what remained and what needed to be done.

Hearing her enter, a man in his seventies shuffled out of the apartment on the main floor. "*Fräulein*, may I help you?"

"*Ja*, my name is Elke Baur. My parents had an apartment on the
third floor. I was hoping it might be available for me to live in for a
while. I grew up here; my parents were Viktor and Else Baur. I also
had a brother named Fritz." Elke knew she was rambling but was
petrified he wouldn't believe her, because she had nowhere else to go.

"*Ja*, the Baurs. I didn't know them but have heard they were very
nice people. I think I heard they moved somewhere in Germany. Did
they survive the war?"

"*Nien*, they were killed in Dresden in '45. I miss them terribly. I
also lost my brother on the Russian front, but I know little about it;
the army doesn't give much information."

"My name is Walter, Walter Gürtne, but please just call me Walter.
Come, I will take you up to your apartment. I have kept it locked as
I didn't know who may be coming back for it, or the things in it."

As the old man moved slowly up the stairs, wheezing, she said,
"You look like you survived the war reasonably well. Were you in
the army?"

"*Nien*, the army didn't want old men like me, so I stayed here and
worked in the aircraft factory. We made the Heinkel bomber. I was
injured, and they gave me a small pension. My supervisor knew a
caretaker for this building was needed and suggested I apply. I was here

long before the Soviets came. It was terrible when they did; I could tell you stories. I understand this used to be a nice quiet neighborhood, but the Russians, they didn't care about people, just liquor, rape, and revenge. Many women were raped over there in the park, young girls, old women, it didn't make any difference. It was awful!"

Finally reaching the third floor, Walter regained his breath and unlocked the door to Number 7. Elke saw that much of the furniture was gone, including father's books and Fritz's piano. This made the apartment seem large, cold, and dark. There remained some chairs in the living room and a chest of drawers and small bed in her old bedroom; even a few of her parents' pictures were still there.

The old man said, "*Bitte!* I have several potatoes and was going to make some soup. Why don't you join me after you are settled in? About an hour?"

"That would be wonderful Walter," Elke replied. "*Danke!*"

An hour later, a bit refreshed, she was looking forward to a meal and conversation. The familiar smell of potato soup and Walter's sparse but cozy apartment put her at ease. The old gentleman seemed to want to talk—and little wonder. She'd seen few people on the walk from the train to the apartment and it seemed there were few residents in the building. Perhaps also, the Viennese wanted to remain indoors in February.

While he served the soup and bread, Elke asked, "What was Vienna like during the war?"

"Well, until we came in range of the British and American bombers the late summer of 1944, Vienna was spared. Before that, our main problem was food. Most went to our soldiers, so getting even potatoes and onions was rare. We still had our music and plays at the Burgtheatre, and opera performances continued. The Jews were all gone, so the quality of the performances were not up to our standards. But the deepest wound was the day the Opera building was hit. I didn't go to the opera much, but that building was Vienna to me. It represented the city I knew before the war. When the Russians took over, every day became a battle with hunger. We stood in long lines waiting for someone in authority to give us a little food—some dried peas, black bread. For breakfast, we ate a watery soup mixed with a little salt. Soon, no dogs or cats remained in the city.

"I suppose we were fortunate that Hitler didn't get a chance to destroy Vienna. I heard he ordered our complete destruction, but the German army was in no condition to carry out the order. I laugh, because the 6th Tank Army got its name because it had only six tanks. No soldier had more than a few rounds of ammunition.

"Now I am afraid you will find the city very dark because there is little electrical power available, and the black market rules everything. Almost anything is available, not in stores, but from a local black market representative; if you want bread, meat, coal, liquor, it is all available for a price."

Elke was disappointed in what she was hearing. She knew the war was wrong, but England had left Germany with no choice. Now England was doing the same wrong to us, there was no difference, she thought. They want to enslave Germany exactly the way Hitler wanted to enslave the Poles; now we are the Jews, the inferior race. They are letting us starve intentionally, a long slow death. She didn't believe the stories about gas chambers told by the Americans, but at least, she imagined, that death would be quick.

Walter continued, "In the early years, we supported the German *Anschluss* because we believed combining our countries would bring us jobs. The jobs came, and for many of us it was good. Then the rumors came of former government officials being sent to Dachau and the brutal revenge of anyone who had been a threat to the Nazis. Then our soldiers began dying on the Russian front, and finally, our cities were bombed. For months after the war there was no order, no transportation, no electricity, and no water in the tap, not even light bulbs available anywhere. Everybody was stealing, shivering, and starving on the streets. I remember the burnt-out center of St. Stephen's Cathedral, the shattered baroque facades, the boarded-up shops, the ruins. Our parks and squares had been dug up for air raid shelters. Wherever there is a patch of grass you see a scattering of white crosses of the graves of the Russians who died in their assault on the city. This is what Hitler and his National Socialism brought us."

This was not what Elke was accustomed to hearing about her country and leader. Her first impulse was to argue, but she was tired, it had been a long day, and she was anxious to spend the night in her old apartment. She bade Walter good night, thanked him profusely for the soup, and walked up the dark stairs that creaked noisily with each step.

At last, she was alone in the apartment. The walls themselves seemed to bring back memories of a conversation she had had with her parents when she visited from her job resettling Germans in their new homes in Poland. The question of German atrocities toward the Poles had come up. Father had viewed these an aberration. However, Mother saw the future in catastrophic terms. Elke could still hear her father's voice saying that even though some Germans were brutal, Germany was a cultured country and would not tolerate the mass slaughter of Poles or Jews. This controversy was not unique; Father refused to believe what seemed unreasonable, while Mother relied upon her intuition.

With sleep beginning to overtake Elke, the weird little man with the sable coat she had seen at the train station came into her thoughts. Why had he popped into her mind again? Sleep remained elusive during the night and Elke awoke to a cold February morning. She continued to lie in bed for some time, because it was the warmest place in the apartment. Her thoughts turned to her present state. She had no money, little chance of getting work, her parents were dead, and probably her brother, too. The future was as dark and bleak as the featureless territory of the Poland she had left.

Elke couldn't keep relying on Walter to feed her; he probably had little more than she did. Elke was fortunate to have shelter in the apartment, but she didn't know where to turn next. A couple of her friends in the BdM had committed suicide.

How difficult could that be? She could take poison. Would that be quick and painless? How about the gas stove in the kitchen? It would be painless, but how long would it take? A gun would be quick, but where would Elke get one? She could ask Walter, but he might know what it was for. Maybe, like Anna Karenina, the best would be to jump in front of a train?

She tried to put these thoughts out of her mind and think instead of Walter and a cup of hot coffee.

* * *

After a bit of coffee and a small piece of dry toast with Walter, Elke drew her old wool coat close around her and stepped outside into a piercing north wind. She walked with head down toward the Strassenbahn stop two blocks away along the familiar cobblestone street. She had taken this tram to school and the *tabak* store, it was a familiar place to get tram tickets, candy, or other small items. There were a few others waiting at the stop. They gave her curious looks: Who was this stranger in their neighborhood?

Soon the Number 38 tram rolled to a slow stop. Elke stepped up on the high step and found the one available seat. She looked at the other passengers and felt they could see her inner thoughts. "Can they tell how miserable I am? Do they see I'm thinking of ending my life?" The tram jerked into motion and began to move slowly and evenly. She felt the warm morning sun on her face through the window. The swaying motion of the train made her forget her fellow passengers and the dreadful thoughts from earlier. "Was I really created to be miserable for the rest of my life?"

She got off at the University stop and began to walk along the Ringstrasse that was once the major boulevard of a vibrant, beautiful city. She passed many other walkers enjoying the cold, sunny day. Women were bundled in colorful coats of red or blue; men wore business dress, with white shirts, ties, and jackets under heavy winter coats. Her spirits lifted a bit. She decided to continue walking to see what damage had been done. She passed the University building, which appeared untouched. She came to the gloomy neo-Gothic Rathaus (City Hall), a building she had always hated, but which, unhappily, she thought, had not been decimated by Allied bombs. However, the Burgtheater across from the Rathaus was nearly destroyed.

She had heard it had not been bombed, but during the street fighting for the city in April, a fire had started near the stage. With no firefighting brigade in Vienna, it had spread to the entire building. She had seen many Mozart arias performed there. She continued toward the Parliament building, which she had loved as a little girl. Built in the classical style of white marble that recalled the Greek cradle of democracy and guarded by a statue of the goddess Athena, it stood out in shining splendor and breathed neo-classic serenity compared with the Rathaus next door.

She walked across the Ringstrasse toward the Augustinian Church, a Gothic church where weddings and funerals of the Habsburg family had been held since the fourteenth century. Here Elke had heard the works of Mozart, Hayden, and Schubert. She had looked forward to visiting this church on special occasions, especially for Christmas and Easter Masses, but upon entering the church she felt melancholy, and paused. Gathering her courage, she sat at a pew in the back and gazed at the east window of stained glass she had enjoyed in the company of her family. Overwhelmed with sadness, she left and went onto

Josefsplatz, a small area among the huge buildings of the Hofberg Palace which honors Emperor Josef II.

She had, of course, learned in school about Josef, who had ruled the Austrian empire toward the end of the eighteenth century. She stopped to admire the statue of him in the center of the square. He was dressed as a Roman Emperor, wearing a toga and crowned with a laurel wreath. She remembered the toga was meant to tie Josef to the Roman Emperor Marcus Aurelius, who had ruled Vienna and died there centuries earlier. While in school, Elke had loved reading Aurelius's *Meditations*. She decided to go to the nearby National Library to look for a copy.

She smiled as she caught sight of the classical facade of the building, one of the largest and most beautiful libraries in the world. Memories came back of the many school days spent here surrounded by the high windows in the domed Great Hall, a dream in marble, gold, and sunlight, with an unbelievable number of books; they stretched to the ceiling.

With apprehension, she asked the gentleman at the desk about *Meditations;* surprisingly, they still had her membership card on file. Some things in Vienna had not changed. She chose a table near the back of the hall for privacy. She opened the book to a random page, hoping to find comfort in reading the stoic philosopher about whom she had written a report during her last year at school. Her thoughts of death this morning had frightened her. Even though she feared death, she also feared life, not knowing where it would take her. She began to read:

> *All that you pray to reach at some point in the circuit of your*
> *life can be yours now—if you are generous to yourself. That is, if*
> *you leave all the past behind, entrust to Providence, and direct*
> *the present solely to reverence and justice. To reverence, so that*
> *you come to love your given lot: it was nature that brought it*

*to you and you to it. To justice, so that you are open and direct
in words and action, speaking the truth, observing law and
proportion in all you do. You should let nothing stand in your
way—not the iniquity of others, not what anyone else thinks or
says, still less any sensation of this poor flesh that has accreted
round you: the afflicted part must see to its own concern.*

Elke began to feel comfort from the book, and from the books
on the shelves surrounding her. She continued to read, finding other
passages that moved her, including this one:

*Has something happened to you? Fine. All that happens
has been fated by the whole from the beginning and spun for
your own destiny. In sum, life is short: make your gain from the
present moment with right reason and justice. Keep sober and
relaxed. No, you do not have thousands of years to live. Urgency
is on you. While you live, while you can become good.*

She closed the book. Leaving it on the table she walked back outside
through the great doors. The afternoon was almost gone; she realized
she was hungry. At a soup kitchen near the church she had a bowl
of hot potato soup, then walked toward the tram stop to wait for the
Number 38. Unlike in the morning, people hurried past her without
notice. A little further on she came across a group of people huddled
in front of a billboard. Most were silent, but some shook their heads
and walked away. The sign read: "Who is guilty?" Beneath those words
were photographs of human skeletons, charred bones, prisoners in
striped uniforms hanging from gibbets, and dead children, obviously
from starvation. Some in the crowd moaned and one or two stifled a
cry, but generally they looked on in silence before moving away. Elke
walked on, telling herself that she was indifferent.

Getting off the train, Elke felt the cold wind and found herself dreading the loneliness of the empty apartment. The snow was ankle deep on the pavement. As she walked toward the apartment building, she noticed four men wearing worn Wehrmacht army coats warming their hands around a fire in a metal oil drum. It crossed her mind that maybe one had known Fritz. She walked over to them, but before she could say anything, a bearded man offered her the bottle of vodka they were sharing. With no hesitation, which she could tell the men appreciated, she took a long pull.

Elke noticed the regiment insignia on their coats, and said, "Were you all in the Eastern front? My brother was in the Stalingrad area. His name was Fritz Baur." The oldest man, about forty, said, "Was he in the Wehrmacht or the SS? We tried to stay far away from the SS."

"I think he was in the SS, but I don't remember his regiment. That was a long time ago," she said sadly.

A younger soldier added, "We were all on the Western front, in France and Belgium. We were luckier than the guys that went east. Few of them survived. Even if they were taken prisoner, the chance of survival was not good."

Elke knew she couldn't stay long with men she didn't know. "I really must get home to my husband," she lied.

"One more drink for the road, *Fräulein*," the bearded soldier said, handing her the bottle back. "It will be a long night."

"I really must go, but I do need this," she said, and took another long pull.

Walter's door was closed when she returned. The creak of the floorboards was now familiar as she approached the apartment door. Again, she thought of Fritz: *It has been two years since the war ended. The Russians would have released him by now if he were alive.* She knew even lucky soldiers would not survive a Russian prison camp. She started to put her key in the lock when she noticed the door knocker. Nothing unusual about it except Fritz had made it out of metal and installed it on the front door. *Why am I thinking of him now?*

It was not a spacious apartment, but it seemed especially large with most of the furniture missing. She remembered the long solid-oak dining room table where she loved to sit and talk with her mother after school . . . the overstuffed chair her father would sit in at night, to listen to the radio or read the newspaper and complain about Hitler . . . the bookshelves with father's precious books. These were all gone, giving the place an even gloomier feeling.

The vodka was making her sleepy, and she changed into her flannel pajamas. It may have been the vodka, her fatigue, or her loneliness, but she thought she could see that strange little man from the train station—not an actual person, but a transparent image. Yet she could see the shapes of the long sable coat, the red hat, even the crow-handled walking stick.

"Who are you and what do you want with me?" Elke asked this without expecting an answer from what she felt was some sort of apparition.

"Who I am is not important. I have come to bring light into your life." A mischievous grin spread across the apparition's face, as though he knew something she did not.

"Well, I don't believe in ghosts; I choose to believe you are really a bit of undigested potato soup or that second drink of vodka."

"Oh! My dear, I don't know if I am a ghost, as you say, but in life I was a writer, and I was able to bring justice to some in need."

"My life isn't worth changing and I don't know why I am talking to a funny-looking old man."

"Ah, I have learned in my long existence that all lives are worth saving."

"Isn't that what Jesus was sent on earth to do, to save souls?" Elke said this with a hint of disdain.

"My dear, your heart is filled with hatred, hypocrisy, superstition, and intolerance; you are a special case."

"How long have you lived in the spirit world? Did I read your writings in school? Why am I talking to a figment of my imagination?"

"If you read my writings, you learned nothing from them. I am not blaming you alone, but your generation and your homeland. I know the hatred and intolerance that consumed your people. You yourself have been spared the true horrors of the past, but you still burn with the same hatreds and superstitions that have consumed your fellow Austrians. I have come to help you make your world better, for you and for others. Your world is *not* the best of all possible worlds. You can make a better life for yourself by cultivating your own garden, but first you must overturn the old dirt of hypocrisy, pull out the weeds of superstition, and cut back the brambles of intolerance. Only then can the beautiful flowers and delicious fruits of life be yours."

"Why do you come to me? I have hurt no one." Elke almost shouted those words. Tears formed in her eyes. She fell to her knees, almost begging the apparition to believe her.

The specter seemed to move closer. "Are you sure you bear no responsibility for the millions killed? What did you think when Jews were being carried off from their homes and businesses? You thought, 'I am not Jewish, so I don't care.' When you saw troops of Brown Shirts swaggering their way down the streets looking for trouble, what did you do? Nothing, because you felt it wasn't your concern. I am afraid I see in you the hypocrisy and madness of all Austria."

Elke, almost hypnotized by what she was seeing and hearing, said, "I was but one person, what could I do?"

"It became easy for you and your fellow Austrians to turn your heads and pretend you do not see. Why must you follow the blind who cry out for you to hate, persecuting all who are rash enough not to be of the same opinion as yourselves? A spirit of indulgence would make us all brothers; a spirit of persecution creates nothing but monsters.

Remember, your garden will not be cultivated on its own. You must work to cultivate that garden."

Before Elke could reply, the specter seemed to fade through the wall and into the night. She ran to the window to see if this ghost could fly, but was greeted by darkness and the cold, frosted glass. She crawled into bed, trying to make sense of what she had experienced. Maybe it was the vodka. The day had been too much for Elke; a morning spent contemplating suicide, a walk around a now-ravaged city she loved, and finally, a strange fantasy of an old man.

But what if he was right? Could the war have been prevented if she and others had acted differently? Why did we simply ignore what was going on in front of our eyes? She thought of her parents, especially her father, and how bravely he had fought in the first war, and how proud she was of him.

5

Captain
Viktor Baur

1918

The mostly European conflict known as the Great War was winding down. The adversaries had exhausted themselves after more than four years of futile attacks on each other's trenches. To the dispassionate observer, the final winners appeared to be Germany and Austria, which had hardly been touched by the war. Towns, buildings and farmlands were serene, even peaceful.

By contrast, northeast France, where most of the war had been fought, appeared like a wasteland. Entire towns had been obliterated. Exploded and unexploded artillery shells rendered the farmlands unusable.

Like Germany and Austria, France and her ally England had each lost a generation of young men. Though America had not entered the war until 1917, it had sacrificed 117,000 young men of its own. The end to the fighting came on 11 November, 1918. All of Europe faced a difficult future.

Capt. Viktor Baur, of the Sixth Austrian Infantry Regiment, awoke on his cot to another hot July day in northern France. His regiment had been assigned to the German First Army for additional support in what most believed were the final weeks of the war. The front line was quieter than usual, and Viktor wondered if the end of the war was indeed near, or if this was merely the quiet before the next storm. Rumors were flying that they were to be part of a major offensive to try to break the French line held by the Second and Fourth French armies. The prize was Paris, less than a hundred miles to the west. After four years of bloody war, the German Army was exhausted. Germany asked for help from her ally, Austria.

Capt. Baur had received no orders for another attack on the French trenches, but sometimes things happened quickly. It was about an hour before dawn, always the worst hour of the day for Viktor. He found sleep impossible. To take his mind off the war, he forced it back to better days. He had been a student at university when the war began in 1914, and had been allowed to finish his degree in economics before joining the army in early 1916. He had spent those years training at the officer's school and later in the Quartermaster Corps. With the war dragging on, he was called up to replace casualties on the front lines. Viktor considered himself fortunate to have survived thus far. But no one wanted to be the last man to die in this awful war.

Capt. Baur was a handsome young Austrian with blond hair cut short in the fashion of the day. His bright blue eyes sparkled when he spoke. He stood about six two and carried himself proudly as a member of the Austrian Army.

As an officer, he took his responsibilities to his men seriously. He made sure they had the appropriate equipment, were fed as well as possible, and were properly outfitted. He believed that in return, his men respected him and felt they were treated sternly but fairly. His best friend, Capt. Christian Müeller, had command of another company within the regiment. Christian was also tall, yet gangly; someone who always seemed a bit undone but whose charming personality made him a favorite with his teachers and fellow officers.

Christian had been Viktor's best friend since gymnasium; they'd grown up together in Vienna's 19th District. Viktor admired Christian; he appeared fearless, and was the school athlete Viktor aspired to be. Although not what one would call good-looking, Christian attracted all the girls. He'd always known he wanted to be a career army officer. Upon graduation from gymnasium, mostly on the strength of his athletic ability, he was admitted to the Military School and commissioned in June 1914.

Capt. Baur had something different to live for. His wife, Else, in far-away Vienna, was due to give birth to their second child in November. She was living in a small apartment with their four-year-old son, Fritz. After seeing the misery of war firsthand, Viktor was hoping for a daughter who would never have to experience what her father had during the last two years. He offered a small prayer for the health of his wife and new baby, and that Fritz would be spared from war. His mind drifted back to his brief leave in February with Else and Fritz. They had spent a wonderful day at the Prater, Vienna's vast public park along the right bank of the Danube, watching Fritz sled down hill after hill. He especially remembered another day with Else in the wine country outside the city. Four-year-old Fritz was staying with Else's parents so they could have some time by themselves. How beautiful were the vineyards in the Austrian winter, the white snow contrasting with the bluish-green acacia twigs with their red thorns. Along the roadside, hidden among the trees and hedges were tunnels with stone-vaulted ceilings and steep steps leading straight down into abundant wine cellars. The lovers were greeted by the owner of one such cellar with a *"Grüss Gott Herr* Captain," a greeting that expressed the comradeship of those who work the vineyards.

"Ja, danka, un wein, bitte?" replied Viktor.

A white candle softly illuminated a few small round tables and chairs, and wine glasses hanging from hooks on wooden racks. The wine they drank warmed their bodies and hearts. The cavern, surrounded by warm earthen walls, was restful. Else looked especially beautiful, with her blond hair bright in the candlelight and her playful grin that Viktor loved. His fears of returning to the battlefield were forgotten during that idyllic afternoon, when the world shrank to what lay within reach of the flickering light.

Sadly, his leave was short; he was soon to return to the front lines. Viktor remembered the morning he left Vienna. He and Else let little Fritz sleep to spare him their emotional farewell. They looked at each other, afraid to speak, realizing they might never see each other again. Tears were beginning to form in Else's eyes. Viktor reached for her hand and said, "Sweetheart, let's be brave. I will get through this. I want to help win this war so that Fritz will never see the same in his lifetime."

"Oh Viktor, if anything good comes from this war, it will be the betterment of our children's world. God keep you safe."

"Take care of Fritz. I am sure I will be back soon," he said, holding her close.

After five more grueling months, those words seemed hollow. Viktor's men no longer wanted to fight and kill, but to go home to family and friends. What kind of Austria would he find if he was fortunate enough to see Vienna again?

Viktor roused himself from thoughts of home, put on his grey service uniform, and went to the Orderly Room for breakfast. Today it was potato pancakes for the officers.

"I am sure today is the day for the offensive," Christian said, as Viktor sat down beside him.

"Why today, when you have been saying this for a week?"

"Gen. Ludendorff asked me if this was a good time," Christian said, laughing.

"Ludendorff is probably safe in Berlin," Viktor grumbled.

"*Nein*, actually we have a company commander's meeting at zero eight hundred and First Army's Gen. Rethel is conducting it. I would be there if I were you."

"Gen. Rethel himself, huh? Maybe you are right for once. Hope he won't mind if I don't change my uniform, I have nothing cleaner than this."

"*Nein*, Rethel is a good guy. He taught me mathematics at military school. If he can teach me math, he must be a good guy."

"All right, but first I must eat," Viktor said.

At exactly 0800, the Orderly Room, which two hours earlier had been filled with the aroma of coffee and pancakes, now held chairs and war maps, and the faint smell of coffee. The officers came to attention when Gen. Rethel entered. Viktor was pleased to see that the general was in a mud-splattered uniform, similar to his and Christian's.

"Gentlemen, I won't keep you long. Things will get serious very soon. Ludendorff has decided to shift our effort south against the French," he said, slapping his wooden pointer against the large map behind him, which showed battlefront of northeast France and Belgium. "Our Sixth Army can hold the British First and Third Armies at bay while Blücher with the Seventh Army and our First Army will attack the French Sixth here, along the Marne River. This area is favored because of the grain fields along the valley of the Oise River. Also, Paris is just seventy miles away. If we succeed here, we will be able to renew the offensive in the north." He pointed to the village of Ypres. "We will deploy our long-range guns, our "Big Bertha's" as the British and Americans call them. Their range of seventy-five miles will force the British to move south to defend Paris. Our six thousand artillery or so and two million shells will give us the advantage.

"Gentlemen, today is July 14th, a holiday for the Frenchies." The officers in the room laughed nervously. "We have fifty-two divisions lined up for attack tomorrow. We will be in Paris by nightfall. Let's help the Frenchies celebrate their holiday. That is all, gentlemen. Good luck."

The officers rose to attention with smiles. The feeling in the room was that this was Germanys last role of the dice to win the war, with Paris the trophy.

The Second Battle of The Marne

The night was unbearable. At 0300, Viktor was wide awake, staring at the ceiling of his tent. He had given up trying to sleep, knowing the big guns would begin their pounding at dawn. He had spent the last two years in the trenches, and he knew tomorrow was not promised to anyone. His anxiety heightened with each moment. Finally, he walked over to Christian's tent under a heavily overcast sky. He whispered, "Christian, are you awake?"

"Well, I am now, thanks to you."

Despite his sarcastic remark, Christian was happy to see his friend and glad for the company.

"I have heard so many rumors that this war is finally about to be over, yet many will die today," Viktor said.

"*Ja*, and you don't want to be one of them. Your problem, Viktor, is you have never accepted the fact we are both already dead. To be a "good German" we must believe we are already dead, only the time hasn't come yet. If it does, it was destined. And if it doesn't, we will go on with our lives. That way we will be able to do what our ancestors expect of us."

"I keep thinking back to the memories of our good times together. When I first met Else and you were seeing Ilse. She was a beautiful girl, so outgoing and personable."

"*Ja*," replied Christian looking down at the floor of the tent, "I was not ready for marriage. Else has made a good wife for you. I hope, more than anything, you get through this to see your new child. When is Else due again?"

"In mid-November."

"Let's hope the war is over by then."

"My hope is that Fritz will never see war."

"Ah, Viktor, we must think positive. This war will soon end and we will find good jobs. I will find a woman who will provide me with children who will grow up in a peaceful, law-abiding world, one with no Bolshies or Jews, only good God-fearing Christians who work together for a unified Europe."

"It is a nice dream, Christian, but such a dream will never happen" replied Viktor.

"Well, I will then dream of a large-busted German woman and she will give me lots of sons to fight the Bolsheviks and the Jews."

"I had better get back to my men; the artillery will begin soon." Hurrying back to his company, Viktor noticed the overcast sky had parted to reveal a bright moon. He had a sense of satisfaction seeing his veterans, confident in their trenches, with the moonlight glistening off their helmets. To Viktor, they resembled knights of a forgotten time; the sight was strangely beautiful and arresting.

A few minutes before dawn, balls of light rose high in the sky, where silver and red spheres exploded, then rained down on his men. These French rockets unfolded like silk parachutes. They drifted down slowly and lit up the sky so brilliantly, his men saw their shadows on the ground. Then came the rattling bursts of the machine guns.

Viktor's fears were realized; the French had anticipated the German offensive and opened fire first with their twelve-inch guns. He knew one would hear the explosion of the shells before hearing the sound of the guns.

This was the time when a soldier understood the term "Mother Earth." He would press himself down upon her body and bury his face into her bosom. The earth became his friend, his brother, and his mother. He stifled his urge to cry in his terror, and with each exploding shell he thanked mother earth for giving him shelter and allowing him to live for another second.

Finally, the shelling began to fall behind them, freeing Viktor and his men to hurl their hand grenades at the French and charge out of their trenches. No one would believe in this howling world there could still be men alive, but steel helmets appeared on both sides of the trench. Not fifty yards away a machine gun barked; this time it was the German guns responding. Viktor recognized the distorted faces and smooth helmets of the French, who had suffered heavily by the time they reached the barbed wire. Their whole line had gone down before the German machine guns. Viktor saw a Frenchman fall into the barbed wire fence, his body collapsing against the wire, his hands remaining suspended on the fence as if he were praying. Then his body dropped clean away, with only his hands and the stumps of his arms left hanging onto the wire.

The sky lit up again. This time green rocks and fragments of mud whizzed by. Viktor crawled along the ground until he fell into a bomb crater, thinking that rarely do shells land twice in the same place. His men paused to reload and the French advanced, attempting to outflank his men from the right. He ordered his machine guns to sweep the area in front of them. Now the cooling water for the guns had evaporated. A container was hastily passed around for the men to urinate into, to provide liquid to cool the guns. All of this happened in seconds.

So preoccupied had Viktor been that he only now noticed a fair-haired young recruit sitting beside him in the shell crater, crying from sheer terror. The boy's helmet had fallen off. He buried his head in his hands and like a small child, crept under Viktor's arm, his head nestled against Viktor's breast. Wanting to give the boy comfort, Viktor at the same time cursed the war that involved young boys.

Attacks alternated with counterattacks. Slowly, the dead piled up in the field of craters between the trenches. By late afternoon, the battle had moved on to other sectors. This allowed Viktor and his men to begin the grim task of retrieving their wounded. Many would have a long wait.

Viktor had been fighting so long, he could tell how seriously a man was wounded by the sound of his voice. If the soldier was severely wounded, his body would soon exhaust itself and he would segue into a dream state. It had begun to get dark when they heard a cry for help. Men were sent toward the sound of the voice, but no one was found. This occurred three times; when the men got to where they thought they heard the cry, the voice would seem to come from somewhere else. Some men searched all night. The next day the area was searched with field glasses. The man's voice slowly got hoarse and fainter; obviously his lips and mouth had become dry. Viktor promised three days leave to anyone who could find the soldier. That was a powerful incentive, but Viktor knew the men would continue the search despite the reward, because the cry was painful to hear. At first, the man had cried only for help. By the second night he had become delirious and talked to his wife and children. By evening his voice dwindled to a croak.

That summer of 1918 was the bloodiest and most terrible of the war, Viktor thought. It seemed every man knew Germany was losing, but the fighting went on. Wild rumors of an armistice and peace were constantly in the air. Never was life on the line more bitter and filled with horror than when, with each bombardment, men clutched at only one thought: *No! No! Not now!*

Letter to Father
28 OCTOBER 1918

Dear Father,

*I hope this finds you well. Physically I am fine, but men-
tally it is a different story. We continue to hear rumors the
war is nearly over. It is a miracle from God that it looks like
both Christian and myself may survive this war.*

*Else is due to give birth in about three weeks. I am hoping
for a daughter, since no one's son should have to experience what
Christian and I have. With the grace of God all will be healthy
and never see another war. I think of you often and hope your
health improves, as I look forward to seeing you soon. I hear
this flu is a serious thing, so take care of yourself.*

*I don't know what kind of Austria Christian and I will be
returning to or what jobs we can find. Christian is determined
to stay in the army and the army will benefit, because he is a
first-rate officer. I, for one, am sick of the army and would like
to put my degree in economics to work at a bank in Vienna.
However, my experience since my graduation from university
has been far away from economics, unless you are talking about
the economics of staying alive.*

*Oh father, the weapons are so much different from when you
were in the army. The bayonet has practically lost its importance.
It is now the fashion to charge with a sharpened spade and
bombs. The sharpened spade is handier, because it can be used
to jab a man under his chin. And because of its weight, if one
hits between the neck and shoulder it easily cleaves as far down
as the chest. The bayonet frequently jams on the thrust and a*

man must kick hard on the other fellow to pull it out again; in the interval he may easily get one himself.

The battle aeroplanes don't trouble us as they are not very accurate, but we hate the observation aeroplanes; they put the artillery onto us. A couple of minutes after the planes appear, shrapnel and high explosives begin to drop. We lost eleven men the other day from this. One man had the lower part of his body and legs torn off. His chest was leaning against the side of the trench, his face, a lemon-yellow color. In his beard was a still-burning cigarette.

The tanks are also terrible weapons. They roll into bomb craters and climb out again without stopping. It is like a fleet of smoke-belching, armor-clad, invulnerable steel beasts come to crush the dead and wounded. Men are no longer men but 'manpower'; humans are being replaced by machines and human values no longer matter. The war has become a machine to which human lives are inconsequential.

Our greatest fear, however, is when you think the bombardment is over, you just begin to relax, thinking you have made it for another few minutes when someone yells, "Gas, gas, pass it on." I grab for my gas mask. Inside the mask my head booms and roars—my lungs are nigh bursting. We breath hot, used-up air, and the veins on my temple swell! Sitting in the hole and waiting for the gas to clear, I feel as if I am suffocating. At the "all clear" I climb out over the edge of the shell-hole. In the dirty twilight my eyes fall on a leg that is torn clean off; the boot looks like it has not been touched.

A surprise gas-attack carries off many young soldiers who have not yet learned what to do. We found one shell-hole full of them, with blue faces and bloody lips. They had taken their masks off too soon; they didn't know the gas lies longest in the hollows. When they saw others up top without masks they pulled

*theirs off to help and swallowed enough to scald their lungs. They
choked to death with hemorrhage and suffocation.*

*Another horror are the rats. They have become much more
numerous because our trenches are no longer in good condition.
The rats are particularly repulsive because they are so fat—we
call them corpse rats. Almost every man in my company has had
his bread gnawed. Some put the bread under their sheet and
then under their head but can't sleep because the rats run over
their faces to get at the bread. We can't afford to throw it away
because we have so little to eat. In the morning we carefully cut
off the bits the rats have gnawed.*

*Father, please understand why I am writing all this. I finally
feel Christian and I will survive, so I feel more comfortable telling you what I have seen. It's not what they put in the war news
about the good humor of the troops, how we are arranging dances
and such. We are often in good humor; otherwise we would go
to pieces. If we didn't find some humor we could not hold out,
but our humor becomes more bitter with each passing month.*

*Why does no one tell us the enemy are just poor devils like
us, with the same dying and the same agony, and their mothers
are just as anxious as ours? How senseless this all is; it must all
be lies and of no account when the culture of a thousand years
could not prevent this stream of blood that has flowed. Go to
any hospital and you will see what war is about.*

*Our meal tonight is ham and pea soup. I had only a portion,
because some say if you are wounded in the stomach with a full
belly, that is more dangerous than having an empty one. I eat
what my men eat, but we are all emaciated and starved. The
food is bad and mixed with so much substitute stuff it makes
us ill. The Jewish factory owners have grown wealthy while
dysentery dissolves our bowels. Some say it doesn't make sense*

to pull up one's trousers after using the latrine because you will soon be back.

We are short of everything. For every German aeroplane there are at least five English and American ones. For every German soldier who is hungry and wretched, come five of the enemy, looking fresh and fit. For the German soldier with one bread loaf, there are fifty tins of canned beef waiting to feed our enemy. Father, as soldiers we are better, more experienced than the other side; we are simply crushed and driven back by overwhelming, superior forces.

We can't bring in all the dead that lie unburied. Even if we could, we wouldn't know what to do with them all. The next shells will bury them anyway. We see men lying with their skulls blown open; we see soldiers run with their feet cut off, they stagger on their splintered stumps into the next shell hole. I saw a man come into the dressing station and over his clasped hands bulged his intestines; we see men without mouths, without jaws, without a face; one man held the artery of his arm in his teeth for two hours to keep from bleeding to death.

Despite all that, yesterday I saw two butterflies playing in front of my trench. They were brimstone butterflies, with red spots on their yellow wings. What could they be looking for here, when there is not a plant nor a flower for miles? I watched when they finally settled on the teeth of a skull. The birds also are accustomed to the war and are just as carefree. Every morning larks ascend from "No Man's Land." A year ago we watched them nesting; the young ones have grown up now.

Oh Father, everyone talks of peace and armistice. I fear the people will not go on like this forever and may someday resort to revolution. Winter is getting close. The skies have turned grey with almost constant rain. When shells explode, they throw up frozen clods of earth, just as dangerous as shell fragments. Our uniforms are caked with mud. I so want this to stop, I dream of our home in Vienna. I want to see again the clear Austrian mornings, the Sunday afternoons when we would stroll through the country and enjoy the green vineyards, the small alehouses. When I was a child you made me feel so grown-up having wine with you and mother in those wine-cellars.

I know nothing now but despair, death, and fear. I see how people are set against each other. I know I have rambled on, but I need to put down on paper what war is truly like. If I don't make it to the end of the war, at least you will have my view of what I have seen.

Give my love to mother and hopefully, I will see you both soon.

~Your homesick and loving son, Viktor

6

Christian Müeller

1913–1918

Looking at a map of the Austro-Hungarian Empire in 1913, one would see lands that stretched from Switzerland in the west halfway to the Black Sea in the east, from the Russian and German empires in the north to the Balkans in the south. Within this vast area lay mountains and lakes, vineyards and fishing villages, snow and sun. The land yielded iron and coal from Bohemia, a Galicia that produced its own oil, and thousands of acres of farmland to feed the population, which made these particular lands self-sufficient. Some areas were rich and industrialized, like Germany; others were poor, like Russia. The empire was as varied as the world itself. It traded with itself and invested in itself; it really was its own world.

The map became more complex when one considered language. Near the Italian border, Emperor Franz Josef's subjects spoke Italian. German was spoken along the Swiss border to the Danube, and then along the German border. In the heartlands of Bohemia and in Prague, Czech was predominant, but not exclusive. Moving further east, the main language became Polish;

moving south, Slovak was spoken. At the eastern extremity, the peasants spoke a dialect of, essentially, Ukrainian, while Polish was spoken in the large cities of the region.

Each of these groups differed in attitude toward the empire and the places within it. At the Austrian Parliament in Vienna, ten languages were spoken yet there were no interpreters, and all writing was in German only. It was an unusual session that didn't witness the throwing of insults and inkstands. It seemed a miracle that such a variety of lands could be held together under this structure. In 1914, the Viennese satirist Karl Kraus called the empire a "proving ground for world destruction."

The week of 13 January 1913 was Carnival time in Vienna; a time for the residents to revel in what they were not. A glacial wind blew down the Ringstrasse and snow capped the hundreds of rooftop statues that adorned the boulevard's palatial edifices. While ice flowed on the Danube, gala affairs sparkled inside baroque portals. At the Vienna Bank Employees Club, several ladies appeared in costume as balance sheets, displaying voluptuous assets curving up from two slender debits. Others came costumed as deposits, and fat men as withdrawals. The merriment increased steadily until 5:00 a.m., when the orchestra leader promptly stopped the music in the middle of the *Emperor Waltz* to announce, to great laughter, that since the musicians had not been paid there would be no more music.

This fairy tale of Habsburg splendor, choreographed with pomp, precedence, raised trumpets, white stallions, and bowed heads had been enacted and reenacted for over 500 years. During Carnival, everything Viennese seemed to celebrate what was no longer. In the Vienna of January 1913, illusion and reality embraced, elegantly and seamlessly. However, under the surface seethed a witch's brew of nationalism.

Six million Czechs attacked ten million Germans for underfinanc-
ing Czech schools in Bohemia and Moravia. Five million Galician Poles
banged on Parliamentary desks to demand greater administrative
independence. Three and a half million Ukrainians stamped feet for a
Russian language university to counter the Poles' cultural domination.

*   *   *

On Friday evening of the first week of January, Christian Müeller,
a young officer kadet at Austria's military school, was walking with
his latest love interest, Ilse Dietrich, whom he had first met, quite by
chance, only yesterday at the open-air dance in front of the Rathaus.
Christian was captivated by the pretty petite brunette with the lovely
smile. The evening was quite cold, and her figure was hidden by a
heavy wool coat of a quality that made Christian assume that she, or
someone she knew, had money. The two drank a beer at one of the
stands and enjoyed each other's company enough to agree to meet
the next evening at the parquet dance floor, which was laid down for
the Carnival celebration.

"Are you warm enough?" asked Christian while they strolled the
perimeter of the dance floor, trying to avoid the merrymaking crowd
surrounding it. Ilse was obviously impressed with the young soldier in
the light blue uniform. His shoulder boards signified he was a second
class with one year until graduation. As they turned a corner on the
dance floor, a voice rang out, "Christian, Christian Müeller!" Christian
turned to see his friend Viktor Baur with a tall blonde on his arm.

"Viktor, how are you?"

"Christian, I am fine! I want you to meet Else Heusinger, very
soon to be Else Baur," said Viktor with pleasure.

"Well, well, well, you damn bastard. I will soon be an officer and
you will graduate from university. We could get all the girls we want
and you are going to be married," Christian said with a laugh. He

quickly added, "I am kidding, Else. I tried to get Viktor into all kinds of trouble in school, but he is much smarter and more mature than I. You have a good man here."

"*Danke*, Christian. Viktor has told me a lot about you," replied Else.

"Well, I hope he hasn't told you too much," said Christian, adding quickly. "You are still at university, Viktor?"

"*Ja*, it has been slow, because I am studying economics; it will take me another couple of years to graduate."

"Let's talk about it over drinks at the Café Central. I really like that place; some very interesting people go there."

Vienna was a city of cafés, and with the current political climate, each had its own style and special clientele. Each was a place where cake, newspapers, chess, and above all, talk, were passions. And Vienna was teeming with passion, especially when it came to the political discord between the Social-Democrats (left wing) and the Christian-Socialists (right wing).

A few days earlier, Franz Schuhmeier, the prominent and popular deputy of the Social-Democratic Party, had been shot and killed at the Nordbanhoff train station. A slight figure in a torn raincoat had yelled, "My revenge!" and fired a bullet through the back of Schuhmeier's skull. The gunman, Paul Kunschak, was the brother of a leader of the opposing party, the Christian-Socialists. He turned out to be a mumbling paranoiac who had convinced himself that Schuhmeier had persecuted him personally. He had planned the murder without his brother's knowledge.

The significance of the tragedy lay less in the politics than the timing. Carnival was about to end. The incident brought home to a reluctant Vienna that the levity and conviviality of Carnival make believe were also over. The Viennese could no longer play-act away the reality of their city's politics.

*   *   *

During the next several days, the political environment provided a pull to the two young friends who began to spend more free time together, mainly at Café Central. Rumors had it that several Russian spies were regulars. Both Christian and Viktor were intrigued by the strange-looking clientele.

"Did you go to the Schuhmeier funeral?" Viktor said, pulling out a cigarette and offering one to Christian.

"Hardly, the army didn't want any part of that mess," replied Christian, lighting up. "I understand over a quarter of a million men and women accompanied the coffin to the gravesite. I heard whole families streamed out of the tenements to join the crowd."

"We have some real problems coming," Viktor said. "In that district of Vienna, Ottakring, only five percent of all people have a room of their own. Nearly half the houses have no running water. More than a third of the staircases are without gaslight, never mind electricity. The mortality rate is twice as high as the upper-class districts where you and I were brought up."

The Schuhmeier burial had not been a traditional Viennese funeral. Called *Schöne Leiche*—the Beautiful Corpse—a funeral was often the only "opera" a proletarian could afford. When dead, he became a star. At the Schuhmeier burial, there was no one draped in sable, no opulence of wreaths, no black-clad band trumpeting a majestic succession of dirges. There was just a simple hearse with a virtual ocean of people following along behind, the men wearing frayed caps; the women in wrinkled head scarfs. Some people pushed prams, some thumped along on crutches, all walked in silence. Most were well aware that a few weeks earlier, the Austrian Parliament had killed a bill that would have subsidized the installation of plumbing in apartments with no sanitation. Most families in the district were forced to use outside toilets. In the late winter of 1913, Vienna had not awoken to the simmering discontent of its citizens.

*   *   *

As the winter turned to spring, the city came alive again, although due to a lack of rain, the leaves and flowers had not yet budded. Demel's, a favorite place known for its pastries and chocolates, signaled the season with iced coffee topped with a tiara of whipped cream.

There was a new entertainment in the city, called the cinema. Christian, Ilse, Viktor, and Else were among the first to attend. *Dante's Inferno* was showing at the Graben Kino, a theatre with comfortable seats, walls of silk, and an orchestra of two pianos and three violins to add lyricism to the shadows on the screen.

The four lovers walked out of the theatre and headed to Stadtpark to enjoy themselves on a warm day. The park was crowded with people. Peacocks strutted under trees ready to explode with leaves at the first rain. White roses garlanded four-wheeled carriages that brought children to their first communion. The girls were like flowers in their snowy lace dresses; the boys wore white carnations in the buttonholes of their dark suits. In the midst of this, the four sat around an outdoor table enjoying the weather and some new wine. The conversation had been lighthearted until Christian broke in with, "You know, we may be at war soon. If Montenegro [a country next door to Serbia on the Adriatic Sea] doesn't pull their troops out of Albania, we will have to go in and force the issue."

"How will that affect you?" asked a worried Ilse.

"Well, they can always commission me early. My grades have me near the top of my class. I have found my calling with the army, and I am anxious to prove my skills as a warrior and a leader. Austria has a fine army, led by fine officers who can easily defeat any army in Europe."

"Oh, Christian, his Majesty will force Montenegro's forces to move out," Viktor said with a slight wave of his hand. "The problem is Serbia. Montenegro is merely at Serbia's beck and call, but we must have stability in the Balkans, regardless of Serbian repercussions. What do you think Russia will do?"

Christian's eyes brightened. "We've just heard a lecture from a colonel, Alfred Redl. He is an intelligence specialist, a really brilliant man, and he gave us an analysis of the growing underground movement in Serbia directed against the Austrian Empire. He says that the Russian blunders concerning Serbia have drawn Austria closer to Germany against the claims of the Serbian nationalists. I tell you I was so impressed by this officer. Col. Redl is a leader that men will follow and learn from. I hope to be that kind of officer."

"What more did he say?" Victor asked.

Christian glanced around to be sure no one was within hearing distance. "Well, Redl is in charge of Austrian counterintelligence. Austria and Germany work together exchanging mutually relevant information. Redl said there is a growing movement in Bohemia directed against the Habsburg Empire. He also gave us an assessment of Montenegro's army and showed us how potent this small force actually is. It all made me realize we are closer to war than anyone thinks."

"Oh, Christian, I hope you are misjudging," said Else with obvious emotion.

"I just don't want anything to start until I can be in it. I have dreamed about leading men into battle since I was a small boy. Great battles with swords, helmets, and high castles with their sweep and fire. If I am to die, I wish it to be in battle. A hero's death is how I want to die, not in some hospital, slowly wasting away."

The two couples separated, but thoughts of a possible war lingered. On the walk back to Else's small apartment, she asked Viktor what he would do if war came.

"Unless it is a long war, I am sure I would be allowed to stay at University. Serbia is a small country and no match for our armies."

"Viktor, if Germany and Russia get into this, and maybe even France, it will be a long war." Viktor could hear the fear in her voice.

"That will never happen, those countries would never get involved in a Habsburg dispute." Viktor gave Else one last kiss and hug. They began to part, reluctantly, when Victor, holding her at arms-length, said excitedly, "Let's get married!"

Else was stunned, but didn't say no. "You mean now?"

"*Ja*, I mean as soon as we can put it together."

"Oh Viktor, that is so exciting! *Ja*, that would be wonderful."

Viktor went back to his classes at the University and Christian to military school, both with renewed vigor.

* * *

Col. Redl was widely thought to be one of the most capable officers in the Austrian army; many believed he would soon earn a field marshal's baton. A rising star, he had been described in character reports as "very companionable, with excellent manners and frequenting only elegant society."

One day in early April, the German counterintelligence unit in Berlin noticed a large envelope addressed to *Herr* Nikon Nizetas c/o General Delivery, Vienna. The package, which went unclaimed in Vienna, had been sent back to the place of postmark in Berlin. The package's unusual bulk attracted the German Secret Service. When opened, it was found to contain six thousand Austrian kronen (crowns) and two addresses, one in Paris and one in Geneva, both known to be used by Russian spies. This was an exciting find, because in recent years there had been considerable concern about a leak of Austrian military secrets to Russia.

The German office handed off the package to their Viennese colleagues. It was carefully resealed and returned to the General Post Office. In a building across the square from the Post Office, two detectives from the Austrian Secret Service set up to wait for *Herr* Nizetas to claim the package. A wire was run from their room to a button under the desk at the General Delivery Office across the street.

The sergeants stood watch during the hours the General Delivery Office was open for business. The days went by slowly. The men were encouraged when two more packages arrived addressed to *Herr* Nizitas containing another six thousand kronen. The detectives were well trained to keep patient vigil by the bell that would not ring. Their chief, Col. Redl, had instilled good habits in his men, the principal trait being patience.

The detectives waited day after day for six weeks in their small room for the bell to ring. Then, at 5:55 p.m., just minutes before closing, on Saturday, 24 May, the bell did ring—but in an empty room. One man had gone to the privy; the other was in the lobby getting coffee. Both men were returning along the corridor when they heard the ring through the door. They ran across the square; *Herr* Nizitas might still be outside. The two reached the street in time to see a cab pull away and vanish around the corner. One of them was able to get the license number, A3313. They ran back to General Delivery. "What did he look like?" they asked the clerk. To their disappointment, the clerk replied that he couldn't help them; Mr Nizetas had worn a gray hat pulled down over his face.

"Nothing, six weeks of work for nothing," uttered one of the sergeants. Dejected, they walked back out to the square. There, by chance, they saw a cab driving by with the license number A3313. They screamed at the cab to halt. The driver said he had dropped the man at the Café Kaiserhof, a short distance away. The gentleman was in such a fearful hurry, the driver said, he had forgotten the sheath of the penknife he had used to open the mail. The detectives grabbed the sheath, got into the cab and ordered the driver to go back to the Café Kaiserhof—and hurry.

They were met with disappointment at the cafe. The head waiter had seen no one enter in the past few minutes. However, another cab driver described seeing a man hurriedly get out of a taxi and get in another. He'd called out the Hotel Klomser. Back in the cab and off to the hotel went the two sergeants. The concierge, however, did not recognize the knife sheath and said there was no *Herr* Nizetas registered at the hotel. The sergeants asked who had come through the lobby during the last half hour. The concierge read the names of every guest registered for that night. The names meant nothing, until he said the name Col. Redl. The men looked at each other in astonishment. They asked in unison, "Col. Alfred Redl?"

"Oh *Ja*, he always stays with us when he is in town from Prague. Always room Number 1," said the concierge.

"When he comes down, ask if he has lost this knife sheath," said one of the detectives.

The men began to wait. The prior six weeks had been nothing compared with this. They moved behind a potted plant for the next hour. Shortly after seven, a man in his forties, slim, with a well-brushed blond mustache, came down the main staircase. He was dressed in the light blue uniform of a colonel, with silver buttons and red cuffs on the sleeves.

"*Guten abend* Col. Redl," said the concierge. "*Bitte, mien heir,* but did you happen to misplace this knife sheath?"

"Why *Ja*," Redl replied. He extended his hand for the sheath, then, realizing what was up, retracted it fast. But it was too late.

At 1:00 a.m. on Sunday, 25 May, four officers walked past a dozing night clerk at the Hotel Klomser. One carried, folded up in his breast pocket, a white sheet of paper. It was a statement signed by the occupant of room Number 1. In exchange for the signature the occupant received a loaded pistol.

The following day, Vienna's major newspaper, the *Neue Freie Presse,* carried the following:

> *Vienna, May 26. One of the best known and most able officers in the General Staff, Colonel Alfred Redl, Chief of the 8th Army Corps in Prague, committed suicide Sunday night in a*

hotel in the Inner City. The highly gifted officer, who was on the verge of a great career killed himself with a shot in the mouth, an act prompted, it is believed, by mental overexertion resulting from severe neurasthenia. Colonel Redl, who served for a long time in a military capacity in Vienna, and who was equally popular in military and civilian circles, had only arrived from Prague on Saturday night and had taken quarters at the hotel.

That same day, the army announced that Col. Redl would be buried with full military honors.

This article was devastating news to Kadet Christian Müeller, but the news that followed was even worse. Egon Kisch, a journalist who happened to captain the Prague football team on weekends, was upset with their star player for missing the game Sunday. That player was Hans Wagner, by trade a locksmith. On Sunday morning, Wagner was getting dressed to play when a detail of soldiers approached, practically threw him into a military car, and drove at top speed to his shop. He was ordered to collect his tools, then driven to Corps headquarters. There, he was commanded to break into a private apartment. Entering the apartment, the men saw a strange sight: perfumed drapery, pink whips hanging from the walls, and lewd photographs in snakeskin frames. Hearing Wagner's story, Egon Kisch's investigative instincts kicked in.

Within twenty-four hours, Kisch did all the right leg work, ferreted out all the right people, and asked the right questions. More importantly, he managed to outmaneuver the long arm of Habsburg censorship. Kisch knew the *Neue Freie Presse* article was a coverup, and wrote in his paper, *Bohemia,* a "reverse disclosure":

We have been requested by official sources to deny the rumors particularly current in military circles, that the Chief of the Prague Corp., Colonel Alfred Redl, who the day before yesterday committed suicide in Vienna, has betrayed military secrets and spied for Russia. The Commission sent from Vienna to Prague was accompanied by a Colonel, and this past Sunday they broke open the apartment, closets, and drawers of Colonel Redl during a three-hour search, investigating irregularities of quite a different nature.

Prague censors thought Vienna had authorized the story and let it pass. Kirsch now sent the real story to a Berlin paper. The news swept across the Austrian border, forcing the Austrian Army to admit that Col. Redl had carried on a homosexual liaison, which created financial difficulties for him, which led to him selling official information to Russian agents. These facts sent shock waves through Vienna. The colonel stood unmasked as a criminal who had spent a fortune on a secret homosexual lover and filled his closets with women's dresses, hair dyes, fragrances, and cosmetics. He had bought his male paramour, a young cavalry officer, an expensive automobile and an apartment. He'd financed these expenses by selling to Russia data on Austrian mobilization plans, army codes, border fortifications, military transport facilities, and supply structures.

Although the Redl affair hit the city like a hurricane, the army sustained the most damage. The only commoner among the counts and barons of the General Staff, the colonel turned out to be a traitor.

*   *   *

Sunday, 8 June, 1913 was Derby Day in Vienna, ordinarily a sporty affair that belonged to Vienna's new generation. For young bloods it was an annual celebration of fashion. Young men wore derbies only until Derby Day. Afterward, they sported summer boaters.

Derby Day provided a stage for young officers to strut about in their light blue coats with red cuffs, silver buttons and white gloves, with

casual cigarettes in their mouths and ladies on their arms. The Redl
Affair changed all that. Instead of pride in the uniform, many seemed
to cringe. There was less flaunting of their new officers uniforms by
lieutenants, less flirting, and hardly any dining afterward in the Sacher
Garten in the Prater. Col. Redl had dishonored the tunic they wore.

The name "Redl" became an emblem of decay; the inevitability
of degeneration in an ancient, but seemingly still vibrant monarchy.
Would the Habsburgs ever be able to develop their realm into a great
modern power? Serbia, its adversary, was small, defiant, and pulsing
with the young passion of nationalism. Until now it had yielded,
however reluctantly, before Austria's warnings. But it never yielded
for long. This was the mood of the Austrian Army when Christian
Müeller was commissioned a lieutenant on 1 June, 1914. By August,
Europe was at war.

The Redl Affair affected the entire Austrian Army and nation, but
it was devastating to the young officer kadet. From a distance he had
idolized the man as young officers often do—his looks, his intelligence,
the way he wore the uniform—these were all impressive to a young
officer who had longed to make the army his career. Christian never
really got over 'the affair'. This was partly because of the dishonor to
the uniform he was about to put on, partly that Redl was a traitor to
his country. And the sexual aspect played a major role. Christian had
only begun to explore the mysteries of sex with girls, most of whom
knew even less than he did. He enjoyed the smell of their perfume
and the look, softness, and scent of the female body. Christian's greatest fear, which often kept him from going too far with a girl, was the
thought of pregnancy. For this reason, he took all precautions. However,
homosexual desire was something he knew nothing about; the idea
of sex with another man was repulsive.

*   *   *

In August of 1914, Austria was at war with France, England, and Russia. Christian now had his chance to prove himself a good officer, but as the war dragged on from year to bloody year, He began to have the same doubts he had felt when he first heard of Col. Redl's betrayal. He knew Viktor's feelings about the hopelessness of the war and felt that there was no future for him after the conflict. Christian knew that if Germany and Austria lost the war, which seemed likely, the army would be broken up, if not disbanded. What would he do, with no other training? If he died in the war, at least he might be honored as a hero.

By October 1918, the war was winding down. Near the end of the month, Christian caught a bit of shrapnel in his right thigh from a stray shell; it seemed almost an afterthought. He felt lucky to be sent to a Catholic Hospital, they were noted for excellent treatment and good food. But the constant noise of the hospital ward made sleep difficult. The first morning there, at dawn, Christian began to doze a little. He was soon awakened when the door opened and loud noise came from the corridor, rousing anyone who had managed to sleep. Deiter, the fellow in the next bed, turned to Christian. "Every morning," he said, "the Sisters say prayers. They call it "Morning Devotion." To be sure we get our share of devotion, they leave the door open. I'm sure they mean well. We are all light cases; they think we may live long enough to be saved."

"This is absurd," grumbled Christian. "Just when I was getting some sleep."

Another man yelled loudly, "Be quiet out there."

Soon, a Sister appeared in her black and white habit. Scowling, in a stern voice she said, "We are saying prayers. Prayers are better than sleep."

From the far end of the room another man yelled, "Shut the door, Goddamn it!"

The Sister left quickly but returned with three more nuns. They demanded to know who had defiled God's name. The room became quiet. The four women turned on their heels and disappeared but left the door open. Another voice rang out, "Shut the door!" Then a bottle flew through the air and crashed to the floor at the spot the Sisters had just vacated.

There were seven other men in the room with Christian. There was Hans, who had the worst injury, having been caught in a gas attack, but none were in good shape, including Christian. As the days went by, he felt weaker and weaker. Franz, another gas attack patient, became thinner and more pallid each day. One day he was taken away and did not return. Deiter said to Christian, "We shan't see him again. They have taken him to the 'Dead Room'." Deiter had suffered a bullet to his right arm and infection had set in.

"The what?"

"A small room at the end of the building. Whoever is about to die is taken there. That way, they won't have so much work afterward, because it's close to the mortuary. They may also take a man there for the sake of the others in the room. They can look after him better, too, if he is by himself."

"Does everybody know about it?"

"Anyone who has been here long enough knows."

Often, soldiers' relatives came, sat by a bed and wept or talked softly. One old woman wanted to stay the night but was forced to leave. Early the next morning she returned, carrying apples, but was directed to the mortuary. With tears, she left the apples for the others in the ward.

Meanwhile, Christian was slowly deteriorating, mentally and physically. Despite the Sisters' efforts, his wound became infected. After a week, it was determined the leg would need to be amputated. At this low point for Christian, a bright light walked up to his bed—Viktor, who approached with one of the Sisters.

"Christian, it is good to see you. How do you feel?" Viktor asked, having heard the news of the impending amputation and not knowing what to say.

"Viktor, it is good to see you—and looking so well. I bet you are anxious to see Else and Fritz. Is the new baby born yet?"

"Not yet, but soon. Christian," he said, "you know they do wonderful things with artificial legs today. You will be like new soon."

"Viktor, I wish you were right. But I don't think I will make it to see the war's end. Things here are as bad as in the trenches. Yesterday a man tried to kill himself with a fork. It took three men to get it away from him. Days go by filled with pain and fear, groans and death gurgles as fellows die during the night. They go fast. Two died of tetanus. Their skin turned pale, their limbs stiffened; only their eyes showed signs of life. Intestinal wounds are constantly full of feces.

"What saddens me the most is above the shattered bodies are human faces in which life goes on. And this is only one hospital; there are hundreds of thousands of wounded in Germany, hundreds of thousands in France, hundreds of thousands in Russia. How senseless this all is. I am glad I will soon not have to see the lies, the blood, the horrors, and the industrialist traitors that have gotten rich while soldiers die. I won't have to witness the end of our Austria anymore."

Viktor listened with concern. "I won't have you talking like this, Christian. You will get through this. Else and I will be there to help you—always. Besides, you have too much to live for."

Christian stifled a laugh. "Like what? Unlike you, I have no wife, no children. Our army is defeated, and with it goes my future. I know only fighting and war. You will muster out soon and have a career in banking. A respectable career."

"Christian, remember the good days before the war with Ilse? You will have those days again."

"Viktor!" Christian looked at him, resolute. "It is probably too much to ask for your help. I can't expect you to understand my depression. Your family and university degree give you optimism for the future. Austria needs men like you to lead our country through the difficult times ahead. I can't go on like this, and I won't. They want to take my leg off from the thigh. I told you years ago, I wanted to die in battle. And now, here I am about to die in this God-forsaken hospital."

"*Nein*, Christian! You will survive this, and the new Austria will be full of promise."

"Promise, ha! We have heard promises before."

"But democracy will change all that. The Habsburgs are over; the middle class will throw out the aristocrats and the Jews, and we will have a pure Germany, one run for the true working people, not rich Jewish industrialists."

"Viktor, there is one thing you can do for me, and I am serious." Christian pulled Viktor closer. He said, quietly, "Bring me a revolver."

Viktor's eyes widened in shock. He was unable to respond; he didn't want to. He stared at Christian for several seconds then slowly backed out of the room, still locking eyes with his friend. He heard Christian say, "Goodbye, Viktor."

He felt ashamed that he could not even say goodbye to his friend, but he thought he had seen an expression of calm on Christian's face, as though he was glad the end had come.

On 11 November, news went around the camp that an armistice had been signed; the war was finally over. On this day, a sergeant came to tell Viktor that Christian had died in the hospital, of a gunshot to the head. Two days later he received a telegram that, also on the 11th, Else had given birth to a daughter, and her name was Elke.

7

Else Baur

1919–1926

Hyper-inflation is defined as prices rising 50 percent or more in one month. It was natural for most Austrians to assume that goods were becoming more expensive, not that their money was falling in value. Money, after all, is no more than a medium of exchange, and can be used as such only when its value is acknowledged by multiple parties. The wider the acknowledgement, the more useful money is. So with prices climbing, people demanded more wages to buy what they needed rather than asking for stable purchasing power. When the Viennese lost trust in their currency, they spent money faster, until they learned their money had no value—except for papering walls. There was no means to measure the worth of anything, and this shattered their society.

It may be hard to grasp what the sudden end of the Habsburg Empire meant to the Austrians, and above all to the Viennese. Some great capitals, like Carthage, perished with their peoples. Most, like Rome, were occupied by their conquerors. But Vienna was a city in ruins, one condemned by the 1919 Treaty of Versailles

to linger in isolation. The end of the war saw the disintegration
of the empire, destroying with one blow the Austrian way of life.
The spirit of the nation, as well as its pride, the roots as well as
the blossom, were swept away.

November in Vienna is cold and dreary in the best of times,
but this was perhaps the worst of times. The city was held fast in
the claws of runaway inflation, which had been building since
before the end of the Great War. The Allies' naval blockade of
Germany and Austria continued until 1919 in order to force
the two Central Powers to approve the armistice imposed upon
them by the Allied Powers.

W ith each passing year, Else Baur felt the previous year would
be the worst and the following year would be better. To her
disappointment, each year seemed more brutal than the previous one.
This year, 1923, had been grueling.

When she married Viktor in 1914, she was a strong woman, a big-
boned Nordic blonde with a pleasant smile and a positive outlook. After
all, her Viktor would have a bright future as an economist. The war
that had begun in August was bound to be short, much like the war
with France in 1870, which had ended quickly with a great German
victory. It was widely believed that the current war against France
would be no different. However, the fighting dragged on until even
Viktor was called up upon graduation. Fortunately, he had survived,
but his friend Christian had not. Christian was one of the last soldiers
to die in the war.

Viktor had come home embittered toward the governments of
Germany and Austria. He felt his men had been let down by government officials, the generals of both armies, and especially the large
industrialists, primarily Jews, who had made fortunes from the war.

The horrors of the battlefield had been replaced by the daily burdens of people starving. There was little milk to drink or flour to bake bread. Meat was almost nonexistent. It fell to Else to find food for her family. As the years slowly passed, she felt herself getting weaker, as she wasn't getting enough sleep. If she didn't survive, who would keep her family together? She was lucky to have a husband with a steady job. Most women she knew had lost their husbands in the war or were trying to feed a disabled spouse who couldn't work—even if there was a job to be had. Else was sustained by the feeling that it was up to the women of Vienna to hold society together—because so many men had died or were handicapped.

On this cold November morning, she was awakened at 5:00 a.m. by her housekeeper, Helga. "*Frau* Baur, I was told to wake you so you could be in line to get the horse meat."

"Oh, Helga, it can't be time already. I feel like I just went to sleep. Is Viktor up yet?"

"*Nein*, madam. He said it would be a difficult day at the bank and asked to sleep until six."

Else groaned, "Oh God, when will this end? Is it still raining?"

"Only a light sprinkle, but it is cold. You should dress warmly. And horse flesh is better than no meat at all. Fritz and Elke need the protein, even horse meat."

"I know, it has been weeks since we have seen any meat."

Helga was an extravagance, one they could barely afford, but a great help to the Baur family. Besides, it was important for Viktor's image as a rising young bank executive to have household help.

* * *

The distribution of the meat was not to begin until 9:00 a.m., but one needed to queue early to have any chance of getting into the hall where the meat was distributed. Else had set a time of 7:00 a.m. to be in line. While she walked hurriedly in the cold, steady drizzle, she cursed this miserable situation. Four years of war followed by four years of starvation rations, and the only way to get rations was to barter something valuable for something outlandishly expensive on the black market.

Viktor had a good job at the Länderbank as a loan collector, but his pay could not keep up with rising prices. They had sold some of their prize possessions, including the gold watch Viktor had inherited from his father. The watch had been traded for enough potatoes to last through the previous winter. They had talked of selling their fine piano. Viktor knew a farmer who would trade another winter's worth of potatoes and several pounds of hog meat for it. But Else had refused.

As with most Viennese families of the time, music was the center of family life. Most middle- and upper-class families had a piano and would gather around it after dinner to listen as one of their number played Mozart, Beethoven, or Strauss. Little Fritz, while only nine years old, was considered a budding Mozart by his family and friends.

His mother loved his beautiful dark blue eyes and sunny disposition. Little Elke had just turned five and was a joy. She enjoyed life as if there was no tomorrow, but she especially loved small animals, and had boundless energy. However, Else worried that Elke was not getting the nutrition she needed.

When Else arrived at the queue, she was joined by at least two thousand other Viennese, mostly women wearing worn shawls, which gave some protection from the cold but not the rain. Lined faces told of years of desperation and deprivation. The women were eager to get this horse meat, now a delicacy. No one seemed to mind the rain. They were all wet clear through and shivering from the cold, but hunger will make one endure significant inconveniences. The police were examining the ration cards of everyone in the queue to be sure they were entitled to the meat.

"*Guten Morgan*, Else. Can you believe we are standing in this line for one pound of horse flesh?" Else recognized her neighbor, Hanna Mallmann, a short, heavyset woman who lived in an apartment building down the street from hers.

"I don't know, Hanna. It seems as if we will go on like this forever. The krone seems to have stabilized, but now we have no money to buy anything."

"I read in the newspaper we should see the end of this situation early next year."

"They have been saying that every year for five years. I don't read the newspapers anymore."

"Well, maybe you should. They have passed a decree that no one can hold more than a half kilogram weight of coal per week, and it can be used only for cooking."

"Oh, my God! Do they realize winter is just beginning? I am going to have to hide coal. How can I warm my family and cook what little food we have?"

After uttering these words, Else realized Hanna might inform on her to the authorities. This would mean her family would be fined and their supply of coal taken away. Without it they could not make it through the Vienna winter with the little coal they were authorized to obtain.

Else quickly changed the subject, hoping Hanna would forget her rash words. "My husband, Viktor, and I talked about converting our saving into Swiss francs back in 1919. But it was illegal and with his job at the bank, we couldn't risk it. Now I wish we had. At least we would have money with value today."

"Did you hear Ingrid Bock traded their grand piano for three months of potatoes from a farmer near Lintz?" Hanna said.

"Oh, I could never part with our piano. Fritz loves to play, and it has become our only entertainment. I would die before parting with it."

"Better a lost piano than a dead child."

Hanna's words landed like the sting of a dart.

Else gasped. "This can't continue much longer."

"This will continue as long as we let the Jews run everything. Yesterday I went into the Dorotheum, the city-owned auction house. I heard unbelievable stories of what was happening there. There were lots of good people like us selling, for any price they could get, their precious jewelry, paintings, furniture, and pianos. The auction items were selling at far higher prices than the auctioneer had expected. It was the Jews who were buying, because they have all the money. While we were fighting the war, they were making fortunes selling to the government. Lawyers, bankers, and doctors staying at home while our boys fought and died. They shouldn't even be allowed into the Dorotheum or any place else where good Austrians are. The Jews are greedy, and the day will come when we will take back what they have stolen from us."

"But Hanna, aren't they Austrians just like us?"

"Else, I once believed that rubbish, but after what we have been through, I have nothing but contempt for them. I don't believe any good Austrian believes that all human beings are born equal. I have come to believe the prime relationship between people is based on contempt, not love."

These words stuck with Else while she waited. Time seemed to drag interminably. The steady rain showed no signs of letting up, and the crowd grew impatient. Then, before the police could prevent it, those at the front of the line attacked the hall. Men seized whatever meat they could get their hands on and pushed aside any women in their way. In moments, everything edible had vanished, as though devoured by a swarm of hungry animals. Those behind, many of whom had been waiting much of the night, were angry and refused to move off. Else, in fear, fled to a nearby park, disgusted.

Walking home with nothing to show for her efforts, she considered the near-riot and what Hanna had said. She had just seen how easy it was to upset the moral equilibrium of whole classes of people. Folks had been forced out of their ordinary habits and were now falling prey to the influence of political agitation.

What had become of humanity and love of one's neighbor? The growing lack of consideration for one's fellow man depressed her. She understood the human instinct for self-preservation, that when one's existence is threatened, all moral laws are lost. She had recently seen on the streets of Vienna a warmly clad man who was robbed of his coat and shoes and had to walk home barefoot.

When Else arrived home, Viktor was waiting there, frantic with worry. "I heard about the riot and all I could think of was your safety." The two hugged each other tightly. "Oh, my love, what are we to do? We can't afford to buy food at these prices."

"Things are even worse, Viktor. Hanna says the authorities plan to confiscate all coal over a half kilogram per week, and coal can only be used for cooking, not for heating homes. Besides, we also need milk for Elke."

Viktor slammed his fist on the counter and took a deep breath. "We have time to move the coal later. The government is only sending out warnings now. The bank will let me have next Saturday off. I have a farmer client with a dairy farm near Breitenfurt, he will get us milk. It is some distance away, but he will help us."

Breitenfurt was a small village west of Vienna, accessible by train. Viktor knew of it because he had made loans to the farmer. He had promised the farmer further loans as well as a box of fine cigars he had received from the bank as an award for collecting delinquent loans. Collecting such loans was easy in these hyper-inflation times; debtors were anxious to pay their creditors with inflated krones. He had a good relationship with the dairyman, and a box of fine Trabucco cigars was a small price to pay for milk.

They took the train to Breitenfurt, where all went well on a sunny Saturday. They had their milk in a bucket and were anxious to get it home. As they walked back to the train station, the streets began to fill with an agitated crowd of angry men. They surrounded an elderly officer. Because he was an officer of the Imperial Army, he would pay for the defeat. Someone grabbed his officer's cap and tore off the imperial eagle. A man near the Baurs yelled out, "It is men like him that have grown fat on the war while we starve; he needs to die."

Viktor and Else cringed against a nearby wall. A man standing beside them sensed their fear and said, "The difference between officers and soldiers has vanished with the war. In the future there will be no privileged class. No emperor, no princes, no counts, no barons."

Viktor said, "Where did you get these anarchistic ideas?"

"My ideas are not anarchistic. I am a Communist."

* * *

The war and its effects hit the middle-class the hardest. It destroyed their savings, including the war bonds people had purchased out of a sense of patriotism. Former civil servants and officers had become the poorest of the poor. Most were too proud to press their claims and could get no employment. It became a daily occurrence in Vienna for an elderly person or retired official of high rank to collapse on the street from hunger.

Winter now began to tighten its icy grip around the city. When the temperature plunged below freezing, Viktor and Else decided to ignore the new coal restriction. They had always saved coal during the summer so the family would have plenty for the colder months. If the authorities found out, however, their supply would be confiscated. Christmas was approaching when they resolved to hide their coal. They knew the *Volkswehr* would search the cellar, so they decided to move it to the veranda. Secrecy was paramount. Neighbors now informed on neighbors; it was impossible to know whom to trust.

About 11:00 p.m., when everyone was asleep, Viktor and Else began to move, bucket by heavy bucket, their precious supply of coal. They lugged it up two flights of stairs and out to the veranda on the second floor. They finished just before the dawn, exhausted. They hoped the *Volkswehr* would be friendly. Two days later, when Else heard a knock on the door, she crossed herself, said a short prayer, and opened the door. Two officers asked to see her supply of coal. Fortunately, their exam was cursory, and the coal in the cellar was under the legal limit.

Victor and Else knew they were breaking the law, but if they didn't, it meant begging or starvation. Necessity was now the basis of everything from barter to behavior. When life is secure, people can enjoy nonessential luxuries, but when life is threatened and conditions harsh, values change. Without shelter or clothing, it is difficult to sustain life, and without food, life cannot exist.

*   *   *

For Viktor and Else, Christmas 1923 was going to be bare, but they were determined to make it a happy one for Fritz and Elke. Else thought back to a typical Christmas before the war. The Baurs had always decorated a silver fir tree as tall as the ceiling, beautifully adorned and bearing seventy little white wax candles. A traditional Christmas dinner was fried carp with potatoes and bean salad, along with a poppy-and-nut pancake, beer, and a light Moselle wine. Afterward, there would be punch, pastries, and fruit. Christmas in 1923 would be far different. They placed a meagre little fir tree, hardly as tall as Fritz, on a small table. Even this poor excuse for a tree was purchased with a box of expensive cigars, once-cherished by Viktor. The decorations were from pre-war days, but only lit with a few unsightly tallow stumps cut from one of their rationed candles. The Christmas menu would consist of a few Portuguese sardines, a good loaf of bread from the farmer in Breitenfurt, and eight ounces of butter. Christmas day swept in with a sharp frost and icy winds. Their little iron stove could not bring the temperature in the dining room above eleven degrees Celsius. The family had to wrap themselves in blankets, so there was no question of festive attire.

By the time 1924 arrived, the krone was replaced by the new schilling. This was a drastic change. Fifteen thousand kronen now equaled one new schilling. Thousands of Austrians had been reduced to beggary. Food was now available and could be bought anywhere. However, Viktor's income had not kept pace with the tireless printing of bank notes. Their small savings were dwindling away quickly.

An older couple whom Viktor and Else knew well had been worth two million kronen before the war. They were regarded as rich, because these funds in their bank gave them an income of eighty thousand kronen a year. With the currency change, their millions were reduced to only one thousand new schillings. Panic overcame the couple, who committed suicide rather than face a bleak future. Viktor and Else, formerly of the middle class, now found themselves reduced to the proletariat, even though Viktor's job was secure and he received regular wage increases. These, however, consistently fell behind the cost of food and living expenses.

*　*　*

Else's Journal
5 January 1924

Things are getting worse. A mob has attempted to set fire to the Parliament building where large numbers of unemployed, their passions inflamed by the communists, are seething with discontent. When mounted policemen attempted to stop them, the police were torn from their horses, which were then slaughtered in the Ringstrasse. Pieces of warm, bleeding horseflesh were dragged away by the crowd.

The rioters were clamoring for bread and work. We see unimaginable want among most of the population. However, we also see a display of luxury among those benefiting from the inflation, mainly foreign tourists taking advantage of the weak schilling. We read in the newspaper that our misery is due to these tourists who buy up all our food, wine and pastries, because for them, the prices are cheap. New nightclubs are being opened despite the difficulty of obtaining supplies. The profits are so enormous that the owners ignore the penalties the state imposes on them. These clubs greatly intensify the hatred of the proletariat against the bourgeoise. Even the most respectable Austrian citizen now breaks the law, unless he is prepared to starve for the sake of obeying it. A housewife from England with no experience of the horrors of devalued money has no idea what a blessing stable money is, and how wonderful it is to be able to buy, with the note in one's purse, the article one had intended to buy at the price one had intended to pay.

The only joy in my life is watching and listening to Fritz play the piano. He is only ten, but his playing is a delight. I stood in the kitchen this morning and could hear him playing his favorite melody from Mozart's String Quartet No. 19. I peeked around the corner and watched him seated at the piano. He looked very pale; he and Elke have not been getting enough food these past five years.

The dream of listening to my boy lasted only a half hour; then reality intervened as I realized how hungry we all are.

There is more fighting daily. The wage demands of workers force up the price of food. I blame the selfishness of the Jewish profiteers at the stock exchange and the greed of the Jewish industrialists. They all get rich while the good Austrians starve. This is the fault of the Jews, and they will pay someday. I feel my strength is deserting me, even my faith in God. I don't know how much longer I can go on.

*   *   *

But go on she did, and inflation began to stabilize due to the schilling replacing the krone. Viktor, being well respected at the Länderbank, was promoted to junior economist. He could now afford proper nourishment for him, Else, and the children, along with a few small luxuries, such as keeping the maid.

In September of 1926, Viktor came home from work full of excitement. He announced he was taking the family on holiday in Semmering, a deluxe mountain resort fifty miles outside Vienna. He had always loved its breathtaking beauty, and how it basked in currents of warm air above valleys shrouded in cold mist.

Viktor, like all Viennese, regarded the Austrian Alps as their private mountains. The showplace of Lower Austria, Semmering attracted people from around the globe who wished to enjoy the natural beauty and the quiet of the mountains. Viktor was proud that the world's first mountain railway had been built in Semmering; it corkscrewed to the summit via a series of viaducts and tunnels.

They checked into the fabulous Panhans Hotel on a warm day in September. It looked like a castle built into a mountain, encircled by tall pines and beautiful gardens. The hotel offered many activities, including a nightclub where dancing and entertainment were held nightly. The days were golden, the air perfect, and hiking was the favorite pastime of Viktor, Else, and the children.

One day, they left the children with the hotel's nanny and took a romantic hike high into the mountains. When they stopped to rest and enjoy the scenery, Viktor turned to his wife. "Else, we have lived in our small rented apartment since I came home from the war and talked about buying our own, larger place. I have seen a wonderful apartment on Daringergasse in the 19th District; it is large and beautiful and there's a tram stop close by. My job is more secure now; I think we can afford it. Would you be willing to look at it? I know you have been afraid of buying a place before, but I think now is a good time."

"Oh Viktor, it scares me after what we have been through, but it excites me also. Yes, I am anxious to see it."

Viktor took her in his arms. She kissed him deeply and passionately. This surprised and excited Viktor; this was not like Else, but he could feel the excitement in her body. There had been little passion in their lives for the past few, almost unendurable years, but now their pent-up passion overcame them. Viktor took Else's hand and they moved to a secluded grassy area just far enough from the trail. Although they had seen no one all morning, they did not want to be interrupted. They were making a memory that would last far into their future.

*　*　*

Else's Journal
28 SEPTEMBER 1926

We are back from Semmering. The weather was wonderful, the Hotel Panhans was fabulous, and the children were a joy; they had us laughing much of the time. Fritz captured the piano in the hotel lobby to the delight of everyone. Elke spent much of her time feeding the squirrels that seemed to always be around her. Viktor and I are going to look at the apartment on Daringergasse next weekend. At last, our own home. Viktor is sure we can afford it. I hope it will be a good place to raise the children.

A lot has happened while we were away. The papers are full of a trial of a Jew-boy who killed his father while hiking. He claims he had gone ahead of his father and came back on the trail only to find his father, by the name of Halsmann, dead by the brook below the trail. No one believes him, of course, and he will go to jail for a long time. What made it interesting to me was a policeman said the father's ghost had appeared to him like King Hamlet to accuse his son. Also, a preacher said from his pulpit that Halsmann, by not repenting, and by insisting on his innocence, deserved worse hellfire than Judas. I am not sure I believe the story of the ghost, but it shows what the Jews are really like.

I had never really thought much about the Jews before, but in the last few years Vienna seems to be overrun by these dirty, illiterate, immigrant people from the East. They seem different from Jews I have known previously. There is something mysterious, even menacing about them. I even imagine them with some evil power. It is nothing I can see, but I know it is there, an active force of evil, one that caused our inflation and caused us to lose the war. The Jew is dangerous, inferior to us, and lecherous. I must always protect Elke from those monsters. Our Nordic race is superior to any other race in the world. The Germanic culture is superior to any and can be seen by our cultural and military achievements. We have faced a constant struggle for survival in our lands and now my worry is a group of subhumans can ruin what we have built over centuries.

To change the subject, Elke will be eight in November. After all we have been through, I want to give her a birthday party that will be perfect for her and her little friends.

* * *

Else was determined to make Elke's birthday memorable—for both of them. She decided to have a tea party for Elke's friends from school. Else got out the Japanese tea service she had inherited from her mother. The blue-grey, wafer-thin china was decorated with hand-painted geishas. Else served tiny croissants, and crisp poppy seed and crystallized salt rolls bought that morning from Vienna's best bakery, *Herr Fritz's* in the *Naglergasse*. They were cut, buttered, and spread with delicate *teewurst*. There was a second course of a rich, homemade cream cake with nuts, orange, or chocolate, Elke's favorite. The party was a big success and the laughter of eight-year-old girls filled the small apartment.

After the first of the year, the Baur family would be moved into their new home on Daringergasse. At last, a home of their own.

8

Viktor Baur

1927

The currency had stabilized, but unemployment in Austria remained high. Most citizens of Vienna were still hungry. The leading political parties, the Social-Democrats and the Christian Socials, viewed each other across class and social barriers with the same deep-seated suspicion and hatred that had previously divided the nations of the empire. The trappings of democracy were there, but the content was missing. The leaders of the Social-Democrats were mostly moderate men, leading a party of the moderate left, but their language was the language of the barricades, class struggle, and capitalist exploitation. In reality, the majority were highly intelligent, civilized, largely middle-class, largely Jewish. Nor were the Christian Social opponents fascist beasts, but they saw little difference between Social Democracy and Bolshevism (communism).

They felt their bourgeois existence threatened, and extolled Western Civilization and German Christian values. By that they meant anything that was not "Jewish-Bolshevik." Political strife was common and extra-political organizations soon sprang up. The Christian-Socials had their Heimwehr, initially a paramilitary group, which recruited from the rural districts and were conservative in outlook. To hold their own, the Social-Democrats formed the Schutzbund, a paramilitary organization that drew its members from Vienna and other industrial centers. Clashes between Schutzbund and Heimwehr could be counted upon to enliven every political event.

July in Vienna is a beautiful time of year. In the city's many parks, flowers are in full bloom and the air smells sweet from their scent. The residents are full of energy, happy that the icy winter is behind them and the next winter seems far in the future. Vienna is really a product and part of its surrounding countryside. The great line of forest-clad mountains to the west stretches out its arms to the city and almost touches it.

The Viennese landscape appears to have the power to charm the city's residents into turning their backs on urgent political developments. Painters and architects, singers and poets have all drawn creative strength from this countryside. Few cities are as rich in history and suffering, in glory and in adversity, as Vienna. This is what makes Vienna such a fascinating stage for the drama of life.

Vienna is a city of coffeehouses. On a beautiful day, Vienna's coffeehouses are filled with political talk. It had been three years since the schilling had replaced the krone as the currency of Austria. It had done its job and given the citizens monetary stability. However, like the beautiful summer that makes people forget the terrible winter just past, the stable currency was covering up Austrian unemployment; most citizens were still hungry. Austria was an unhappy country.

Neither the rural nor the city folks had come to terms with their dismal circumstances. Most Viennese dreamed of their splendid past, disliked the world as it was, and feared the future. Behind the baroque masonry of superb elegance lay dark, dank corridors filled with the stale smell of over-boiled cabbage and the clearly discernible odor of hatred and envy.

None of this seemed to disturb young Viktor Baur. With the Austrian schilling stabilized, his net pay was beginning to get ahead of the bills. On this mid-July morning, Viktor was just leaving his daily grooming session with *Herr* Josef Lohan, his barber for the last year. Even though the Gillette safety razor had been invented, Viktor adamantly refused not only to use it, but to allow it in the house. He enjoyed his daily routine with *Herr* Lohan. To be dabbed and brushed and fussed over by a true professional and to emerge from the shop clean and smooth-cheeked after enjoying the barber's lather and *Eau de Cologne* made Viktor feel cleaner, smoother, and more prosperous and important. He felt this indulgence was vital to a rising economist in those difficult political times.

In Vienna, a semi-important businessman would be addressed by a title at least one grade higher than actually attained. Thus, *Herr* Lohan addressed Viktor as "*Herr* Direktor," rather than Inspector, to which he had finally been promoted. Viktor could have been the model for the popular Viennese view, expressed in a ditty which went: "No one is as well off as the chap with a secure job with a pension at the end, with a pension at the end."

In the Baur family's comfortable new apartment in the northern suburbs of the city, the living-room was the focus of family life. When one entered through the double doors from the dining room, the first thing visible was the large, black concert grand piano, played beautifully by Fritz. The piano stood against two windows. At the other far wall stood a mahogany bookcase filled with Viktor's books, perhaps his most prized possessions. Viktor often sat in his large overstuffed chair next to the books and dreamed that someday Fritz and his wife and children would live here just as contented as Victor and Else were. Owning an apartment meant he and his family were secure, as were their children and grandchildren, because at that time, estates and businesses were handed down from generation to generation. Viktor never imagined that another war or revolution would interfere with this bright future.

He tried to stay out of any political fracas. He had a family to feed and was concerned with his advancement up the corporate ladder of his very conservative bank. With pride, Viktor looked back on his good luck in being employed by this bank. His military experience had taught him to be humble, and humble he must be to remain an employee of this highly esteemed institution. It had been impressed upon him just how conservative the bank was when he was hired.

As an example of what was to come, the bank issued "The Severe Rules for Employees." This booklet left little doubt as to what was expected of each man. Paragraph ten: "Every employee must serve the interests of the bank during official working hours. If necessary, he will, on the instruction of his supervisor, work additional hours." There was no question of paid overtime or coffee breaks. The book continued with, "Employees will lead a private life giving no cause for annoyance," and further, "No employee can enter matrimony without the explicit consent of the bank. Such consent can be refused without the bank having to state any reason for such refusal." The latter did not apply to Viktor, since he was married with two children when employed in 1919.

Viktor liked the bank and the bank liked Viktor. After his initial six-month trial period, he was promoted to Temporary Employee. After a further six months, he was given permanent status. He then had a good job that offered lifelong security.

On this morning, when Viktor walked through the lobby of the Länderbank, he remembered that everyone in the Economics

Department was to hear a presentation from Dr. Friedrich Hayek. Viktor had heard of him, mostly because as a young man of only twenty-eight, Hayek had earned doctorate degrees in both law and political science, and was becoming known for his views on economics. Viktor was anxious to hear what he had to say.

Viktor found a seat near the front. He was soon joined by his friend in the department, Hans Reinhard. Hans was younger and more athletically fit than Viktor, and single. He had a good head for numbers and was well liked by others in the bank. The two had been close since Viktor's earliest days with the bank. Hans enjoyed their political talks. Both had concerns about Austria's future but differed on solutions to the country's problems. Tensions seemed to be building in the city, as memories of the recent economy were still vivid, especially with bankers.

They both felt this presentation by a controversial economist should be entertaining, if nothing else. Viktor could tell by the quiet comments among his fellow employees that the speaker, who was known for his capitalist views, could be in for a rough time, because most bankers felt that it was the government's job to control the economy.

Dr. Hayek was introduced by the Direktor of Economics, who gave a hearty *Guten Morgen,* gentlemen!" This was followed by courteous replies from the audience. "A few of you are familiar with Dr. Hayek, but I know him well. His father is a professor at the University of Vienna, whom I have known for some time. However, Dr. Hayek is a special academic. At his young age he recently founded the Austrian Institute for Business Cycle Research. He has worked for the government studying the legal details of the Treaty of St. Germain, and we applaud that work. He is recently returned from America where he studied the American economy and the operation of the U. S. Federal Reserve. Many of you may not know that Dr. Hayek was decorated for bravery as an airplane spotter during the Great War and suffered damage to his left ear. So do speak up with any questions. I now introduce to you Dr. Friedrich Hayek."

The professor, a tall man in a dark suit, white shirt, and striped tie, looked the part of an economist, especially with his round rimless glasses and a small dark mustache.

"*Guten Morgen,* gentlemen, and *danka* for that introduction. However, I must correct one thing. I was only a decorated soldier because the army was liberal in giving out decorations near the end of the war [laughter]. I was almost killed once, but it was due to stupidity when I attempted to jump from an observation balloon and forgot to disconnect my earphone [laughter]. I was probably much braver when, in 1922, I moved to New York City with exactly $25 in my pocket. It was still a lot of money, and I managed to make it last almost two weeks. I thought I had a job as a researcher, but upon arriving I found out the professor was on holiday and could not be reached. My money was running out, so I accepted the position of dishwasher in a restaurant on Sixth Avenue. I was about to start the next morning when, to my great relief, my employer contacted me to begin my job immediately. Today, the fact that I never started washing dishes is a source of everlasting regret." The room filled with laughter, which broke much of the tension. "I am very pleased to be addressing you this morning, at a time when our currency is stabilizing and the future seems brighter.

"So, I speak today to the economists of the Länderbank, a bank that has survived and prospered through these perilous times. Do you ask yourselves what has happened to the promises and hopes that liberalism gave us during the nineteenth century? Have not our finest minds incessantly worked to make this a better world? Have not all our efforts and hopes been directed toward greater freedom, justice and prosperity? Instead of freedom and prosperity, bondage and misery stare us in the face—is it not clear that sinister forces must have foiled our intentions, that we are victims of some evil power which must be conquered before we can resume the road to better things?

We are ready to accept almost any explanation of the present crisis of our civilization, except one—that the present state of the world may be the result of genuine error on our own part, and that the pursuit of some of our most cherished ideals has apparently produced results utterly different from those which we expected.

We still believe that until quite recently, we were governed by what are vaguely called nineteenth century ideas or the principle of laissez faire. We have progressively abandoned freedom in economic affairs, without which personal and political freedom cannot exist. We are rapidly abandoning not the views merely of Cobden and Bright, of Adam Smith and David Hume, or even of Locke and Milton, but of the salient characteristics of Western Civilization as it has grown from the foundations laid by Christianity and the Greeks and Romans."

The bankers began to stir; this was not what they had expected to hear. Hans mumbled something to Viktor, who didn't hear him, as he was grabbing a pad from his briefcase to jot down these intriguing words.

Dr. Hayek proceeded with the meat of his lecture. "Socialism began as a reaction against the liberalism of the French Revolution. In its beginning, it was frankly authoritarian; to them freedom of thought was regarded as the root-evil of nineteenth century society. The French writers who laid the foundations of modern socialism had no doubt that their ideas could be put into practice only by strong dictatorial government. To them socialism was an attempt to terminate the revolution by a deliberate reorganization of society.

It was an effort to organize all society along hierarchical lines, for the benefit of all, but nonetheless according to one mind and one will. What the nineteenth century added to the individualism of the preceding period was to make all classes conscious of freedom. The result of this growth surpassed all expectations and man became rapidly able to satisfy ever-widening ranges of desire.

At the beginning of the twentieth century, the working man in the Western world had reached a degree of comfort, security, and personal independence which a hundred years before had seemed scarcely possible. Despite all this freedom, we have been warned by some of the greatest thinkers of the nineteenth century, by de Tocqueville and Lord Acton, that socialism means slavery, however we have steadily moved in the direction of socialism.

The idea of organizing all of a society's economic aspects could not be conceived until after the industrial revolution. The technology simply did not exist previously to exert such control; a society without even the telegraph and paved roads was difficult to organize comprehensively.

The ultimate goal of socialism is not external change of men's lot in life or of their economic order, but internal transformation. The World War and hyper-inflation blew apart the great nineteenth century liberal dream of a peaceful and harmonious world united by commerce and free trade. Laissez-faire of that period was dead or at the very least in a state of suspended animation, and the monetary crisis in Austria and Germany increased support for socialism in Europe. When tens of millions were unemployed it appeared capitalism was a failure, Marx's prophecy of capitalism's demise was accurate, and that a collective state was the best way to achieve a stable and productive economy.

"Nobody saw more clearly than de Tocqueville that democracy, an essentially individualist institution, stood in an irreconcilable conflict with socialism. 'Democracy extends the sphere of individual freedom,' he said in 1848; socialism restricts it. Democracy attaches all possible value to each man; socialism makes each man a mere agent, a mere number. Democracy and socialism have nothing in common but one word: equality. But notice the difference: while democracy seeks equality in liberty, socialism seeks equality in restraint and servitude. I believe there can be no progress without economic liberty. The attempt to mandate interpersonal agreement by requiring all the members of a society to live in accordance with the dictates of one prevents the emergence of the kind of human order in which material and technological advance will occur. The Rule of Law should prevail over individual commands: private property is essential to this order."

By now the bankers were becoming restless. Many were eager to question a man who was raising points most saw as ludicrous and unworkable. A man in the back row asked, "I have been studying Karl Marx, and as I understand him, he says under capitalism workers' nominal wages for their labor will rise, but capitalists' profit will increase much faster, because capitalists are only out for themselves. This disparity will continue to widen with each year, because the workers will be left far behind. Isn't there a better way to reward an individual, maybe physical things like a house or an automobile?"

A chuckle went through the audience. Hayek continued, "If we strive for money, it is because it offers us the widest choice in enjoying the fruits of our efforts. Because in modern society it is through the limitation of our money incomes that we are made to feel the restrictions which our relative poverty still imposes upon us, many have come to hate money as the symbol of these restrictions. But this is to mistake for the cause the medium through which a force makes itself felt. It would be much truer to say that money is one of the greatest instruments of freedom ever invented by man. It is money which in existing society opens an astounding range of choice to the poor man—a range greater than that which not many generations ago was open only to the wealthy. If all rewards, instead of being offered in money, were offered in the form of public distinctions as privilege, positions of power over other men, or better housing or better food, opportunities for travel or education, this would merely mean that the recipient would no longer be allowed to choose and that whoever fixed the reward determined not only its size but also the particular form in which it should be enjoyed."

Another hand shot up. A portly man asked, "Dr. Hayek, isn't planning inevitable because of the technological changes in our modern economy that have made competition impossible in an increasing number of fields . . . and the only choice left to us is between control of production by private monopolies and direction by the government? Doesn't the growth of a large firm give that firm an advantage over a small firm? Will this not continue until only giant firms are left?"

"An excellent question, but the facts don't support that contention. The assertion that modern technological progress makes planning inevitable can also be interpreted in a different manner. It may mean that the complexity of our modern industrial civilization creates new problems with which we cannot hope to deal effectively except by central planning. In a sense this is true—yet not in the wide sense in which it is claimed.

"What the central planners generally suggest is that the increasing difficulty of obtaining a coherent picture of the complete economic process makes it essential that things should be co-ordinated by some central agency. Otherwise, social life may dissolve into chaos. This argument is based on a complete misapprehension of the workings of competition.

"It is the very complexity of the division of labor under modern conditions which makes competition the only method by which such coordination can be adequately brought about. There would be no difficulty about efficient control or planning were conditions so simple that a single person or board could effectively survey all the relevant facts. It is only as the factors which have to be taken into account become so numerous that it is impossible to gain a synoptic view of them. With claims that decentralization is necessary, the problem of coordination arises. The coordination can clearly be affected not by conscious control, but by information to each agent that he must possess in order to effectively adjust his decision regarding constant change of demand and supply of the different commodities. This is precisely what the price system does under competition, and what no other system even promises to accomplish. It enables entrepreneurs by watching the movements of comparatively few prices, as an engineer watches the hands of a few dials, to adjust their activities to those of their fellows. The important point here is that the price system will fulfill this function only if competition prevails, that is, if the individual producer has to adapt himself to price changes and not control them.

"It is no exaggeration to say that if we had had to rely on conscious central planning for the growth of our industrial system, it would never have reached the degree of differentiation, complexity, and flexibility it has attained.

"I have gone over my time, but I would like to close with these thoughts. It is a mistaken assumption that all knowledge can be collected in one mind such as the government direction of an economy. My goal is for the highest standard of living for all people, and this can only be achieved through a properly designed competitive market order, that depends on fluctuating prices, private property, profits, contracts and the ability to exchange goods and services. There are many socialists who have never come to grips in any way with the problem of economics. They invariably explain, in the cuckoo land of their fancy, that roast pigeons will in some way, fly into their mouths. They, of course, omit to show how this miracle is to take place."

This was greeted with much laughter.

As the men were filing out, Viktor turned to Hans. "He does have a good sense of humor," he said.

"He needs it, with those hair-brained ideas. You still up for coffee at Café Künstler after work?"

*   *   *

Later that afternoon, Viktor joined his friend at their favorite café near the University, which also happened to be a favorite meeting place of Viennese economists. It had been a long day even before the lecture by Dr. Hayek.

"How long have you been here?" Viktor said, taking a seat next to Hans.

"Just long enough to order this wonderful wine. Viktor, have you heard about the demonstrations that are planned for tomorrow at the *Justizpalast*?" [Palace of Justice]

"Hans, I have two kids at home. I don't know anything but their schoolwork."

"Well, the Social-Democrats are planning to demonstrate tomorrow morning, to protest the killing of a *Schutzbund* member by the *Heimwehr* at the village of Burgenland last week."

"Oh, another demonstration. How will this be any different than any of the others? Hans, this has gone on before, and we will survive this demonstration also."

"I don't know, Viktor. I think there is a lot of unrest in the city. You don't go out at night like I do. I see things you don't."

"Let's wait for the trial verdict. The judge is a fair man and that will be the end of it." Viktor paused to take a drink of the rich red wine before continuing. "I see the citizens of Vienna as good people that have been through so much—the war, starvation, cold, and no jobs, but now we see an improving economy. I see a better future ahead."

"Unfortunately, Viktor, I see only squalor and misery. I see men going to the streets, breaking each other's heads and a state not strong enough to control them. I believe the only answer is union with Germany. I think this new republic is incapable of survival."

"Hans, I fought in a war. I don't want to go through another one. Also, I have a thirteen-year-old boy, and I want him to see life without war."

Viktor looked up as Dr. Hayek entered the café. "Look, Hans, it's Dr. Hayek, and he's by himself. Let's invite him to sit with us. I enjoyed his talk this morning."

Hans mumbled something that sounded like, "I thought he was a nut."

Without waiting for a reply, Viktor rose and walked up to the economist. "*Bitte!* Dr. Hayek, if you are not with anyone would you care to join my friend Hans and myself? We attended your lecture this morning at Länderbank."

"I thought you looked familiar. I just came in to have a drink, but I would love to have the company of two economists."

Viktor escorted the doctor to their table and introduced Hans, who graciously rose and shook hands while Viktor signaled the waiter for another glass of wine for their guest.

"A speaker is always glad to receive comments, either good or bad, from members of his audience."

"Well, I guess I am a capitalist, Dr. Hayek. I completely agree with you that open and fair competition is best for all the people," Vikor said.

Hans now replied, "Sorry, doctor, but I have read John Maynard Keynes, and I agree with him that it is government's responsibility to get the economy moving again. Government should employ people, perform public works, affect expenditure to the poor, and maintain high spending."

"I know I am a voice in the wilderness," replied Dr. Hayek. "Maybe someday I will write a book and title it the *Road to Servitude*, or something like that. Remember, the Rule of Law was consciously evolved only during the liberal age and is one of that age's greatest achievements, not only as a safeguard but as the legal embodiment of freedom. Voltaire expressed it better than I can: 'Man is free if he needs to obey no person but solely the laws.'

"Nothing distinguishes more clearly conditions in a free country from those in a country under arbitrary government than the observance in the former of the Rule of Law. This means that government in all its actions is bound by rules and announced beforehand. Rules which make it possible to foresee with fair certainty and to plan one's individual affairs based on this knowledge. The individual is free to pursue his personal ends, certain that the powers of government will not be used deliberately to frustrate his efforts. Without law there can be no liberty. Liberty is freedom of individual action and association created through law."

"That can never happen in Austria and I don't think even in Germany," Hans said.

"I didn't want to go into this part with my talk this morning, but I would like to try this theory on you two gentlemen. That is, it is the lowest common denominator which unites the largest number of people. The political dictator will be able to obtain the support of all the docile and gullible, who have no strong convictions of their own but are prepared to accept a ready-made system of values if it is only drummed into their ears sufficiently, loudly and frequently. It will be those whose vague and imperfectly formed ideas are easily swayed and thus swell the ranks of the totalitarian party. Also, it is easier for people to agree on a negative program—say the hatred of an enemy, or the envy of those better off—than on any positive task. The contrast between the 'we' and the 'they,' the common fight against those outside the group seems to be an essential ingredient in any creed which will solidly knit together a group for common action. It is always employed by those who seek an unreserved allegiance of huge masses. Thus giving them greater freedom of action than almost any positive program. The enemy, like the Jew, has come to be regarded as the representative of capitalism because a traditional dislike of the population for commercial pursuits had left these careers readily accessible to a group that was practically excluded from the more highly esteemed occupations. It is the old story of the alien race's being admitted only to the less respected trades and then being hated still more for practicing them. The fact that anti-Semitism and anti-capitalism sprang from the same root is of great importance to the understanding of what may happen here. We have seen how the separation of economic and political aims is an essential guaranty of individual freedom. But centralized as an instrument of political power it creates a degree of dependence scarcely distinguishable from slavery," he said while taking a sip of wine.

"No totalitarian government will ever be a threat to the people of Austria," asserted Hans.

"Never say never, my good friend, and I will go a step further. There will be special opportunities for the ruthless and unscrupulous. There will be jobs to be done in the service of some higher end, and which have to be executed with the same expertness and efficiency as any other. The readiness to do bad things becomes a path to promotion and power."

"I don't believe any of that. At least not here in Vienna, or in Austria," Viktor said with some indignation.

"What to watch for here in Austria as well as Germany, is that it is essential that the people should come to regard the ends of the government as also their own ends. The skillful propagandist then has the power to mold minds in any direction he chooses. Even the most intelligent and independent people cannot entirely escape the influence of a leader who may be guided by an instinctive dislike of the state of things. This leads to a desire to create a new hierarchical order which conforms better to his conception of merit; he may merely know that he dislikes the Jews who seemed to be so successful in an order which did not provide a satisfactory place for him, and that he loves and admires the tall blond man in the novels of his youth."

Dr. Hayek stood to leave. "I am sure I have bored you both to death and I must go. Thank you for your patience in listening to me, but I do worry about my Austria."

"I went through the war as you did, doctor, and then the hyper-inflation that followed. Don't you think that was the worst and the future will be better?" Viktor asked.

"I will leave you with this," Hayek replied. "What our generation has forgotten is that the system of private property is the most impor-tant guaranty of freedom, not only for those who own property, but scarcely less for those who do not. It is only because the control of the means of production is divided among many people acting indepen-dently that nobody has complete power over us. If all the means of production were vested in a single hand, whether it be that of society as a whole or that of a dictator, whoever exercises this control has complete control over us."

"Thank you, doctor! I will give serious thought to what you have said," Viktor said, rising to shake the professor's hand.

Hans and Viktor finished their wine with no further discussion, left the café, and headed toward the Ringstrasse. However, muted conversations in the café had concealed the noise and activity in the central city. The streets were filled with people and no trams were running. There were lots of policemen about, mostly watching the events unfolding.

Hans had to yell to be heard above the din of the street. "Look, Viktor, at that newspaper; the *Heimwehr* men have been let go. I knew this would happen."

Viktor ran over to the Tabac shop to buy a newspaper. He chose the *Neue Freie Press,* which he believed would offer the most detail without lots of propaganda from either side. Back with Hans, he read aloud, "The three *Heimwehr* killers on trial pleaded self-defense, and the jury accepted this. The judge had no option but to let them off."

Viktor lowered the paper. He looked off into the distance and said slowly, "I am going home, Hans. I want to be with my family."

*   *   *

The next morning, Viktor awoke early. He had a feeling that things could get worse, regardless of his optimistic words the day before. He had joined neither party, because his bank would not have approved of active participation in politics. Anxious for news, he walked to the Tabac shop at the nearby tram station. There, he overheard a man say the city electricity workers had decided to strike. Soon there would be no lights. He rushed back to the apartment for his coffee and cream, carrying the Social-Democratic newspaper, the *Arbeiter Zietung*, under his arm. Sitting in his favorite chair, he read the lead article. The paper's editor denounced the acquittal of the *Heimwehr* men in words that sounded incendiary. The political situation, Viktor thought, had reached a combustion point.

Else joined him with the children. Viktor said, "I think the army and the police can keep order, but I want to see for myself."

"Don't be foolish, Viktor," Else exclaimed, as he rose from his chair. She began to cry. "The trams are not even running. It is too far to walk. What are you going to do, run all the way?"

Viktor sat back down, realizing she was right. What was he thinking?

Friday, 15 July, 1927, unfolded much as Viktor had feared. When the jury's verdict became known, infuriated workers left their shops and marched to the Parliament. By mid-morning, the demonstrators had grown into an angry mob, with thousands more streaming into the city. The multitude now stormed the *Justizpalast* and set it ablaze. To the mob, this building symbolized the hateful class-justice system that had let off the *Heimwehr* murderers.

At first, the police merely looked on as the *Justizpalast* burned. However, police reinforcements soon arrived. Armed with rifles, they were led by Police President Johannes Schober and Julius Deutsch, the senior Social-Democrat leaders. But by now neither man was in control, and their messenger, sent with orders for the violence to cease, could not get through the dense crowds in time.

The police, embittered by rumors that some of their comrades had been beaten to death by the mob, began to fire. Shots rang out, spelling death for ninety-four workers—and for Austria as well. The bodies of these men were an unsurmountable obstacle to a path toward reason. Neither the right nor the left had wanted this slaughter, but both were equally responsible for poisoning the political atmosphere.

After hearing about this, Viktor went back to work, but he was displeased with himself. He felt he had let down his family, his country, and most of all, himself for not being there. This was strange, because he wasn't even sure which side he was on. He hurt for the families of the ninety-four Social-Democrats killed, yet he hated the communist element of the Social-Democrats. He saw the Austria he knew and fought for during the war giving way to Bolshevism controlled by Jewish industrialists. His bank was not heavily Jewish, but other banks were. Those, he felt, along with the Jewish department store owners and Jewish industrialists, were sending Austria and Germany down the wrong path. He feared for his Austria-German way of life, now much improved with the end of hyper-inflation. He believed that after the events of this day, his family's future was in jeopardy.

He thought about Hans, who was a perfect Social-Democrat, an idealist, a do-gooder who sincerely wanted to improve the lives of the working classes. Viktor believed Hans felt guilty and ashamed of his inherited educational and social privilege, and thus had turned to "progressive" causes—as long as he could belong to the élite left and enjoy "more" equality than others. Besides, the Social-Democrats were the party of the Jews, of men like Viktor Adler, the founder of the party. Jews were prominent throughout the leadership and few came from working-class backgrounds.

* * *

One day in early September, Viktor came home from work and said to the family, "Let's go walk *Kartnerstrasse* and do some shopping."

"*Ja*, Papa!" yelled the children. He saw a relieved grin on Else's face. She knew Viktor had not been himself since the riots of 15 July, and she worried about him.

"What is the reason for this?" she said, smiling.

"I just think we all need to relax a bit."

The kids bounded out of the apartment. Viktor and Else tried to catch up before they got to the tram stop.

"It is a beautiful day," said Else, "and winter is coming, let's enjoy this while we can."

The tram took the family downtown to *Kartnerstrasse*, Vienna's most elegant shopping street which then met the "Ring" or the Ringstrasse, a tree-lined boulevard shaped like a horseshoe with its two arms meeting the banks of the Danube River. This street showed the true beauty of the old city: the baroque palaces, the old churches, the wide streets where Mozart and Hayden, Beethoven and Schubert had once walked. Along the Ringstrasse, the narrow lanes of the medieval city met the elaborately ornate buildings from which the Empire had been governed for hundreds of years.

But Viktor had something else in mind for his family, something much newer.

"Where are you taking us?" Else said.

Looking at his children, he said, "Where have you two been wanting to go for some time?"

They stared at each other, puzzled, until Fritz yelled out, "The movie house!"

They turned the corner to the *Stadt-Kino* and the kids screamed with delight. The children had heard stories of people moving about on a screen; now they would see for themselves. Throughout the movie, Fritz kept asking how the people on the screen could be moving. Elke seemed transfixed by what she saw.

The movies were all American and introduced the Viennese audience to a slanted impression of what America was like. The movies were usually about cowboys in the "Wild West" or "gangsters" or high society in American cities. They were immensely popular, and all classes of Viennese society could hardly wait to see the next production. Movie stars like Greta Garbo and Tom Mix had become well known to Viennese audiences.

Since the day was still lovely when they emerged from the *Stadt-Kino*, Viktor led the family to the Prater, Vienna's famous amusement park. The main attraction was the giant Ferris wheel, called *Riesenrad*, more locally known as the Prater Wheel, which carried its laughing riders to unbelievable heights overlooking Vienna. The family stood in a large red carriage and watched Vienna's rooftops slowly spin beneath them.

Afterward, they continued to walk through the grand area of unspoiled woods and meadows along the right bank of the Danube. Just on the other side of the city, they saw the mountains and wooded plain with its ponds and pools that stretched right up to the suburbs. One can wander about for hours in this great natural park. The Baur family liked to walk down the *Praterstrasse,* the long boulevard lined with chestnut trees.

It was a beautiful autumn day, still warm and with the fall colors in full glory. Elke gathered ripe chestnuts, which had fallen in their open green shells. The family stopped at an outdoor café for a meal of bratwurst and sauerkraut, with beer for the parents. After they finished eating, Viktor asked the children, "What did you like the best about the day?"

"Father," Fritz said, "I loved the motion pictures and asked myself how they made the pictures move. Someday I hope to understand. But my favorite were the bands here in the Prater. I want to be able to play in a band when I'm older."

Else asked her daughter the same question. Elke answered with the enthusiasm of a nine-year-old, "Oh Mama! The moving pictures. I want to go again!"

They would go again. This was the "Roaring Twenties," an exciting time in Vienna. One found exuberance everywhere, not just at the movies but also at the many nightclubs and theaters. There were many dancing schools in Vienna, crowded with people wanting to learn the latest dances—the Foxtrot, Tango, and Charleston; and the traditional Vienna waltz was not neglected. The more affluent citizens looked forward to Carnival, a time of fancy balls that made some forget the harsh weather that would soon descend upon them. However, in recent years, when Carnival ended, the Viennese faced bitter winters in a sharply divided city. The world was soon to move from the "Roaring Twenties" to the uncertain 1930s.

9

Hans Reinhardt

1931

On 13 May, 1931, The Financial News of London summarized the international standing of the Credit-Anstalt Bank as follows: "The bank has always been considered good for any engagements . . . It has been backed by the Viennese House of Rothschild, and it was known that, if the worst came to the worst, the Austrian government would continue to support it to the utmost to save Austria from disaster." Sir Eric Phipps, minister plenipotentiary of Great Britain in Austria said, "If even the Credit-Anstalt cannot be relied on, everything in Austria must be rotten."

In short, the announcement of the crisis at the Credit-Anstalt rocked the entire economic structure of the Continent and sent shock waves through the rest of the world.

Outside it was a brilliant January morning. But inside Viktor Baur's office on the fourth floor of the Länderbank Building, it was another hectic day of frantically trying to get ahead of the never-ending mounds of paperwork that crossed his desk. Viktor regretted that his children seemed to be growing up too fast while he was working at the office.

Money pressures had finally eased; even the Austrian economy seemed to be improving. His department's forecasts for 1931 predicted increasing employment and earnings growth for businesses. Viktor daydreamed about taking the family to Berlin on vacation that year. Elke would be twelve and Fritz sixteen, in his third year at gymnasium. Viktor wished he could enjoy the cold, clear weather and fresh snow covering the city outside, rather than being stuck here inside his bank office.

His daydreaming suddenly ended when his office door flung open and his friend Hans Reinhardt appeared with a look of anxiety on his face.

"Meet you at Café Central right after work," he said. "I have something to tell you but don't have time to explain."

It was not unlike Hans to be excited and emotional about some unimportant rumor he had overheard. He was younger than Viktor and a bit immature, but Hans was smart and a well-regarded economist at the bank. Viktor hadn't had a close male friend since the death of Christian almost thirteen years earlier. Not a day passed without some thought of his late friend. Viktor loved his family, but missed having a close male friend; one could talk business, football, and increasingly, the politics now on everyone's lips. Hans seemed to be getting more and more involved with the Social-Democratic Party, while Viktor tried to remain aloof from it all. Viktor imagined Hans' big news was that he had joined the *Schutzbund*, the party's private army.

*   *   *

"Welcome to Café Central," a waiter in a starched white apron greeted Viktor. The marble columns and high arched ceiling made the café look more like a library, but instead of people reading in silence, one was greeted by the sounds of clinking glasses, piano music, and carts rolling across smooth floors. Patrons were greeted with the sharp smell of boiled coffee and dark cocoa, cakes and pastries arranged temptingly on plates along a zinc countertop. Waiters wore crisp, white shirts under their white aprons while serving the luscious pastries topped with a fat dollop of whipped cream. The room was filled with men seated around white tables drinking coffee, smoking, reading the newspapers, and arguing.

Hans emerged from the noise and smoke.

"Well, what is your earth-shattering news?" said Viktor with an amused look.

"I am leaving Länderbank."

"What, are you out of your mind? Where are you going to go?"

"Coffee first," replied Hans with a smile, signaling to a waiter carrying a silver tray with coffee, glasses of cold water, and a white bowl piled high with sugar cubes.

Stirring the sugar into his coffee, Hans began. "I received an offer to join Credit-Anstalt. They want me to eventually be their Direktor of Economics. At my age it is an offer I can't turn down, and besides, the money is great."

"You know there are rumors that the bank is not as strong as it appears? Are you sure you want to join a ship which may sink?"

"Those are rumors started by the competition, like Länderbank. Look, I am single with no children. This is my chance. Länderbank is so conservative I will never make it to Direktor. I just want you to know, because I don't want to lose your friendship."

"I assure you, you won't, but I worry about you. Many of the things I have heard seem authentic."

"Look Viktor, this is the largest bank east of Germany and the biggest banking house in all of Central Europe. I don't see anything that can go wrong. Besides, there is always the Rothschilds, who have more money than God, to support us and there is always the backing of the Austrian National Bank."

"The Jew Rothschild, I don't trust that family at all."

"He may be a Jew, but Louis Rothschild, the bank president, has better contacts in the world's financial centers than do any of the large German banks. I mean London and New York. We are at the forefront of international finance."

"Well, I wish you good luck. I hope this will be a great opportunity. When you head up the Economics Department, don't forget your old friend. I don't know if I will ever get a chance to be the Direktor of Economics at Länderbank, but I have too much responsibility at home. Oh, by the way, are you going to the Bankers Ball at Carnival this weekend? Or a better question, did you get a decent girl to go with you this year?"

"Very funny, *Ja*, I have a lovely girl. And since this is a masked ball, I have told her to tease you constantly. Her intention is to totally embarrass you."

"I can always spot your girlfriends; they are fat and ugly."

"Hey, I want a girl with enough to get a hold of, and looks aren't everything. I can't see her with the lights out in bed. Besides, she has other attributes."

"I am a married man; I don't want to know what they are."

Viktor and Else would also attend the Banker's Ball at the House Konzerthaus, a large building that boasted a long hall lined with box seats, and several smaller rooms for other balls. An orchestra played traditional music in the largest hall. Smaller quartets played more modern music in the smaller rooms, where food was served from lavish buffets and all manner of drinks were available.

It was customary for husbands and wives to arrive at these balls separately. While the men wore tuxedoes and were not masked, the women wore lavish evening gowns that had been kept secret from their husbands. The women wore masks to make it difficult for their husbands to recognize them. During the dancing, the women would tease the men as they tried to find their wives or partners. Viktor was asked to dance by a somewhat heavy woman who kept saying, "Oh, *Herr* Baur, you look so lonely here, and your wife is having a wonderful time." Some women could be positively devilish in tormenting their dance partner. Then, at midnight, the women would remove their masks; most men would only then realize they were not dancing with the person they expected.

*   *   *

Surprisingly, the month of May brought a sense of optimism to Vienna. Viktor often thought that the very air in Vienna seemed to contain an answer to all of life's problems. Yet now that vision was like warped and distorted reflections in a poorly made mirror. What one sees is not necessarily reality.

On this May Sunday, the Baur family had spent much of the day walking through the Prater, and the children had talked about nothing but the first talking motion picture that had arrived from America. They begged Viktor and Else to take them to the *Park-Kino* movie house, which had been converted from silent movies to sound. People had lined up for hours to see the first talky to be shown in Vienna, *The Singing Fool*, starring Al Jolson. The Viennese were delighted with this new wonder from America. The Baur family went that very day and were amazed to hear people on the screen talk. This reminded Else of their visit to *Stadt-Kino* to see their first motion picture and how the children were transfixed by it. The tram ride back home at the end of a glorious spring day was filled with laughter.

The next morning, Monday, 11 May, Viktor woke up, had his morning shave with *Herr* Lohan, and arrived at his office a few minutes before nine o'clock. He was met with worried looks from fellow employees milling around in the hallway outside his office. He said to his clerk, Peter Strobel, "What is going on?" Peter, a dependable young man, followed Viktor into his office.

"I don't know. Klaus Schmidt [head of bank operations] has called a meeting of all officers for nine-thirty in the conference room."

"Any idea what it is about?"

"All I know is that it's something to do with Credit-Anstalt. I don't want to guess until we know more."

"*Ja, Das ist gute!* Get me some coffee, I have a feeling I may need it."

At nine-thirty, the bank's officers assembled in the large conference room with the massive mahogany table. It had never been used to accommodate all of the bank's officers before, thus there were not enough chairs and most were standing. The only sounds were subdued whispers.

Even the whispers ceased when Hans Niemeyer, the president of Länderbank, strode in. Those seated immediately came to their feet. Though a small man, Niemeyer's piercing eyes made him look as if he were angry at the world. Niemeyer was followed by Klaus Schmidt.

"Gentlemen, thank you for coming this morning," Niemeyer said. "I want to address what seems like a widening of rumors about the strength and stability of Credit-Anstalt. Please remember how dangerous and hurtful unfounded rumors are, not only to Credit-Anstalt, but to all banks. So if you are circulating rumors, they affect us also.

As you know, each bank in Austria is required to publish its annual balance sheet at the end of this month. Austria has a new bank Direktor, and I have heard on good authority that he has refused to sign the first draft of Credit-Anstalt's balance sheet. I don't know if this is true, but spreading unfounded rumors will not do our bank any good, either.

I have been through a depositors' run on banks before; it is not a pretty sight. A run will quickly turn into a panic. If the public panics, this can affect every bank. I have seen deposits pulled from strong institutions when every bank is tarred with the same brush. Also remember, Credit-Anstalt was the first European stock company to be introduced onto the New York Stock Exchange, thus it occupies a very special place among European banks. Each of us must defend its excellent reputation. Are there any questions?"

A heavy man sitting at the table near the president asked, "If these rumors are true, and if we receive questions from our clients, can we assume the Austrian National Bank will become a lender of last resort and would we be able to offer any assistance?" This drew subdued laughter from the men in the room.

For once, the president smiled. He replied, "Of course, if the situation is that severe, the Austrian National Bank would come to their aid. As to your last question, remember who owns Credit-Anstalt. I don't think we would care about the Jew Rothschild and his Jew business associates. Maybe those Jew bankers weren't as smart as we all thought." This last remark brought unrestrained laughter. Viktor looked over at Heinrich Weinstein, the lone Jew in bank management. Again, Weinstein looked concerned.

"This is why I don't put much stock in these rumors," Niemeyer continued. "Because the Rothschilds and their business partners own a great deal of Credit-Anstalt stock, they can manipulate its value. However, don't lose sight that during the last few months the Austrian economy has been greatly improving and the long-awaited recovery seems to have arrived. Also, the large domestic bond issue, the Austrian Housing Loan, is a great success. It is more than fifty percent oversubscribed. Even the *Times of London* heralded the bond issue as a sign of better times approaching. Also, the stock market has been experiencing a healthy recovery thus far this year, and I fully expect this to continue. I think we can relax and look forward to better times ahead both for Austria and the Länderbank. Thank you, gentlemen."

The meeting broke up with relieved smiles all around.

This same Monday morning, another meeting was taking place a bit further down the Ringstrasse, at Credit-Anstalt. Hans Reinhardt was seated next to friends near the back row of a small auditorium. Hans had heard the wild rumors concerning his bank, where he had only been employed for four months. He was not concerned with these wild rumors. He had heard them before but knew he was working for the bank financial people referred to as the "unsinkable" Credit-Anstalt. Besides, the past weekend he had attended the major annual Viennese horse-racing event, the Traber Derby. He had seen both the Chancellor and the Minister of Finance enjoying themselves in the grandstand. Surely if there was a crisis, they would have better things to do—like attending a meeting the press had been writing about, which was said to be held over the weekend.

Hans had been accompanied to the derby by the beautiful Karin Lothian, a woman he had known for some time, but only recently had he become more serious about her. She seemed impressed by his title of Assistant to the Economic Direktor of the bank, and he was impressed with the vitality with which Karin carried herself. In her bright pink dress, she was the object of attention for many at the Derby.

The main reason Hans wanted to work for this bank was because it was owned by the most important Jewish families in Europe. At its head was Louis Rothschild, followed by several Austrian aristocratic Jewish families. This gave Hans comfort in his belief that his new employer was in solid condition.

The senior Rothschild would not attend this Monday meeting. It would be held by Gerhard Mayer, his administrative assistant. The look of acute distress on Mayer's face worried Hans. Mayer got right to the point. "You may have heard that over this past weekend several meetings have been held with officials of the government and the Austrian

National Bank. It will be announced today that our balance sheet for the year 1930 will show a loss of 140 million schillings, which is 7.5 percent of our total balance sheet, and about 85 percent of our equity."

This news sent groans throughout the room.

Mayer continued, "The reasons for this loss are bad loans which financed some risky speculation. The management of the bank cannot gloss over the fact that this is indeed serious. The bank will ask for assistance from the government and the Austrian National Bank, the Rothschilds, and the shareholders. The management feels this plan will prevent any interruption in our ordinary business, and the bank will be secure in its future with a new capital base.

"This news is due to be released at noon today. We probably will see a brief run because some will want to withdraw their funds. However, I want to emphasize that we have the reserves available and will take care of our customers. When the public sees this, any initial panic will subside, and everything will be over shortly.

I recommend each and every one use the telephone and call as many clients as possible as quickly as possible. You may tell them about the loss on the 1930 balance sheet, and that the bank has financing in reserve to cover it. That is all, gentlemen, it is time to get on the telephone. This is not a time for questions but a time for action."

Many in the room sat in stunned silence before jumping to their feet to call their clients. Hans, because he had been sitting in the back, was one of the first out of the room. He ran into his office and closed the door. These were going to be difficult calls, but he had faith in the Credit-Anstalt and felt he could show this confidence in his voice over the telephone. The first calls were met with stunned silence and few questions, but he thought the news must be getting around, because his later calls were met with difficult questions, then angry voices demanding to get their deposits out, and: "My money had better be there!"

It was getting close to noon when Hans had made most of his calls. He decided to go to lunch, but when he opened a door he was greeted by the raised voices of hundreds of people frantic to get their funds out of the bank. A long line of customers, desperation on their faces, was beginning to form outside. Hans walked outside through a back door and across the street to better watch what was happening. He saw an unimaginable scene. Some people were yelling obscenities, others were crying. This brought back memories of his mother standing in line to receive a small amount of bread or meat during the hyper-inflation days. Back then, people wanted to get rid of their Austrian krone and buy food or any hard asset. This time, people wanted to get all their Austrian schillings from the bank holding them.

Within the first few days after the bank's announcement, it became apparent that doubts of the public had not been eased by the bank's reconstruction plan. In fact, for four days not only did the Credit-Anstalt witness a run on its reserves, but so did most Viennese banks. The Credit-Anstalt even extended its business hours until 8:30 p.m. to handle all the withdrawals. In just two days it lost about 16 percent of its deposits, and after two weeks, about 30 percent. These withdrawals would have rendered the bank illiquid had not the Austrian National Bank covered the losses. However, the Austrian National Bank, by accepting promissory notes from the Credit-Anstalt, was in violation of its bank's charter. As the days went on the situation grew worse.

In the days immediately following the Monday morning meeting, Hans felt that he—and the public—were both in the dark about the goings-on within his bank. He became an avid reader of magazines and newspapers in a futile effort to discover the latest news. On Saturday, 16 May, he picked up the London *Economist* and read, "Financial opinion is mainly disposed to congratulate the bank for avoiding a very delicate situation." Hans respected *The Economist,* but the signs he had seen all week told a different story.

When the bank's true losses, much larger than originally reported, began to come out, withdrawals continued at an even more desperate pace. Hans did know that the Austrian government, which had no funds at its disposal, had approached the Bank of England for a loan, and been rejected. The government now approached the Bank of International Settlements in Basil, Switzerland, which agreed to a loan of 150 million schillings ($21 million). Many felt the pressure had been lifted. All this begged the question: Where were the Rothschilds and their money?

Hans had seen what was likely coming, not from the phony reports he received from management, but what his eyes told him as he walked the city streets and overheard agitated conversations. People were blaming Jewish bankers for what had happened. The people didn't trust the government reports any more than he did. He realized that as a new employee at the Credit-Anstalt, his days were numbered. It was time to protect himself.

* * *

Letter To Viktor
5 SEPTEMBER 1932

Dear Viktor:

I know it has been sometime since we have talked, but you can guess my life has been one crisis after another since May 11th. I didn't realize a large bank like Credit-Anstalt could be managed so poorly. You were right that day at Café Central, and I should have listened. As a banker and competitor, I felt we could not be seen talking, but now that I have left Credit-Anstalt, I feel comfortable explaining what I know of the crisis.

First of all, the initial reported loss of 140 million schillings was nowhere near the actual loss of over a trillion schillings, more than seven times the reported amount. The largest part of the loss was due to bad loans. These came to 700 million schillings, not the 40 million originally reported. The Bank for International Settlements in Basil said it could loan 150 million schillings, but it took over two weeks to arrange the loan, and then for only 100 million. Meanwhile, Austrians and foreigners began to convert their schillings into foreign currency, leading to a large-scale reduction in the Austrian National Bank's reserves. When the Swiss loan finally arrived, it was far too little, too late. The delay proved disastrous. In under a week, the 100 million was withdrawn by the public, which distrusted the Austrian currency.

Remember, at this time a customs union between Germany and Austria was being discussed and France was fighting this to the point of pulling French short-term deposits out of all Austrian banks. Now the Bank of England decided to extend an emergency short-term loan. By short-term, I mean only seven days, renewable on a week-to-week basis. As bad as these terms were, Austria had no choice; non-acceptance would mean the withdrawal of all foreign deposits from all banks. So now the Austrian state was guaranteeing 1.2 trillion schillings of bank deposits, yet the government had a budget of only 1.8 trillion schillings. The government believed this guarantee would induce foreigners to place additional funds into Credit-Anstalt. This proved optimistic. Withdrawals continued; even an interest rate of 10 percent could not stop the capital flight. There was still no permanent settlement with foreign creditors and, of course, I was out of a job.

Most of us felt the crisis could have been avoided by the timely intervention of some authority—one strong enough to be the "lender of last resort" and lend freely but at a penalty rate.

This lender would be able to stand ready to halt a run by making money available. It would thus prevent each market participant trying to save itself but ending up ruining almost everyone. The financial distress of the few became a financial crisis for all. The president of the Austrian National Bank, Richard Reisch, seemed unconcerned and overly optimistic to me. I always wondered, since Credit-Anstalt was considered the "Jew bank," what effect this would have on government decisions. And where was the House of Rothschild? Their money backing the bank was the reason the bank was so successful.

The chance of international help was slim, especially since the possibility of a customs union with Germany was in the news. Someone told me Austria's position in 1931 "was like a victim on the international altar, tied and bound, and with a knife at her throat." However, there were many knives; not just the French, but the international bankers wanted to get all they could from Credit-Anstalt or from Austria.

The reserves, which were meant to provide stability and the securities were a large part of Credit-Anstalt's portfolio, which at the time gave the impression of potential liquidity. However, as the crisis showed, this liquidity was an illusion because of the large size of Credit-Anstalt. When they needed to sell securities, the amount to be sold was greater relative to the market and the mood of the market was bearish. Liquidity can only be bought at a very high price, by selling assets at a very low price.

I have gone on longer than I expected, but I felt you needed to hear the reasons from someone inside the bank. You should be proud of your bank. I understand Länderbank suffered no losses during this crisis. Don't feel sorry for me. A few days ago I learned that Chancellor Dollfuss needed an economist on his staff.

I applied for the job and I am now working for the Chancellor.
I really like him and think he will do a good job.
    Let's get together soon at Café Central?

Sincerely,
Hans

*   *   *

Café Central was bustling when Viktor approached a waiter wearing the standard white, heavily starched apron, who directed him to Hans' table. Victor was surprised to see that Hans looked older than his forty-years and a bit heavier. Still, he greeted Viktor with his usual cheery welcome.

"*Grüss Gott,* my friend," said Hans with a big smile.

"And you, my friend. It has been too long." They reached out to each other for a hug. Viktor continued, "So, you have gone to work for *Millimetternich?*" [A term the Socialist press used to disparage the new Chancellor, whose height was only 4 foot 11.]

"Well, we are in interesting times, Viktor. I worry about my Austria. I believe the Republic is failing. I feel we are moving gradually to authoritarianism. Inflation has embittered the middle classes and pensioners, the very people whose savings were wiped out by the Credit-Anstalt crisis. Is it any wonder the German Nazis are appealing to these Austrians?"

"Hans, I saw enough of war. I don't want to see more, but I believe that soldiers like myself were stabbed in the back by Jew industrialists and bankers. After seeing the devastation of France and coming home to see Austria and Germany virtually untouched by the war, it makes one wonder what my friend Christian Müeller died for?"

"Viktor, why don't you join me in our Jaeger Battalion? I believe the National Socialists when they promise to do away with unemployment and with it, poverty in Vienna. I believe them when they say they will unite the German nations."

"What?! The last time we talked you were upset because some *Heimwehr* men had killed some poor Socialists. You were pissed off that a judge let them go after they pleaded self-defense. What has changed?

"As much as anything, it was probably the Jews that were running Credit-Anstalt into the ground with their lousy loans to their Jew friends. I never should have left Länderbank, I should have listened to you, but their offer was too good. I was as blind as a newborn baby to what they were hiding."

"Hans, I will think on this. I grew up in right-wing, middle-class surroundings. My parents were avid newspaper readers. Political opinions would begin over breakfast, so I knew about political parties before I knew my multiplication tables. I despise the racially inferior Jew-ridden Freemasons. And the greatest threat of all is Marxism, promulgated by the Jew, Karl Marx. However, I have wanted to stay out of politics, mostly for my banking career."

"You may have to start, Viktor, because the Communists are getting stronger. They and all the Socialists are nothing more than a bunch of fools who believe in democracy, socialism, Marxism, and racial mixing. They believe in the Parliament they created. They need to be introduced to our fire and sword, and then kept in their place or utterly rooted out."

"I have heard this before but can't remember who said it."

"Prince Starhemberg," Hans said with a large grin.

"*Ah, ja*! Prince Ernst von Starhemberg; you can't be serious about him. As a leader of the *Heimwehr* he is a joke, nobody takes him seriously."

"Well, I wouldn't make him a loan. He is, however, the darling of the young Fascists. He's aristocratic, good-looking, has an unfair amount of sex appeal, and possesses far more intelligence than his birth and upbringing would lead you to expect. There are rumors, I think true, that as a boy he got himself mixed up in Hitler's 'Beer Hall Putsch' in 1923. He also has an easy manner, probably because he believes he is superior to everyone he has ever met, including the entire House of Habsburg."

Hearing this, Victor recalled another false hero.

"This reminds me of Colonel Redl, a traitor to Austria before the Great War. My friend Christian idolized him, partly because he looked great in uniform. I have learned it takes more than a uniform to make a man."

"Prince Starhemberg merely keeps himself amused with politics. What 'going on a binge' means to an alcoholic is politics to Starhemberg."

Viktor thought for a moment. "I like that he has called for all German races to unite in a Teuton realm and to exclude all foreign flat-footed parasites from the East."

"Viktor, I desperately wish to join the *Heimwehr,* because its members believe the politics of today are a matter of life and death. I want to attach myself to something great and fundamental. We are united by one thing only—that the misery of Austria is due to the Jews. The Jewish spirit is seditious and Jewish blood is corrupting. People who pity the Jews still don't understand what the Jew is. To allow Jews to continue living in the German body politic and to have pity with them is like having pity on tuberculosis bacteria. Pity is the great danger facing the German people."

Viktor signaled for another glass of red. "I understand Dr. Joseph Goebbels from Berlin is going to speak in Vienna. I would like to hear him. Are you interested?"

An excited Hans replied, "There are rumors of Hitler himself coming, and I would really like a chance to see him. I know Dollfuss and the government don't want either of them here, because Austria doesn't need the disruption but *Ja,* I would like to. It is at the football stadium tomorrow night. I will come by at six and pick you up."

Viktor got up to leave, then turned to Hans. "I think I would like to join your *Heimwher.* What do I have to do?"

"After we hear Dr. Goebbels we will talk about it further."

With those words, the men parted. Viktor knew he was beginning to tread an unfamiliar path. He knew these private armies, the *Schutzbund* of the Socialists and the *Heimwher* of the Christian Socials, regarded themselves as arms of the law. They were a product of the chaos that had followed the Great War and the collapse of the Austrian krone. At first, the government welcomed these groups because they were local and defensive, and the Austrian army, along with the central police force, had ceased to exist. The obvious result was that they were unable to maintain order. Chaos was almost constant in Vienna and many other Austrian towns. As time went on, these men, who previously had waited for blazes to extinguish, now were lighting fires themselves.

Viktor felt he had no choice, he had to declare himself for one side or the other. He was a Teuton through and through, but he knew in his heart his beloved Austria could not survive on its own; there must be an *Anschluss* with Germany. He loved his country but his service in the war, especially when his unit was attached to the Wehrmacht in the last months in France, had taught him Germany was stronger and better organized than Austria.

The future belonged to the strongest. He knew the Germanic people needed to grow while preserving the purity of German blood, and to do that they would require more living space. Because of this, he knew that his feelings had changed. Terrible street violence was erupting within the city, people were dying every day over who would run Austria, Hitler or Dollfuss.

Viktor felt there could be no coexistence between race-conscious people and the Jews. These thoughts darkened his mind as he hugged his wife and children. He looked around the apartment. A life of hard work and struggle had provided a good life for the family he loved. Viktor knew he had to do everything he could to preserve that life.

10

Prince Starhemberg

1933

*Engelbert Dollfuss, small in stature at "five foot nothing"
but full of energy, became Chancellor of Austria in May 1932,
with the world Depression at its height. His finest quality was
his dauntless personal courage, a quality he would need from
the outset. His first success as Chancellor was to secure a loan
of 300 million shillings through the League of Nations for his
struggling country. However, this aroused the bitter opposition
of the Austrians who wanted union with Germany, as well as
the pro-Nazi wing of the Heimwehr. In March 1933, Dollfuss suspended parliament and launched his own brand of dictatorship.*

The Baur household was quiet on this spring afternoon. Viktor
was absorbed in the morning newspaper. For a change, Fritz
was home and sitting at the piano working on a Mozart sonata. Elke
was now fifteen and into her schoolwork. She liked school, especially
the literature classes. She told the family she would like to work for
a newspaper someday. Else was concentrating on her sewing. The

political news seemed to be worsening; she worried about her city, her country, and most of all, her family.

She knew Viktor had joined the *Heimwehr*, although he had tried to keep it from her. She knew he was attending meetings in the evenings with his friend Hans, not meeting bank clients as he had told her. Even Fritz was putting pressure on them; he wanted to join the Austrian National Socialist party. Fritz had begged his father for the brown shirt uniform he needed in order to join. Thus far, Viktor had refused.

The economy had destroyed any chance of employment for a nineteen-year-old who couldn't stay in school. There were no jobs, regardless of the field of study. But Else knew her husband, and she knew that in time, Viktor would relent. The ascendance of Adolf Hitler was already a grave threat to democracy. In Austria, the noisiest prophets of Germanism were the Austrian Nazis; Else worried that they were gaining ground. Brown shirts and Swastika armlets had broken out like a fungus all over the streets of Vienna. The rhythmic throbbing of the senseless reiterations, which Hitler had learned and used to intoxicate the Germans, began to deprive lower middle-class Viennese youth of their reasoning faculties.

Else did not want an argument with either Fritz or Viktor, but she feared for her country and placed the blame on the Austrian Chancellor, Engelbert Dollfuss. He had ended Parliamentary government back in March. She could see nothing positive coming of that. She was certain now that Viktor was convinced that Anschluss with Germany was inevitable as Austria was too small a country on its own. The Social-Democrats of Dollfuss, who were manning the barricades, were largely middle-class and Jewish while the Christian-Socials who wanted Hitler saw the Social-Democrats as only communists and Jews. Else spent her day shopping and talking. She could feel the tide turning toward Hitler and the Nazis.

"What's for dinner, Mother?" Fritz had stopped playing. She was startled by his words, as if she'd heard a clap of thunder.

"I have a pork cooking. I had almost forgotten. Thank you, Fritz." Viktor didn't look up from his paper and Elke was engrossed in her schoolwork.

Else was glad to get back into her small kitchen where she felt comfortable and removed from the political talk. Any conversations that might arouse anger or controversy were ordinarily barred from the kitchen and dining room.

At dinner, this rule was adhered to until Fritz broke in with, "I understand Dollfuss has called for a rally of his Austrian Front at Schönbrunn. Father, can I go?"

Else interrupted. "No politics at dinner time."

Fritz persisted. "Father, can I go?"

"Else, let me address this, it is a good question," Viktor said. He thought for a long time before he answered. "I have been feeling lately that the ground is slipping from under me. It is like standing in a bog. The seizure of power by Hitler in Germany and the violent propaganda campaign which has followed has upset me. I feel we must show the people there is strength in Austria; that there is a power that can protect them from the Nazis. The people are wavering; army officers and police are left guessing whom they can trust—Austria or the Nazis. We must organize things in Austria so individual citizens will find it extremely inconvenient, and even dangerous to be a Nazi. We must meet National Socialist terrorism with even worse terrorism. There has never been a big patriotic demonstration in Vienna. A march of twenty-thousand or twenty-five thousand armed *Heimwehr* would prove the current conditions in Vienna by no means represent the real spirit of the country. *Ja,* son, and I will go with you. We will go and see this for ourselves."

The family sat in shocked silence until Else blurted out, "Viktor, you are scaring me."

"No, Mother, I think Father is right. This is why I want to participate in the Austrian Front demonstrations at Schönbrunn."

"No, I will not allow it." Else stood up and stamped her foot, which, coming from this usually quiet lady, surprised everyone around the table.

Viktor took his wife's hand. "I know this is a difficult time, but we have been through worse, and we will get through this."

"Oh Viktor, when will the bad times stop? I don't want to lose my family." She broke down in tears and fled to the bedroom. Viktor, Fritz, and Elke looked at each other.

"She will be okay, she is tough," Viktor said, following her. He found her sobbing into her pillow. "Sweetheart, nothing will happen to Fritz or to me. I promise," he reassured her.

She raised her head and looked at Viktor. "You don't know that; people are dying in the streets every day. I am sure they all felt death would happen to someone else. Viktor, how would Elke and I live if you and Fritz were gone?"

"Else, please. You worry about things you have little control over. Fritz is nineteen and someday will probably be in the army. You can't control that. Hopefully, we will get through this and Austria will be stronger and the better for it."

"Viktor, I think you are wrong. This will not end well, and I feel so helpless."

"Have faith, my dear. Have faith in God. He will see all of us through."

"Viktor, I pray all the time. I just don't see things getting any better."

Elke, who had been quietly watching from the doorway, said, "Sometimes Mother, God works in strange ways. We must trust in His judgement."

*　*　*

Of all the splendors Vienna had to offer, the Schönbrunn Palace and gardens were Viktor's favorites. The Palace was a grand building set amid the quiet woods and meadows of the Wienerwald, a glittering, fairy-tale edifice commanding a view of the whole countryside. However, this was not a day to take in the scenery. The area in front of the palace was filled with a reported forty thousand peasants, citizens, and workers, many of whom were armed. To Viktor it was both picturesque and depressing. The *Heimwehr* regiments in their green uniforms were flanked by Tyrolean defense volunteers in colorful traditional native garb. For the first time since the war, soldiers and officers of the Austrian army were represented, wearing their old uniforms. Even retired colonels and generals had dusted off their old outfits, polished their spurs, sabers, and medals and marched proudly at Schönbrunn.

The crowd began screaming "Heil" when the diminutive Chancellor traipsed up to the speakers' dais to address the excited multitude. In his grey-green uniform of the *Kaiserjager,* the Imperial Alpine Regiment, a military cape over his shoulder, wearing immaculately shined boots and a white feather on his cap, he inspired a sudden wave of nostalgia as the crowd yearned for an earlier time. Dollfuss announced he had outlawed the Nazi party, and it was now illegal to wear the brown shirt uniform. The thousands cheered and hailed the new era.

Fritz, who was caught up in the excitement, had to yell to Viktor to be heard. "Who is that on the dais with the Chancellor, Father?"

"I believe it is Prince Starhemberg, the head of the *Heimweir.*"

At that moment, a familiar face appeared next to Viktor.

"I don't see you *Heiling* with all the rest?" Hans said, turning to admire the mass audience. "I am pleased so many have turned out to see this wonderful moment. I am so proud of Austria right now I could burst." Hans beamed with satisfaction.

"I don't know, I am not convinced this is what is the best for Austria," Viktor answered.

"It may not be for the best, Viktor, but for now it is the only way."

"What are you doing now, Hans? It has been a while."

"I am still working for the Chancellor. I am his economic advisor, but my primary duty is to be an administrative assistant to Prince Starhemberg."

"I almost forgot. Hans, this is my son, Fritz. He is nineteen and hot to wear a uniform, really any uniform."

"Good to meet you, Fritz. Your father is a fine Austrian, but I am afraid things are changing a bit too fast for him. When you get a littler older and Viktor lets you, come and see me. I will get you in the proper place."

"My son is asking about the Prince. I told him he's someone Dollfuss can rely on. Do you agree?"

"I trust him completely, but don't believe everything you hear about him. He is a colorful personality."

"Tell me more about your job."

"I guess I have become a kind of channel between Starhemberg and Dollfuss. Things are unsettled. Dollfuss doesn't know who supports him on Austria and who wants to give in to the Germans. By the way, do you have time for coffee tomorrow? I have lots to tell you."

"Looking forward to your stories. I will see you at Café Central at noon."

On the tram back to the central city, Fritz said, "Do you think I will ever wear a uniform like Prince Starhemberg?"

"I don't know, Fritz. When I was in the war I hoped and prayed you would never have to go to war. But Austria is sick, politically. I am afraid only some wonder drug can heal the festering wound which resulted from suspicion and hatred, inflammatory speeches, and the bullets of July 1927. I am afraid our Chancellor does not possess such a wonder drug. I do believe Dollfuss has the courage of his convictions and believes in an independent Austria."

In bed that night, Victor replayed the day in his mind; the forty thousand voices screaming for Austria and Else's fearful words. He thought, *A fanatic terrorist would not be deterred by imprisonment, but he is afraid to fall into the hands of men who also have no scruples, either from bureaucratic training or a respect for the law, and will inflict on him a sound beating or maybe death.*

*   *   *

While Viktor sat reading the *Neue Freie Presse* at the Café Central, his eyes caught the words of his friend's new boss, Prince Starhemberg.

Herr Hitler, you are the greatest liar Germany has ever known, for you pretend to fight against Bolshevism, whereas in reality, you are leading the German people into Bolshevism. Your National Socialism is nothing more or less than the German form of Bolshevism. It is brown Bolshevism.

Hans soon approached Viktor's table. He looked stressed.

"Dollfuss drives me crazy," Hans said. "He cannot make up his mind. He is upset with the Prince for his words to Hitler that, I assume, you were just reading. I guess Dollfuss' idea of diplomacy is to bend over and take it in the rear."

"Did you remind the Chancellor that Hitler is not only the German Chancellor but the leader of the Austrian Nazi terrorists?"

"*Ja*, I recognize Dollfuss is in a difficult spot. He is not sure how to resist Hitler when it is impossible to know, even of the highest executive officials, that they are not secretly helping the Nazis to power . . . when the deputies of Dollfuss' own party cannot be trusted and even ministers may have gone over secretly to the enemy."

"Are things as bad as all that, Hans? How does Starhemberg fit into this?"

"The two fight like cats and dogs. Dollfuss is always looking for compromise solutions. He actually begged the Prince not to attack

Hitler, even though it is well known Hitler is behind those who, in his name, have murdered Austrians and destroyed Austrian property."

"Hans, you said Dollfuss isn't sure who to trust in his own government. You don't mean Starhemberg?"

"Heavens, no! Ernst loves Austria and hates the Nazis. Now, this next thing must stay between the two of us. You must promise." Viktor was taken aback at Hans referring to the Prince by his given name, but agreed. "Hans, I promise."

"Well, here is what Starhemberg himself told me. Back in October, Dollfuss asked for his recommendation for Secretary of State for Public Security—a man with plenty of push and few scruples, particularly regarding the Nazis. Ernst said Dollfuss wanted Major Emil Fey, currently the head of the Vienna *Heimwehr*. Starhemberg agreed to go along, although he had had some unfortunate experience with Fey. Ernst knew Fey was extremely ambitious but should have realized an ambitious man was potentially dangerous. Ernst says the day may come when he will deeply regret that decision to go along with the Chancellor."

"God, Hans, what do we do?"

"Let's see what happens. The Chancellor is a good man who loves Austria. Other than that, we have to do what is best for ourselves."

* * *

For Hans, the days seemed to fly. Despite the hours spent as Economics Direktor, more and more time was spent with Prince Starhemberg. He took notes in each meeting the Prince attended and followed up to ensure decisions were carried out correctly.

In 1934 things became even more serious. In January, Dollfuss called a meeting of his cabinet for 9:30 in the evening to announce that he had entered into negotiations with Theo Habicht, Hitler's envoy, who had been expelled from Austria only the year before. Dollfuss justified this on the grounds that Nazi terrorism was damaging the Austrian economy, and he wanted peace, but not at any price.

Starhemberg exploded, "What do you mean peace, but not at any price? Just talking with that scoundrel would compromise us."

Dollfuss replied, "Naturally, there would not be the slightest concession on our side that affected the independence of Austria. I just want to appease the National Socialists."

Starhemberg was quick with his opinion. "It is incompatible with your dignity as the Austrian Chancellor to sit at the same table with such a contemptible person, a man you yourself expelled from Austria. I consider it an insult on Hitler's part to suggest you negotiate with Habicht."

Stockinger, the Minister of Trade, agreed. "For the Lord's sake, do nothing of the sort. All we have accomplished, all we have sacrificed, will have been in vain. Whoever persuaded you gave you bad advice."

Hans noticed that Major Fey was quiet during this discussion.

Dollfuss defended his plan. "The talks tomorrow with Habicht are of secondary consideration. What comes out of it is all that matters."

Starhemberg, almost red in the face, burst out, "You don't know the Nazis; they are only entering into negotiations to compromise you, even if they end by you throwing Habicht out of the room. The fact that you, the Austrian Chancellor, even discussed matters with the leader of terrorists and the organizer of bomb outrages, will compromise your position hopelessly. No one in or outside the country will understand it. If Hitler were honest in his desire to end the conflict, he would appoint a more reputable delegate."

Dollfuss was quiet as Starhemberg continued, "I am afraid, Chancellor, our ways must part if you hold this discussion with Habicht; I do not doubt your loyalty or your wish to fight for Austria, but I will not follow you on this ill-advised course."

The meeting ended after midnight. Dollfuss had been convinced to disinvite Hitler's representative, and a wire was sent to Berlin.

Habricht was already on his way when instructions reached him to turn back to Berlin.

*   *   *

In February 1934, violence and terrorism between the Social-Democrats and the Christian-Socialists seemed to ratchet up. Now, anti-Semitic tendencies became more noticeable within the Christian-Socialists, but Dollfuss needed them in his struggle against the Nazis. The leaders of the party were aware that Dollfuss was wooing subordinate groups in order to split the party. Hans found himself in the middle of these events. He admired the Prince and Chancellor Dollfuss, but felt the situation was a powder keg, one that needed only a spark to ignite it.

Until that spark came, Hans needed to let off some steam. He chose to do so at the bar at the Hotel Sacher. On this cold February evening its patrons were enjoying a small band playing some of the new jazz music from America. This music took Hans's mind off the tensions and fears obsessing him. He sometimes wished he had stuck with the piano lessons his parents had forced upon him when he was young. But in those innocent days all he thought about was becoming a football player. Today, fears of the outside world were always on his mind. A soft female voice broke through his thoughts.

"You are Hans Reinhardt, aren't you?"

"*Ja*, I am. Have we met before?"

"Probably not. I work for Dr. Stockinger in the Trade Ministry and I have seen you around. I don't mean to be forward, and I'm sorry if I am interrupting anything. Are you waiting for someone?"

"*Nein*, I am not, just trying to get my mind off current events."

"Let me know how that works. By the way, my name is Inga Bonhoeffer."

"Please sit down, *Fraulein*. Do you like the music?"

"I really don't know this music. I was brought up on Strauss, Beethoven, and Mozart."

"I am learning to appreciate it; there is something about the beat I like. I just wanted to get away from the tension at work and in the country."

"Do you think the Chancellor can bring everyone together?"

"I hope so, but with the current interference from Germany I am afraid it may not happen. But I came here to forget that. And now a pretty girl has introduced herself to me, and I don't want her to leave."

Inga was tall with dark brown hair that came to just above her shoulders. Her skin had a tint of an olive color that might indicate Italian heritage. She wore a charm bracelet on her wrist and small gold earrings. She spoke well, and since she was working for the Trade Ministry, which was a bit unusual for a woman, Hans guessed she was very bright.

"I feel as though I was too forward by interrupting you, but yes, I would like to stay. Maybe you can teach me to appreciate this new music."

The evening went well. Hans found himself wanting to get to know Inga better. For some time he had been thinking of looking more seriously for a female companion. He wasn't ready for marriage, but it would be nice to have an intelligent woman to talk with.

About an hour later, the evening ended with Hans asking Inga to dinner, and her accepting. When she left, Hans felt there was a glimmer of light on his otherwise gloomy horizon.

However, those dreams were rudely interrupted the following morning by a phone call from an agitated Prince Starhemberg. Little did Hans know that he was about to help stop a civil war.

"Hans, I need you here, and quickly. Dollfuss wants us to go to Linz as soon as possible."

The line went dead. A quick glance at the clock by Hans's bed said it was 5:30, and the urgency in the Prince's voice was real. He quickly dressed and, without shaving, hurried to the Prince's apartment near the *Ballhausplatz* (the Chancellery). The door was opened by the Prince himself, already dressed in his green *Heimwehr* uniform with brilliantly polished boots which came to just below his knees and his *Heimwehr* hat with the cock's feather atop.

"Sorry to wake you. Major Fey called that there is trouble in Linz and I am the only authority to muster the *Heimwehr*. I did, however, tell him I think calling out the *Heimwehr* will further inflame passions. I have asked to see the Chancellor; we will all meet with him at his apartment."

They hurried over to the Chancellor's office at the Hofburg. Major Fey was already there, pressuring him about the *Heimwehr*.

Dollfuss looked pale and depressed. He said to Starhemberg, "This situation is damned unpleasant."

Fey explained to the Prince and Hans that a Socialist uprising had been initiated by the Reds in Upper Austria, and a party of police had forced their way into the Hotel Schiff, known as a Workmen's Club of the Linz Social-Democrats, to search for arms. Also, there was news from Steyr: Unemployed men had forced their way into a factory and killed the managing director. And at Ennsleiten, a workers' colony near Steyr, a *Heimwehr* man and his fiancée had been murdered.

"That's not all," Fey said. "At a crossroad between Linz and Wels, four army officers who knew nothing of these events were shot by the Socialist *Schutzbund*. The *Heimwehr* must put an end to this."

The Prince glanced at Dollfuss, who looked blank. "I must call my people in at *Heimwehr* headquarters in Lintz," Starhemberg said. He turned to Hans, who had anticipated his request. A brief conversation between Starhemberg and the official confirmed Major Fey's report. The *Schutzbund* had occupied the section of Linz situated on the north bank of the Danube. By occupying the bridge, they had cut off communications.

As soon as Starhemberg hung up the phone, it rang again. The news was even more discouraging: The rebels had occupied the town of Steyr. This meant the occupation of its large arms factory was only a matter of time, with the rebels getting their hands on large stores of rifles, automatic pistols, and machine-guns. This greatly alarmed Dollfuss. He begged Starhemberg and Hans to go to Steyr.

The situation was too dangerous for the two to go alone; the road to Steyr led through country in which revolt was likely to spread. Starhemberg called out about a hundred of his most loyal *Heimwehr* troops to accompany them. It took time to procure motor-buses for the trip, thus it was not until late afternoon that four buses left Vienna. One took the lead, followed by a car with the Prince, Hans, and the driver, while three buses brought up the rear. Above all, they had to prevent the arms from being seized and handed out to the rebel groups.

Hans appraised the situation: The worker's colony of Ennsleiten, on the right bank of the Enns River, dominated the arms factory and the town itself, which was in the hands of a well-armed and well-disciplined *Schutzbund* unit. Rumors circulated of atrocities committed upon the inhabitants by the *Schutzbund* rebels, but most turned out to be grossly exaggerated. Now that the *Heimwehr* controlled the high ground with trench mortars that could fire upon the town, the rebels capitulated with little resistance.

Accompanied by twenty men, the Prince and Hans drove to the Steyr arms factory to see the situation for themselves. To their surprise, it was deserted. Not far from the head office stood a small car. Reaching it, they gasped and tried not to throw up. In the driver's seat was the managing director. His hands gripped the steering wheel, but where his head should have been was a shapeless mass of skin and clotted blood. He had been shot at point-bank range with a large-caliber revolver.

The men pushed on to the office, where they were met by a frightened employee who was much relieved when he recognized their uniforms. He led them into a large room where the office staff and some of the higher officials were barricaded. They must have spent some unpleasant hours, knowing the fate of their director. But the arms were intact. That the rebels had made no effort to seize them, showed they had no offensive intentions. Also, the factory workers had no part in the uprising, even though they knew of the existence of the arms and would have realized their importance.

That evening, they called Dollfuss to tell him order reigned in Steyr, and they would come back to Vienna the next day. The Chancellor urged them to hurry back because riots had broken out in the workers' apartments in the Karl Marx-Hof (a building complex created to provide low-cost housing for the working class, completed in 1930). After an all-night dash back to the city, they learned that the Minister of Security, Major Fey, had taken over the government.

The men immediately went to the modest apartment of the Dollfuss family on *Stallburggasse*. They were dismayed to find a pallid Dollfuss pacing between the drawing-room and the bedroom, where his telephone was fixed to a wall. "I cannot control Fey," he cried, "he has become a megalomaniac and there is no talking to him. Starhemberg, you must help me manage the man."

The Chancellor's concern was to stop the fighting immediately—not merely to avoid a full-scale civil war, but to avoid giving Hitler a pretext for intervening "to restore order." His first thought was to use, not howitzers, but tear gas. He ordered the main military arsenal to collect all available supplies of gas for immediate use. To his astonishment and anger, the arsenal's apologetic reply was that the Austrian Army had no tear gas, because all forms of gas warfare had been forbidden by the Treaty of St. Germain. Dollfuss jammed the receiver back on its hook and began pacing again.

Suddenly, he stood still. "There is another way to bring them to heel quickly. Bring up artillery and fire on the houses they are fighting from. We could save countless lives, and the houses can easily be rebuilt. I must do it, even if I'm condemned for it. Everyone will shout 'artillery against the people,' but it's the only way to get the business over quickly and with little sacrifice. I must take it on my conscience."

Hans, hearing the pleading in the Chancellor's voice, felt the crisis was out of control, and he was not sure the government had the will or the strength to restore order.

*   *   *

As Hans and the Prince left the Chancellor, they were shocked to see notices on building walls (undoubtedly posted by Fey's cronies) hailing him the savior of Austria. During lunch in a local cafe, people were talking about the bravery of Fey during the storming of the Red "citadels." It was rumored Fey had even promised his own troops rewards for their victory.

When Hans finally left the Prince that afternoon, he called Inga and arranged to meet her for dinner that evening.

It had been a horribly hectic day for Hans, but as he walked into the restaurant he relaxed when he saw the lovely lady waiting for him.

"Where have you been? I have been worried sick," said Inga in a low voice. She was interrupted with a warm embrace and a deep kiss.

"I am sorry, but Starhemberg dragged me to Linz to help secure the arms stores. I missed everything here in Vienna."

"Well the fighting is not over, and it may go on for days. Your friend, Major Fey, is bombarding the workers in their apartments in the Karl-Marx-Hof, as well as their women and children."

"He is not my friend. In fact, both Prince Starhemberg and I think he is working behind the government's back with the Nazis."

"Well, regardless, your trip to Steyr was all Dollfuss needed to bombard women and children."

"We had to secure the arms inventory in Steyr."

"Well, did you?" Her tone was a bit softer.

"It hadn't been touched, and it looked as if the Socialists hadn't even thought about taking the weapons. I don't think either side wanted to start a civil war. The right wing fears what will happen with Germany if they win, and the left knows victory is impossible."

"I think you are right about Dollfuss. He knows no matter who wins this civil war, the real winner will be Nazi Germany, thanks to Major Fey. This is exactly what Fey wanted."

"Look Inga, we are just guessing about what is going on. Let's take the Number 39 tram to near the Karl Marx-Hof at dawn tomorrow and see for ourselves what this looks like."

The next day the two met at the tram stop near the university. The tram was there, but its crew was standing in the street next to it. "Don't bother to wait," one of the conductors said. "There is no electricity, we don't know ourselves what's going on." Hans and Inga began to walk along the tram line, hoping to find one running. However, they soon passed many stationary trams, some with their crews, others without them. There was hardly any traffic about, and the few pedestrians they saw all seemed in a hurry. Lorry-loads of armed, steel-helmeted police passed them. The sound of howitzers and machine gun fire could be heard on that cold Sunday morning in February when they arrived at a barbed-wire barrier that blocked them from going further. The streets were full of spectators. They looked as if they were attending a football game. Most were cheering on the "home-team," that is, the "players" manning the artillery. The thud, thud, thud of shells dropping into apartments packed with workers and their families never stopped. The two were standing near some *Heimwehr* soldiers. They overheard one say, "Parquet floors and shower-baths for workers, indeed—you might as well put Persian carpets in a pigsty and feed the sows on caviar."

Inga motioned she wanted to leave. She and Hans walked until they could be heard better over the noise of the shells slamming into the building. Once away from the noisy crowd, he saw she was crying. When they reached a park bench, they sat down. She began to shake, tears running down her cheeks. Hans put his arm around Inga, who laid her head on his shoulder.

"I can't believe the ruthless destruction, by unintelligent, unimaginative, selfish people. These buildings were a beacon of hope for people who had grown up in a jungle of slum living. There, life was only dirt, disease, and dependence. These buildings offered my fellow human beings some of the good, simple things life has to offer: a clean home, sunshine, pure air, a glimpse of green from at least some of the windows, decent sanitation and opportunities for personal cleanliness. A corner of safety from traffic for their children to play in. Medical attention in case of an emergency. Now these dream cities are being trampled back into the jungle by beasts who cannot tolerate their existence."

Pent-up emotion poured out of Inga. Hans was silent, knowing this was a time for tenderness. "Hans, hold me! I feel the worst is still to come. There will now be executions."

"No, that will not happen. Dollfuss has promised amnesty for all but the leaders, if they lay down their arms. The Prince and Chancellor have both agreed this is a conflict neither side wants. Dollfuss knows mercy to the vanquished is the best course."

Inga said grimly, "We will see what Major Fey does. I don't want to be on the wrong side of this, but I am afraid the only side remaining is the Nazi side."

Hans walked Inga to the tram stop where, miraculously, a lone tram was running. He put his arm around her and gently kissed her on the cheek. "You take care of yourself and stay safe." As the tram pulled away, Hans could not help but feel Inga was a better woman than any he had met before.

The brief civil war came to an end on 16 February, 1934, with 193 civilians and 128 police dead.

11

Putsch

1934

The Austrian historian Gordon Brook-Shepherd accurately described the difficulties Dollfuss faced as follows: "Indeed, the new Chancellor, probably the youngest Head of Government in the Europe of his day and certainly the shortest in both stature and experience, had been summoned to rule a country which seemed politically, morally and financially bankrupt beyond repair. The causes of this mortal sickness were largely rooted in that Empire from which the new Austria had been forcibly torn in 1918; but, by her own mistakes and mishaps, the young Republic had steadily aggravated her case. All that need be mentioned here is the general picture of government which Vienna presented when he took office.

"It was that of a creaking merry-go-round, revolving wearily in some deserted corner of the fair. Almost all the figures on the different Cabinet horses had been riding the merry-go-round for the past fifteen years, one hand stretched out in front to try and unseat the passenger ahead and the other stretched out behind to ward off similar attacks against themselves. For some

time it had been of little importance which rider was up and which rider was down, since the whole apparatus was anyway revolving in the same fixed and vicious circle of intrigue. But, by 1932, not even this monotonous circular motion could be guaranteed. The motor was running out of fuel, the organ was running out of breath, and the real interest in the Vienna fairground had already shifted to the lusty side-shows. The name of this badly-built contraption which was now grinding to a halt was Parliamentary Democracy, Austrian style."

Inga Bonhoeffer was working at her desk in the office of the Minister of Trade, but her mind was on the howitzers that had bombarded the Karl Marx-Hof along with innocent women and children. Her thoughts were torn between those unfortunates and her job with a government that felt the need to use force to control the violence in the streets. *Surely there was a better way!* Yet she had confidence Dollfuss had explored every option. She also knew the responsibility for ending the civil war rested squarely with the government.

It was not Dollfuss's crime to be Austrian Chancellor on 12 February 1934, but rather his supreme misfortune. What he was called on to put an end to was not so much a rebellion against his own person or policies, but rather a sickening domestic crisis that had been mounting steadily in Austria for the previous fifteen years. Hans had told her the real force behind the violence was Major Emil Fey. She wondered if the Minister of Security was secretly working with the Nazis. If so, *Finis Austria* was not far in the future.

These thoughts were interrupted when her boss, Trade Minister Fritz Stockinger, appeared at her desk. "Inga," he said, "there will be a memorial service for the dead in front of the Rathaus (Town Hall) at 1:00 today. Would you come with me? We will be on the speakers' stand with the Chancellor. He will say a few words, and I think it would be good to have more government people present."

"*Herr* Stockinger, this situation has really upset me, but I want to hear the Chancellor's words."

Stockinger sat down across from her, his expression compassionate. "Inga, you know I have been involved in many of the decisions," he said. "Please understand, the alternative was to send in soldiers, which would have cost more lives on both sides. Also, the bombardment itself was a series of single shots, preceded by appeals to surrender."

Inga flashed back to the sights and sounds of the day before. She vividly remembered the unrelenting thud of mortar shells slamming into the workers' building. Was her boss lying to her, or just repeating what he had been told?

At noon the two walked over to the Rathaus and to the adjacent open area, now with a bit of snow on the ground, that a few weeks earlier held the Winter Carnival, with all the gaiety the event brought to the people of Vienna. She thought, *How can this place have held so much joy, only to be followed by so much sorrow?*

In front of the steps to the Rathaus, lined up in neat rows, were the open coffins of all 321 men of both sides who had given their lives in the brief but violent civil war. She followed Stockinger to the front steps, joining Dollfuss and others. She found herself close enough to Dollfuss to hear him mutter to Stockinger, "To order that shooting was the most terrible decision of my life, but it was the only way to cut short the fighting." Inga felt genuine grief in those words, but no sense of remorse or guilt.

Inga's suspicions about Fey were confirmed when she saw him on the speaker's stand along with the, until now reclusive, President of the Republic, Wilhelm Miklas. She was shocked to hear Miklas thank Fey for his "wise moderation in the defensive battle forced upon him." Miklas then awarded Fey the Great Insignia of Honour of the

Republic. After this, Dollfuss spoke briefly. In a fatherly way, he told the defeated workers that he admired their courage, but the fighting was over. Like the good fellows they were, they should accept defeat and move on to make a better Austria.

After the brief ceremony, Stockinger led Inga toward the Ringstrasse. They saw Hans walking toward them, looking worried. Inga asked her boss if he knew Hans.

"Oh, *ja* we have had our small battles, but a good man you are, Hans."

"Dr. Stockinger, would you mind if I talk with Inga for a moment?"

"Of course not, I need to get back to my office anyway. Thank you, Inga, for accompanying me."

"What is the matter, Hans?" Inga said. "You seem upset."

"You were right, Inga, the trials have already begun."

"But the workers have barely surrendered."

"I know, but the first trial is starting at the *Justiz Palast*. A married shoemaker of forty-three, with three children. Would you come with me?"

"Hans, how can I after what we saw at the Karl Marx-Hof yesterday?"

"Inga, please. I don't want to be there alone."

"Shouldn't these men have time to see their families, to see a defense council?" Inga thought for a moment longer. "All right Hans, if you think we should see this."

At the *Justizpalast* they found a surprisingly small group of people in attendance for something so important. Watching from the gallery, they soon realized the trials were a sham; conducted quickly and with no mercy. They were in time for the trial of the shoemaker, Karl Münichreiter, who was accused of being the leader of the *putsch*. The man was so badly wounded he was brought into the court on a stretcher while trying to hold his bowels in place. He was condemned to death in less than an hour.

The next accused was Georg Weissel, the fire brigade commander in Vienna's Floridsdorf district and a *Schutzbund* officer. He had been arrested for giving the order to fire on the forces attacking a Floridsdorf workers tenement block. Inga and Hans felt his bearing was remarkable. When he declined to incriminate others, the judge said, "After your manly admissions concerning yourself, I shall not press you to involve others. Did you act in accordance with your inner convictions?"

Herr Weissel answered with a strong "*Ja.* And we surrendered because we were outnumbered, otherwise we should never have done so."

By late afternoon the executions began. The shoemaker was first. The judge, a priest, and a police-surgeon were present, as was the executioner in his black suit with black top hat and black gloves. The sentence was read once again. The corners of the convicted man's mouth began to twitch as the hangman drew the noose tight around his throat. Münichreiter shouted a Marxist phrase like, "Long live Social Democracy-Freedom," as the hangman's assistants pulled the steps away from beneath his feet. After an interval of seven and a half minutes, the police-surgeon announced he was dead. Thirty-five-year-old George Weissel didn't face the gallows until midnight, but he marched with pride to his fate and shouted as the noose was placed around his neck: "Long live Revolutionary Socialism!"

Hans and Inga later learned that the trial judge, having watched Weissel's hanging, drove to the humble dwelling of the widow, placed his hands on her shoulders, and said in a broken voice, "It is I who judged your husband, and I have come to tell you that he died like a man and a hero."

Seven more were executed, after which Dollfuss promised there would be no more hanging in Vienna. He kept his promise, for when they caught Koloman Wallisch, national secretary of the Austrian socialist party, in the Alps a week later, they hung him in Styria.

*   *   *

The end of the civil war brought an uneasy truce between Vienna's warring factions. Even the German leader of the Austrian Nazis, Theo Habicht, issued the following order: "During this period no party member is allowed to attack the Austrian Government by word of mouth, in writing, or by any other means." In the meantime, however, members of the Austrian left were treated like outlaws. They became free game for the *Heimwehr* and the largely Nazified police. The Party itself was immediately suppressed, including those in Parliament. The trade unions were dissolved. The worker's communal property belonging to the union members was confiscated overnight; most of the plunder was handed over to the *Heimwehr*. This was known as "restoring order." By May, German airplanes were crossing the frontier and dropping leaflets inciting the Austrian population to refuse to pay their taxes, urging them to start a run on the banks by withdrawing their deposits.

Soon, railroad stations were being blown up, rails uprooted, phone lines cut, and power stations bombed. These things became daily occurrences, which made life in Vienna dangerous but still exciting to Hans. One day in mid-July, returning from lunch to his office in the Chancellery, he was greeted by a nervous colleague.

"Hans, are you all right?" said his secretary, Wolfgang Holsweher, or Wolfie, as Hans called him.

"Wolfie, I didn't know you cared, but I appreciate the thought."

"Did you hear the Nazi Gauleiter [the leader of a regional branch of the Nazi Party] Alfred Frauenfeld, made a radio broadcast inciting the Viennese people to rise up and murder our Chancellor?"

"Oh Christ! I didn't."

"*Ja,* but the Chancellor thinks it is a joke and is not concerned."

"Well, I am taking it seriously," Hans said. "I just saw a crowd in front of a Jew-store. An SA (Storm Detachment) man had put up a sign in front of the store which read, 'Don't buy from Jews.' The owner came out to protest; he must have been in his mid-sixties. The SA man started hitting him, and the crowd cheered him on."

"You didn't try to intervene, did you?"

"*Nein*, I don't care about the Jew. I wouldn't go into his store anyway. But this and the Frauenfeld broadcast, to me indicates things are heating up after the lull since the civil war in February."

"I think those SA Nazis are more funny than serious. I consider them funny little brown-shirt delinquents, more comic than dangerous!"

Hans said, "My job is to protect our Chancellor. Not taking these people seriously is a grave mistake many of us are making. Is Dollfuss available?"

"The last I saw he was reading the papers."

"I bet he is enjoying that," said Hans, hurrying to Dollfuss's office. He burst into the room and cried, "*Herr* Chancellor, have you heard about Frauenfeld inviting people to assassinate you?"

"Hans, you can't get excited about these things. People say things in the heat of the moment. I am the best Chancellor for even the Nazi sympathizers."

"But sir, the Germans are dropping leaflets advocating citizens to stop paying taxes and empty their bank accounts. That is illegal. We are a sovereign nation and Germany is interfering with our citizens."

A seemingly relaxed Chancellor replied, "I am sure our friends in the League of Nations will tell *Herr* Hitler to end all of this. These are merely a bunch of crazies that are in all countries."

"Sir, this is coming from Hitler himself. He wants to take over Austria."

"Oh, I don't believe that. He is Austrian, and our friends in London and Paris would never permit such a thing. They will always have our back."

"Sir, they don't care about us." Hans said, rolling his eyes.

"Hans, everything will be all right. We must have faith in God." Then, Dollfuss's expression changed. He gave Hans a piercing look. "My boy," he said, "just in case, stay close to me. I may need a protector, and I would like for it to be you."

Stunned, Hans was at a momentary loss, then recovered enough to reply, "Sir, you can count on me." Hans turned and walked from the Chancellor's office, shaken.

"How did it go?" asked Wolfi.

"I think the man is in a dream world. He thinks the League, France, England, and God will protect us."

"I don't think anyone will protect us, except Germany," Wolfi said.

"Oh God, Wolfi, Britain's only concern is to avoid any rumpus on the Continent in the hope the dictators might leave something of the Versailles crockery intact. France, all she wants is to keep Austria and Hungary in perpetual check. That said, our only hope is to find a foreign protector who is willing and able to shield Austria from Hitler's blows."

Wolfi shook his head. "I don't think there is a chance with Hungary; we must look across the Alps to Rome. A drowning man is in no position to grumble at the color of his life-belt. We must form an alliance with Rome, because if the Germans have breakfast in Innsbruck, they will want to eat dinner in Milan. Hans, tell me what you know about Fey; he frightens me."

"Ha! I have been trying to tell the Chancellor for over a year that Fey is working with the German Nazis, but you know our Chancellor. "'Let's not be hasty'," Hans said, in a poor imitation of Dollfuss. "I have it on good authority Dollfuss has dismissed Fey from the front ranks of power but, in true Dollfuss fashion, to cushion Fey's fall, has nominated him a 'General State Commissioner for the Suppression of Anti-government Tendencies in private industry.' "

"What kind of title is that? It sounds like some comic-opera position," Wolfi said with a big grin on his face.

"Dollfuss now has direct control of the police, gendarmerie, and the army."

"He sounds more like a garrison commander than a Chancellor."

"Probably fitting, because Austria herself seems less like a state than a fortress with battered walls, undermined by treason from inside." Hans said, with distinct sadness that seemed to envelop the room.

"Maybe the fall of Fey will help that."

*   *   *

The Viennese, according to legend, were always fond of eating and drinking, especially in public places, such as the Prater's large area of unspoiled woods and meadows. One can wander about for hours in this great natural park joined by many thousands of people. The Prater can absorb them all in its wide expanse of ponds and pools. It offers cool shade and relaxation as well as enjoyment and recreation for all social strata. An ice cream from a stand, a cup of coffee at the Sacher Pavilion, or a meal at the *Lusthaus* were within everyone's reach.

The left side of the main avenue of the Prater, when one comes from the city, is lined by café after café. What the writer Adalbert Stifter wrote in 1844 remained true in 1934: "From each of them music resounds. Under the trees stand many thousands of chairs on which the occupants in their Sunday best look like so many flowering bushes, in the air there is talk, laughter and bluster, intermingled with the tinkling of glasses; and before your eyes shining carriages roll up and down the avenue which seems to stretch as far as the eye can reach."

Coffee-houses, of course, are without number in Vienna. This is unsurprising, since it was here that coffee set out to win the world. Great quantities of coffee beans were found after the liberation of Vienna from the Turks in 1683. Vienna has always taken to heart the old Arab saying that coffee must be black as the night, as sweet as love, and as hot as hell. The coffee-house creates an atmosphere of illusion, and the slightest illusion can make the Viennese happy.

It was in this setting, on a beautiful Sunday in mid-July, that Hans and Inga met with Viktor, Else, and Elke, then sixteen, to enjoy one of the coffee-houses while trying to make some sense of what was happening to the country.

As they were seated, Hans asked Elke about her favorite subjects in school. She explained about her love for writing and desire to someday work for a newspaper.

"Well, young lady, there certainly are enough goings on around here to fill a newspaper."

"My friends at school say the Nazis will take over the country soon."

Her mother gave her a pointed look. "No political talk, Elke, this is a day to enjoy the Prater and each other."

Elke said to Hans, "My mother thinks if we don't talk about what is going on in Vienna it will all go away."

"I wish your mother were right," said Hans with a sigh.

Inga rose and said, "Let us ladies walk toward the Prater Wheel and leave these men to themselves."

Viktor and Hans sipped their coffee. Viktor asked, "What do you hear, Hans? You are closer than I am."

"I am under the impression Major Fey is not as important as he was. However, the person I worry about the most is Dr. Anton Rintelen. He seems to be the most ambitious of all."

"Ah, the minister in Rome. How is he involved?"

"Well, first off, he's not in Rome. He's here, residing in the fashionable Hotel Imperial on the Ringstrasse. He is supposedly here to report to the government on Italy's political position prior to the summer recess. However, it is common knowledge that this Styrian freebooter is planning to replace Dollfuss. He seems to appear at every crisis. The man's ambition is limitless."

"More so than Fey's?"

"Here is where I have become proud of our Chancellor. A few days ago he got serious and secretly assigned three detectives to shadow Fey night and day. I think he senses trouble, but not necessarily toward himself. The problem for those who support Dollfuss is we don't know who in the government is secretly working with the Nazis. The other problem, even more difficult, is that so many of our politicians are hopelessly muddled and disorientated. Only Austria seems to have produced such men in a large quantity."

"God, Hans, this seems hopeless."

"It probably is. But unfortunately, in a moment of weakness, I pledged to the Chancellor that I will watch out for him."

"Why? He has security people."

"As unbelievable as it sounds, there is really no one in his cabinet he can truly trust, but he trusts me."

"Well, he picked a good man. But how can you do this?"

"I have an idea, and this may sound crazy, but let me run it by you. I need a mole, someone neither Fey nor Rintelen would ever expect to work inside their group."

"Sorry, but not me," replied Viktor quickly.

"Ha! *Nein*, not you. I am thinking of Inga. She is sexy, smart, has worked in the Chancellery for years and knows everyone. Besides, a woman could gain the confidence of these massive male egos."

"Will she do it?"

"I think so. She's fiercely Austrian. She has had her differences with Dollfuss. The workers' show trials and the bombardment of their quarters angered her. But she dislikes the Germans interfering in Austrian affairs even more. In fact, I was hoping to ask her today. There isn't much time left. I keep hearing rumors Hitler has established an SS commando unit here in Vienna called *Standarte* 89 with the purpose of kidnapping both President Miklas and the entire Cabinet at the same moment. The pro-Hitler government of Rintelen would then replace Miklas. Besides this, they hope to seize the Austrian radio transmitter and the Vienna telephone headquarters. This is all only rumor, so please go no further with it."

"If all this is only partly true, we are in deep trouble. You realize you may have to propose marriage first in order to get Inga to do this? Shh! Here they come now," said Viktor, with a finger to his lips.

"Well, did you two solve the world's problems while we were gone?" Else asked.

"*Nein*, but we are getting there," Viktor replied.

Small talk continued until Hans asked Inga to walk with him. As they strolled along a quiet shaded path, Hans broached the subject. "Inga, I am concerned something dangerous will soon happen in Vienna. I feel great tension in the air."

"What do you think this something is?"

"I've said that Dollfuss is not assertive enough toward the Nazis, and he asked me to stay close to him."

"You think someone is out to assassinate him? That would put the country into turmoil."

"Inga, neither he nor I know whom to trust. Even ministers in high office may be working behind the scenes with the Germans."

"You don't think my boss, Dr. Stockinger, is one Dollfuss can't trust?"

"*Nein*, I don't, and I think you would have suspicions if that were true. I am more concerned with Fey and Rintelen. I need someone to get close to those two especially."

"Whom do you have in mind?"

"I need someone attractive, with a sharp mind and a woman's intuition."

There was a long pause before Inga retorted, "Oh no, not me!"

"Inga, you are perfect. You know them all, having worked closely with each of them."

"I won't sleep with them," she said with venom.

"Look Inga, I'm in love with you. It tears me up even to think about asking this of you. I hope it never comes to such a choice. But I believe Austria's future is at stake, and you are in the perfect position to get the information we need."

*   *   *

23 July began as a normal busy Monday for Hans. He arrived at the office early; he was behind in his work and was determined to get caught up. His phone rang at about 10:00.

"Hans, meet me for lunch at noon at the Imperial Café," Inga said, and hung up.

Her tone was urgent. Hans put his work aside. This must have something to do with Rintelen.

When he arrived, Hans was surprised to see Inga talking with several of the men Dollfuss and Hans did not trust. To his further consternation, Inga made no attempt to acknowledge him. The clock had almost reached noon when a voice behind him whispered, "I am leaving. Follow me, but not too close."

Hans turned slowly and saw Inga moving toward the door. She walked slowly along the "Ring," occasionally looking in shop windows but never looking back to see if he was behind. When she stopped, Hans would pause to glance at a newspaper headline or admire his surroundings like a tourist. Soon she turned toward Stadtpark, a good place thought Hans, with trees and bushes that would afford privacy. She gradually slowed to allow Hans to catch up.

"Hans, this is serious. There is a *putsch* planned for tomorrow afternoon at the Chancellery. They intend to capture the Chancellor and his entire Cabinet."

"The last day before the summer holiday. Who are *they*?"

"This is the scary part. It is almost an entirely German operation. They want Rintelen and his pro-Hitler government to take over."

"You are convinced then, Rintelen is our villain. How do they plan to do this?"

"The SS *Standarte* 89 is real. They were formed at the beginning of this year, made up mostly of Nazis who had been expelled from the Austrian military. As I understand it, they are in the process now of rounding up the lorries to transport this force to the Chancellery."

"What about President Miklas?"

"Ha!" she said. "They wanted to capture him with the Cabinet, but he blissfully sailed off to Velden in Carinthia to get an early start on his holiday."

"So they will settle for the Chancellor and his Cabinet? I must warn Dollfuss."

Inga's face lit up as if she had just seen a light, "Wait, suppose Dollfuss postpones the meeting until the 25th? It would give him time to prepare."

"*Ja*, it would give him an extra day and not tip his hand." Hans paused. "By the way, what did you have to do to get this information?" he said with a wicked smile.

"I will keep you guessing for now," she said, with an equally devilish grin.

Hans hurried back to Dollfuss at the Chancellery. Fritz Stockinger was called in, as he and Hans were the only two Dollfuss could count on. They agreed to postpone the Cabinet meeting scheduled for the next day. Dollfuss ordered a special police guard to watch Rintelen at the Imperial Hotel.

For the past several days, Fey, the *Heimwher* Minister (now without portfolio) was being shadowed night and day by no fewer than three detectives. Dollfuss, although now convinced something sinister was brewing, believed that by carefully watching Fey and Rintelen and having the Imperial Guard monitor him, he would be fine.

For the three men trying to hold the country together, Tuesday the 24th was a quiet day. This gave them the impression the crisis had passed. They didn't realize that by midday the order had been given to start the action. The lorries were rolling to the rendezvous point, laden with weapons and Austrian Army uniforms when, just before 3:00 p.m., Rintelen was informed the Cabinet meeting had been postponed until noon the following day. However, Vienna Police Headquarters, which had been aware of the movement of the lorries, never thought to inform Dollfuss or issue orders for extra protection at the *Ballhausplatz*.

The *putschists* were up until 3:00 the morning of the 25th, revising their plan. A new assembly point was needed. The gymnasium in the *Siebensterngasse* less than a mile away from the Chancellery was selected.

*   *   *

Inga had spent the night with Hans in his apartment, but it had been more stressful than romantic. Each felt the tension surrounding that day's Cabinet meeting. They agreed that if the *putsch* was going to happen it would be at this time. The government must assemble prior to the summer recess beginning next week.

Breakfast on this Wednesday, July 25th, was coffee and a pastry that Inga had bought the afternoon before. She reached for Hans's hand. "I am worried about you. I have a bad feeling about this."

"*Ja,* I feel the same. Rintelen seems to be laying low at the Imperial Hotel, and I have heard nothing about Fey."

"Do you really have to go to this meeting?"

"Well, first of all, I am his economist and this is the last meeting before the summer recess. Second, and more important, he asked to me to help protect him. He should be in the office early, and I need to be there."

"Please be careful, don't try to be a hero. Austria is not worth dying for."

Hans reacted with a slight laugh. "This is not what you said when we first met."

"I know, but I feel Nazism is inevitable. I guess, if you can't beat them, join them."

"Now that is the girl I fell in love with."

After a passionate kiss and embrace, Hans started for the door. He turned to Inga. "You are going to work, aren't you?"

"Oh *Ja*! I wouldn't miss this, and I just might be the hero to save *you*," she said with a mocking smile.

After one last kiss, Hans walked to the *Ballhausplatz*. A slight breeze that ruffled the trees went unnoticed. His mind was on what he was sure would be a momentous day for his country. When he approached the Chancellery, he was confronted by the presence of the military guard in their fine uniforms, which gave the impression the building was secure. He walked across the courtyard and entered the Chancellery through a great oaken door, which could quickly be closed in case of an emergency.

Hans entered the large cream-and-gilt office on the first floor of the Chancellery and adjacent to the Cabinet Room where the last meeting of the Cabinet was to be held before the summer recess.

"How are you, sir?" Hans asked.

Without acknowledging the greeting, Dollfuss replied, "I have changed the meeting from noon to 11:00 a.m., Hans. If there is anything going on out there, this should disrupt their plans."

"Will everyone be here, sir?"

"*Ja*, but mostly I want the Security and Defense people, General Zehner, Baron Karwinsky, Fey, and Stockinger. We need to get a real handle on these rumors."

"I have checked on the guard in the courtyard and the doors can be closed quickly. How about Major Fey, sir?"

"I don't trust Fey, but he does have powerful control over the *Heimwehr*. If something is coming down, we will need him."

While Hans settled in to await the 11:00 a.m. meeting, Inga decided to wander into the Café Weghuber and keep her eyes and ears open. It didn't take long for her to become aware of Johan Dobler, a district inspector of the Vienna police, who was busy telling anyone who would listen of the plot that was scheduled to assemble at 12:15 p.m. at the *Siebensterngasse* gymnasium. This she wanted to see firsthand. After finishing her coffee melange, she walked to the *Siebensterngasse*. Arriving at 11:45 she was stunned to see Austrian policemen in league with the conspirators and members of the SS *Standarte* 89 streaming into the assembly point. Some were already dressed in stolen army uniforms and carried weapons. At a café across the street, she used a public telephone to call Hans at his office.

*   *   *

After learning of the plot, Major Fey went straight to the Chancellery, but did not join or contact his colleagues in the Cabinet Room. Instead, he ordered a *Heimwehr* regiment maneuvering that morning in the Prater, three miles away, to march immediately back to town. It was now nearly noon. He entered the Cabinet meeting an hour late. After apologizing for his tardiness, he maneuvered Dollfuss into a corner and whispered something in the Chancellor's ear.

Dollfuss shook his head, as if in doubt, then moved to the conference table. He addressed the Cabinet members. "Fey has just informed me of something alarming. I don't know if there is truth to it. But it's perhaps better we interrupt the session and every Minister goes back to his office. I will let you know when we can continue."

When they were alone, Fey explained that he'd heard an action was planned against the *Ballhausplatz* that might involve a gymnasium in the *Siebensterngasse*. However, because he wished to keep the details to himself, he revealed no other information—no mention of the time, the proof, or of his own actions.

Hans spoke up in anger. "You have to tell us more than that. What are you hiding from us?"

Fey glared at Hans. "Baron Karwinsky and I are responsible for security, both of the country and the Chancellor. You, an economist, are of no help. I ask that you leave now."

Hans glanced over at Dollfuss, but the Chancellor did not look back. Hans stormed out of the room. Back at the office, Wolfgang told Hans he had an urgent message from Inga and gave Hans the number in the café, where she was waiting.

"Hans," she said, "I am seeing hundreds of men in army uniforms loading lorries with cases and sacks. Hans please, there is no time to lose."

Hans hung up and raced to the courtyard. He wanted to be sure the guard was on duty and would close and lock the building's main door. He arrived there at exactly 12:50 p.m., the time the relief detachment of the military guard appeared outside the main gate. The doors were opened to admit them. Suddenly, in roared the lorries of the SS *Standarte* 89. These bogus soldiers immediately began to disarm the genuine guard as they were carrying out the formalities of guard-changing. The rebels need not have bothered. It was the ultimate lunacy of the day that the Chancellor's military guard was considered ceremonial—and therefore the rifles they carried were unloaded. Hans ran toward the door but was struck by a rifle butt to the head by one of the rebels.

It was now 12:53 p.m. The seat of the Austrian government, which until then had been occupied by a strange assortment of people who did not quite know what to do, was now under the control of 154 armed Nazi *putschists* who knew precisely what they wanted to do. The rebels broke into the Chancellor's office and found Dollfuss, unprotected, along with Fey and Karwinsky. The Austrian Nazi Otto Planetta rushed up to Dollfuss and, without uttering a word, fired two shots at him from close range. The bullets lodged in the Chancellor's neck and armpit and he fell, bleeding heavily, to the floor. It was now 1:00.

The dying Dollfuss was allowed to bleed slowly to death on a sofa by his assailants, who refused all pleas for proper attention and rejected medical aid when it became available. (A doctor with an ambulance made two attempts to gain admittance to the building during the afternoon. On the second attempt, he was told it was too late for his services.) Dollfuss's grief as a devout Catholic can only be imagined, as he begged his captors to be allowed to see a priest. He died without Catholicism's final consolations.

However, Dollfuss' greatest pain was not physical; he was tormented by the feeling everything he had striven to achieve for his country during his two years in office had been destroyed in less than two hours by the handful of desperadoes hovering over him. He died believing Rintelen, the embodiment of ruthless evil, was at Austria's helm and that, behind that power-crazed puppet, Hitler's shadow loomed over Vienna.

*   *   *

The rebels managed to control the national radio transmitter and broadcast a brief message announcing the "resignation" of Dollfuss and the appointment of Dr. Rintelen as his successor. This was their last success. Between 2:00 p.m. and 7:30 p.m., the *putsch* fizzled, snuffed out by an air of half-heartedness and indecision. The Ringstrasse outside the Hotel Imperial was the picture of normality, a July day of unexcitable, leafy tranquility. No delegation came to the Hotel to escort Rintelen to the Chancellery in triumph. After the initial radio announcement, the station began playing light music. The Austrian

SS units that were supposed to be parading in the streets were conspicuously absent.

Whatever hopeful plans Rintelen and his followers had been harboring were dashed, because slowly and somewhat nervously, a counteraction had begun. Kurt von Schuschnigg was the senior minister. After leaving the *Ballhausplatz* at Dollfuss's insistence, he telephoned President Miklas in Carinthia to report the alarming events of the day. Miklas, remote though he was from the scene of the crisis, supplied some badly needed energy and action. He declared he would not recognize a single decision announced by the *Ballhausplatz* captives Fey and Karwinsky, nor would he accept any political conditions demanded by the rebels. He swore in von Schuschnigg over the telephone as the provisional Austrian Chancellor and head of all departments in the Dollfuss Cabinet. He then ordered von Schuschnigg to bring the situation under control by force and punish the rebels. Miklas directed his new emergency Chancellor as follows: "Above all to free the captive members of the government, and liberate them safe and sound from the Chancellery."

At 5:30 p.m. Schuschnigg dispatched Gen. Wilhelm Zehner to the *Ballhausplatz* with an ultimatum to the rebels to evacuate the Chancellery within fifteen minutes, or force would be used to reoccupy it. The Nazi "garrison" were promised safe conduct across the German border, "if no loss of life had been caused among the imprisoned Ministers."

The force outside the Chancellery now numbered several thousand, was heavily armed, and represented the free, legal government of Austria. It waited patiently while the gang of desperadoes bargained for their lives. Only when Hitler's envoy to Vienna turned up in person, even if only to whisper something through a crack in the door, did the rebels feel their necks were safe and opened the Chancellery gates. The attackers, who had never attacked, streamed through in triumph. By 8:00 p.m., the seat of government was again in Austrian hands.

*   *   *

Three days later, the mood in the Baur apartment was melancholy as Viktor, Else, and the children dressed in their darkest clothes for the Requiem Mass for Dollfuss in St. Stephen's Cathedral. There was little conversation. A taxi had been called and was waiting below on Daringergasse.

When Viktor finished tying his tie, he said, "I am going to hospital to see Hans after the funeral. Would anyone care to come along?" Fritz said he would meet up with his friends, but Else and Elke said they would join him in visiting Hans, who was suffering from a concussion caused by the nasty blow from the rebel's rifle.

The crowds were so great that when their taxi had worked its way as close as it could to the Cathedral, Viktor told the driver they would walk the rest of the way. The family walked past the muzzles of machine guns. Troopers knelt beside them, ready to feed the belts. Inside the Cathedral they passed up the aisle between a double row of men armed with carbines, revolvers, and sabers. At each corner of the Cathedral a machine gun detachment was stationed.

Viktor was impressed that the huge crowd appeared to consist of all classes. The middle-class was predominate, as Viktor expected, but to his surprise, a large part was made up of city workers. In this divided and demoralized country, it seemed that in death Dollfuss had become a national symbol, and this was surely a national act of mourning. In the sadness of the moment, Viktor turned to Else and, choked with tears, said, "You know, I think he served his country-men by the martyrdom of his dying. He will remain the symbol of an Austrian way of living and thinking and therefore of an Austrian right to independent existence."

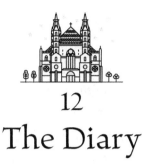

12

The Diary

1935

During the Great Depression, many groups blamed the Jews for their financial predicaments. Among them were university students who could not find jobs upon graduation; small shop-keepers who hated the larger department stores, many of which were owned by Jews; industrial workers who felt abused by the factory owners, many of them Jewish; and the Pan-German nationalists, who seized any excuse to justify the idea of a "pure German" Austria. All these groups believed their way of life was being fundamentally threatened by the economic calamity that had befallen Austria and the world, and they were ready to turn their fear and anger toward the Jews.

Elke's Journal
MONDAY, 11 NOVEMBER 1935

This has been the best birthday ever. Today I turn seventeen, and I feel more like a woman. I know this sounds silly. Father gave me a pretty scarf for the coming winter. My two girlfriends,

Ursula and Helga, came by to wish me a happy birthday and brought nice birthday cards. We laughed all afternoon. I even received a letter from Fritz wishing me a happy birthday. He apologized for not being home to join me on this day, but he is on duty in the army. My best gift was from Mother. She has periodically kept a diary of the family's important events, and she gave me this beautifully bound leather diary, with hopes I will keep it filled with my innermost thoughts. Although I don't have much to write about because my life seems monotonous, I hope I will be glad to read it in the future. Someday, I plan to be a journalist and having the discipline to write in my diary every day will be good for me.

Elke's Journal
TUESDAY, 12 NOVEMBER 1935

Nothing special to report today. The morning was the usual school day. I have a mathematics test tomorrow that I am not looking forward to. I hate math and consider it a waste of time. I enjoy reading and try hard to understand what the author is trying to say by forcing myself to read heavier literature. I have just finished Dostoevsky's The Brothers Karamazov *and really enjoyed it. It was a difficult book—my mind is preoccupied with all kinds of thoughts about life. The story is about a murder, but the reader is inside the mind of the criminal. It is also a courtroom drama as well as several love affairs. The author portrayed Russian life as an ethical debate about God, free will, and morality. I think how soon life passes by and wonder what makes a human being worthy of life and what makes one happy. Diary, am I too young to have these thoughts? I go to sleep with these thoughts.*

Elke's Journal
WEDNESDAY, 13 NOVEMBER 1935

Walked to school today with my friend Helga Eberhard. She told me someone wrote on Erna Echfield's desk, "Jew, get out, go to Palestine!" I know Erna a little bit, but I don't like her because of her arrogance. She is very smart and lets you know it. About a third of my class are Jews, and they are all above average in almost all subjects. They seem well bred and their good behavior is a source of irritation to all of us. Also, what bothers me about them is their physical maturity. They are "ladies" already while they make me feel that I am still a child. Helga is good company. I can talk freely with her about anything. We talked a little bit about the Jews. We feel they have their friends and we Austrians have ours. There is no reason we should mix together since we have so little in common. Our conversation was so engrossing I did not notice when we arrived at school. But I can't write anymore. I am exhausted from all this thinking.

Elke's Journal
THURSDAY, 14 NOVEMBER 1935

Maybe it is ridiculous to write in this diary, because the days are all alike and not interesting at all. But at least I can pin down thoughts that whirl around in my head all day long. Had a long conversation with Ursula at lunch today. She is all excited about Ernst being in her class. She keeps talking about how cute and smart he is. I don't think he is cute at all. I have no boyfriend and don't want any. I have every reason to be content with my life but still, I am not. Something is missing. I am trying to find out what it is. People keep telling me a woman must have a goal, but I refuse to admit this is marriage only. I do not care much about boys, and I would like to keep it so. It is terrible to watch my friends all torn up with love, like Ursula is with Ernst. When I think about it, I'm sure I have too much pride to allow myself to be devastated like that. My goal is to become a journalist for a large newspaper. I want to write stories about events and people who are making history. We are living in interesting times and I do not want to miss my chance to be a part of them. I am looking forward to history class tomorrow. I really enjoy Herr Klinghöfer. He makes history come alive for me and he has interesting thoughts on where Europe is headed in the future. Time to get some sleep for tomorrow.

Elke's Journal
Friday, 15 November 1935

Today's history class was almost scary. Herr Klinghöfer laid out a large colored map of Europe and each country was shown in bright colors. On each country, sat, crawled, or stood, a picture of a naked baby. The teacher explained that each of these children was a symbol of the birthrate of the country. The German/Austrian families had on average far fewer children than say, Polish families. This was why a frightened little girl sat on a patch of blue, which represented Germany and Austria. The yellow patch, just to the right, showed a sturdy little boy crawling on all fours aggressively in the direction of the German/Austrian frontier. Herr Klinghöfer pointed to the boy and said, "Look at the boy. He is bursting with health and strength. One day he will overrun the little girl." That picture is still with me tonight, and I am having trouble going to sleep. Could he be right, that the Poles or the Russians could attack us?

Elke's Journal
SATURDAY, 16 NOVEMBER 1935

This is five days in a row I have written in my diary. I am proud of myself. It is a lovely day, a bit cold but fine for mid-November. Met Ursula at Stadtpark. We walked to the Ring and spent a leisurely late afternoon. All she wanted to talk about was Ernst. I only occasionally listened to her and pretended to agree with everything she said. I love this city and the Ring. We walked by the National Library, one of my favorite places to read. I tried to get Ursula to go inside so I could show her around, but she was not interested. I love her dearly, but we have different interests. I have been thinking of joining the Hitler Youth for girls, the BdM, and was hoping to talk with Ursula about it. But although we are good friends, when I think about it, I can't picture Ursula in uniform. We talked about Herr Klinghöfer's class yesterday, but she didn't take it as seriously as I did. I hope she is right, that Poland and Russia won't invade.

Elke's Journal
FRIDAY, 22 NOVEMBER 1935

Sorry, my diary, I know I have abandoned you for several days. I have been busy. I have done it, I joined the BdM! I hate keeping it from my parents, but I don't want to go through the scene that would develop if I asked for permission. I really feel I will learn more about journalism and writing through the

BdM than through school. I would never consider dropping out of school, because that would really hurt my parents. I respect them so much for what they have been through and how they have managed to do so well in difficult times. I am proud of my father, who was an officer during the Great War, and my mother keeping food on the table during the inflation of the krone. My parents read the newspapers thoroughly and we discuss the news over meals. Listening to the radio is a family ritual, and I have enjoyed thinking of Father sitting in his large wing-backed chair reading his newspaper surrounded by his books and Mother quietly knitting in her favorite chair. But they are living in the past, in the days of the Habsburgs. They are living in an out-of-date world, one which must come to an end. With so many people out of work and poor, radical change is needed. This writing has made me tired. Looking forward to my new adventure.

Elke's Journal
SUNDAY, 1 DECEMBER 1935

Oh, diary, I have so much to tell you. First, my little secret of joining the BdM from my parents didn't last long. Mother found my uniform at the bottom of a sweater drawer while doing laundry. She seemed to understand my desire better than Father. He stormed about the room saying Hitler would be the ruin of the world. However, I love my uniform. It is a dark blue skirt with a brown, long-sleeve blouse and a dark blue tie. I feel it projects an image of a feminine brand of toughness, and I have a real sense of pride when I wear it. They have instructed us not to paint our fingernails, pluck our eyebrows, wear lipstick, dye our hair, or be too thin. I have learned Nazi leaders consider the cosmetic boom as Jewish commerce, which has turned good women into prostitutes. They feel a young woman's glow should come from physical exertion, from being outdoors, and from pregnancy.

Today is Sunday, and I went to Mass with my parents. I am having some conflict between the regimentation of National Socialism and my upbringing in the Catholic Church. The daily prayers, the grace at meals, the biblical instruction I received are in contradiction to National Socialism. I am the only girl in my group who is in secondary school. The others are shop girls, office workers, dressmakers, and servant girls. I really enjoy these ladies. They seem to be there for the same reason as I am, to make Austria a better country through National Socialism.

One more thing, diary, I have met someone, his name is Kurt. I don't want to give his second name yet. He has the same interest in reading I do. He gave me his copy of Tolstoy's War and Peace. *It will take me forever to read it.*

Elke's Journal
THURSDAY, 5 DECEMBER 1935

I was too tired to write when I went to bed, but I am unable to sleep. I spent time today with Ursula and Helga. They wanted to know all about the BdM. I don't think they will join. I like the discipline and the submissiveness to orders and the habit of obedience much more than they would. I cannot imagine those two submitting to the orders I have been given.

I am a firm believer in Adolf Hitler and the Nazi cause. I want to be part of the new Austria with Germany, which will be built by brushing away the old, weak, and decrepit, all those who no longer have the drive necessary to radically transform society. Hitler is my ideal mentor and role model. I love to see him picking flowers, patting the cheeks of small, pigtailed girls.

When children hand him bouquets of flowers he always bends down to receive them.

This is not the only reason I am unable to sleep. The reason Helga and Ursula wanted to talk to me was not my joining the BdM, but because they had seen me walking with Kurt in the park yesterday. They were unrelenting in their questions. Have we been on a date? Have we been alone? Has he kissed me yet? I disappointed them. All we have done is walk in Stadtpark and talk about Tolstoy, which we are both enjoying. He has loaned me other books, which I am eager to read. Afterward I will have the pleasure of discussing the book with Kurt, who understands so well. To tell you the truth, my diary, I am flattered he seeks my company. Maybe now I can sleep.

Elke's Journal
Friday, 13 December 1935

I am so grateful to have you, my diary, a place where I can freely unburden my feelings. Kurt was in an odd mood today. I felt he didn't want to be with me. I can't think of anything I have done to upset him. At today's BdM meeting we were given pamphlets with advice on choosing a prospective mate. The first question was: "What is your racial background?" We have even received instruction on "racial hygiene" designed to identify the obvious characteristics of "subhumans" in facial features and head shapes. One of our teachers told us Jews were ugly, not only on the outside, but on the inside too. And we Germans are a superior race. The only Jews I know are in my school class. Not one comes from a poor home and the ostentatious clothes many of them wear upsets me. They think they are impressing us when their chauffeur sometimes comes to fetch them in their father's car.

Elke's Journal
SATURDAY, 14 DECEMBER 1935

Oh, diary, I am so confused. Yesterday Kurt acted like he didn't want to be with me. Today I saw him at the market, and he asked me to walk with him. I asked him if he was all right. He said he had some trouble at home with his parents. He didn't seem to want to talk about it. We walked and talked and laughed a lot. He asked what I thought of War and Peace. *I said I loved Natasha and her carefree attitude, but I struggle with the Russian names. I told him about Herr Klinghöfer's class last month and how it frightened me to think that strong Poland might attack us. He got a sad look, took my hand, looked into my eyes and said, "My fear is it may go the other way." "But why would we attack Poland? There is nothing there," I said. Kurt said something that made me realize what a deep thinker he is. He said the Nazis want to move the Jews out of Austria and Germany and resettle them in Poland. I asked if that was a problem. After all, the Jews would be together and could build their own homeland. He smiled, like I was so young, and said, "Would you like to be removed from your home?" I didn't try to answer him, but I was glad he was still holding my hand.*

Elke's Journal
SUNDAY, 15 DECEMBER 1935

The whole city is in a holiday spirit, and I love it. After church I met Kurt and we took the tram to the hills on the outskirts of the city, near the Vienna Woods. It is an area everyone loves, even more so this time of year. Kurt makes me see things differently.

He is a year older than I am and thinks beyond his years. This fascinates me. I am not sure I agree with him on everything, but he does make me consider things from a different side.

I have been thinking about what he said about moving the Jews out of Germany for resettlement. I see it as a good thing for both. We have nothing in common with them, nor them with us. He asked again how I would feel being made to leave my home? I said if it gave the Jews a better life with their own kind, so much the better. Besides, moving to a rural area in Poland, the Jews will learn to work with their hands instead of just making money. When I asked him about that today, he said, "What makes you think the government will stop with merely relocating the Jews?" I said the Catholic Church would never let that happen. What he said next really bothered me, that the Catholic Church has failed to fill the emptiness in peoples' lives since the end of the Great War, so people are turning from the Church to the Nazi Party. Kurt claims the Church has created a vacuum the Party is filling, and this is what has made it so strong. Because when people call the Party for help, it always helps—in religious matters, for domestic problems, in everything. The Party has watched over the lives of the people, not spying on them, but caring about them.

My brain hurts, I don't think I can write any more.

Elke's Journal
WEDNESDAY, 18 DECEMBER 1935

I have thought a lot about what Kurt said about the government going further than relocating the Jews, and I don't believe him. I think he is being too negative about Austria's future. I believe Hitler wants to bring greatness, fortune, and prosperity to the German Fatherland, and that includes Austria. He wants to see that everyone has work and bread, that every German is free, happy, and independent. I want to help create a national community in which people would live together like one big family. My friends in the BdM are believers in progress and want to improve the whole of mankind. I am more of a skeptic and believe in educating only the Germanic nation.

I know Kurt has his doubts, especially since suddenly he can't find his favorite Austrian author, Stefan Zweig, in any bookstore. I think he is overreacting. Zweig is a renowned writer, and the bookstores are just temporarily out. Kurt has seen too many American movies; he sees gangsters everywhere. We have a big BdM meeting tomorrow evening and I don't want to miss it.

Elke's Journal
FRIDAY, 20 DECEMBER 1935

I know diary, I have not said much about my relationship with Kurt. I didn't tell you his last name at first because I assumed my interest would be short. I like Kurt a lot, he is very good to me, very patient to the point of humoring me, and I like his sense of humor. His last name is Hoffmann. We have not been "out" or anything like that, my parents still feel I am too young. We go for coffee and walk in Stadtpark. I don't know if this relationship will go much further, but we enjoy being with each other.

Something happened today in the city that confirms my belief Hitler will bring peace and order to Vienna. Some men threw a bomb into a jewelry store owned by a Jew, who was killed instantly. Also, someone vandalized a Jewish cemetery and stink bombs were thrown into movie houses owned by Jews. This is the very thing that will cease when union with Germany takes place. Hitler believes in order, and it is this kind of brutality he and the Nazis will put a stop to.

13

Elke Baur

1947

The American journalist William L. Shirer wrote upon returning to Vienna shortly after the war: "Austrian friends told us of what happened there on the night of March 12, 1945. Swarms of American heavy bombers flying up from Italy turned the city into a fiery inferno. Hundreds of flaming buildings toppled over into the streets . . . The people huddled in their air-raid shelters. Then a rumor began to spread. To the Viennese it was too horrible to believe. 'The opera has been hit!' From all corners of the burning city the citizens converged on the Ring, unmindful that their own homes might be going up in flames or that they might get killed in the street from the falling bombs and collapsing walls. All through the night and the next morning, they tried to save the stately musical shrine that meant so much to them, forming bucket brigades to help the firemen, but it was hopeless. Slowly, reluctantly, thousands of Viennese abandoned the scene, their smoke-blackened faces full of anger, resentment, and heartbreaking sorrow. You could pulverize their homes and

*offices and all the old imperial state palaces, but to destroy this
temple of music—this was barbarous."*

T he morning dawned bright and cold, and the sun shone brilliantly in a room with no curtains on the windows to obstruct
the light. Elke awoke in her old apartment with an awful headache.
At first, she wasn't sure where she was.

As the room came into focus, her fogged mind recalled the four
Wehrmacht soldiers of the night before. She had slept heavily and
dreamed of her parents. In the dream, she saw this room filled with
furniture and heard her mother's laughter coming from the kitchen.
She could even smell sausage cooking in the skillet. And then, a curious old man had appeared before her. As she tried to conjure an image
of him in her mind, all traces of him seemed to vanish.

Slowly, she came fully awake and realized she was in her old apartment in the now-ruined city. The February cold made her shiver under
her old woolen coat that had served as her blanket. She felt very much
alone. Tears formed as she considered her situation. If she was going
to survive, she needed to find a job, and coal to warm her apartment.
Walter was her key to both, but he was not in the best of health. He
was thin and walked slightly bent over. She imagined him carrying
the weight of Austria on his shoulders. She dressed quickly and soon
knocked on his door.

"*Guten Morgen, mein Fräulein,*" Walter greeted her. "I was hoping
to see you this morning. Please come in and join me for breakfast.
I've got coffee and biscuits I made myself."

Elke was grateful for the warmth of his apartment, and the coffee
and fresh biscuits were a true delight. He obviously took great pride
in his accomplishment.

"Walter, I need some coal. It is freezing upstairs."

"*Ja.* The cold doesn't seem to let up. I have read in the newspaper that since the first of December, we've had forty days when the temperature has never gone above zero degrees. Thus, coal is at a premium, but I have a good source. If it is all right with you, I will get your stove going by this afternoon."

"Walter, I also need a job of some kind. Do you know anybody? I will do almost anything."

"*Fräulein,* I wish I could help, but the only jobs I know of are construction jobs, rebuilding the bombed ruins. Just keep your eyes and ears open. You are smart and attractive; something will turn up. You are how old now?"

"I am twenty-nine and will be thirty in November."

"*Ja,* young enough with your future ahead of you," he said, with a slight smile.

"Walter, I am very depressed. The city seems sad and foreign. I know it went through the war and I am sure Berlin is no different, but this is my city. I don't recognize the people; they seem, well, broken."

Walter looked at her appraisingly. "Elke, you are new to Vienna and some things you must know. There are few Austrian men between sixteen and sixty here, and the ones that remain are often invalids, in mind and body. Women between the ages of twenty and forty probably outnumber men by a hundred to one. Many of Vienna's women were raped by the Russians. Morality is loose, and prostitution and disease are everywhere. In this sector many women are hungry and are prepared to have sex with the Americans for companionship, protection, cigarettes, food, or stockings. The people are finally having to realize they are no longer Nazis, yet they still long for Hitler's time, before the bombs fell. They live in a present they wanted before the war, a city without Jews and with *Wiener Schnitzel.* Most are interested in surviving in the here and now, as you are. And I want to help you as much as I can."

"*Danke,* Walter!" Elke reached out to hug him.

To give Walter time to get the coal and have the stove working properly, Elke went for a walk in the neighborhood. This part of the city was in the American zone, distinguished by the number of ice cream parlors that seemed to be on every street. However, almost every street reminded her of her parents. How often the family had walked together here, especially on Sunday afternoons. Father, who loved his Vienna and knew its history so well, would tell them when a building had been built and who had lived there. The buildings stood as firmly as ever because the Allies hadn't bombed this area, but Father and Mother were gone. Thinking of her parents, tears sprang to her eyes.

Stopping in front of a familiar restaurant, she could taste the favorite dishes of her childhood—*Wiener Schnitzel* as crisp and dry as it is served only in Vienna, and *Zwiebelrostbraten,* a pot-roast usually accompanied by *Semmelknödel,* big round dumplings made from rolls cut into small squares and soaked in milk. Austrian cuisine was so good and varied because it took most of its tastiest dishes from the many countries of the Old Empire.

When Elke glanced up, she saw a young Austrian woman and an American soldier walking toward her. They were holding hands, obviously in love. The woman was a full-bosomed female, one the Nazis and her BdM would have approved of; a woman built to bear many children. Elke was depressed by the sight of the couple, partly because of the American hanging all over the Austrian girl. But also, she realized that at almost thirty, she had no one to love her and no one she could give her love to. She avoided eye contact and quickly walked by, but after only a few steps she heard: "Elke, Elke Baur, is that you?"

She turned to see her old school friend from gymnasium days, Ursula Bettauer. Elke had not recognized Ursula in her long red coat and blond hair.

"Ursula, I can't believe it. I didn't know if any of our classmates survived the war."

"I have seen Helga, and I know she would love to see you. In fact, she asked about you just the other day."

"I would love to see Helga. How is she?"

A polite cough from Ursula's companion reminded the two they were not alone. "I am so sorry, William, but this is my good friend Elke Baur. We were together in school."

Elke nodded the briefest hello possible, and William nodded in return.

"Elke, we have to catch up. I will get in touch with Helga. Let's meet soon at Demel's in the Kohlmarket. I love their pastries! Oh wait, how do I get in touch with you?"

"I don't have a telephone but you can contact Walter at my building at this number. He is always there."

The three parted. Elke thought that perhaps by reliving the past with her two school mates maybe she would feel better about her future. And possibly, one of them would know where she might find employment.

*   *   *

Demel's, founded in 1786 and located in the Kohlmarket near the Emperor's Palace, was famous for its pastry and chocolaterie. During the Habsburg Empire it was a favorite of the famous of the day. Even today, it seemed as if time had stood still. The waitresses still wore long black dresses and frilly white aprons. The marble-topped tables and bentwood chairs remained. For Elke and Ursula, the desolate Vienna of 1947 was overshadowed by talk of the better days of their youth.

"I am sorry Helga could not join us right now, but she says she could meet us at my apartment in an hour or so."

Elke was happy to agree. The conversation quickly turned to past friends. Sadly, most had not survived, especially the boys. Ursula asked Elke where she had been and what she had done during the war. "We have often thought of you and wondered how you were doing."

Elke explained how she had gotten out of Vienna ahead of the Russians and spent two years in an American prison camp. "They tried to make me feel guilty about the war, but it didn't work, and they finally let me go and sent me back here," she said.

"Are your parents still here in Vienna?" asked Ursula.

"*Nein*, they were killed in the firebombing of Dresden."

"I'm so sorry; how awful for you. Are you working? I am a nurse at General Hospital, and we can always use assistants," Ursula said.

"But I don't know anything about nursing. Why would they let me work there?"

"Are you kidding? There are way more invalids in this city than people to help them. Come see me in the next few days and I will get you started."

"Thank you so much!" Elke exclaimed. "I will! By the way, I remember, you were dating Heinz Lasky after we were out of school. Have you heard from him?"

"*Ja*, we had a wonderful time before he was called to the Wehrmacht and killed in Russia. It took the government a year before his parents were notified."

"You seemed quite friendly with William the other day. Is that serious?"

"*Nein*, he is just a good friend."

Sadness began to permeate the talk as the friends realized the carefree days of youth were long gone. Elke had said little about her years as a prisoner of the Americans. She didn't want to be questioned about whether she had been loyal to her past. Elke said instead, "Will Vienna ever come back to greatness again?"

"Vienna will never come back as long as the Jews are still here," said Ursula, in anger. "Thank God there are not many anymore. All they want to do is cheat Christians. The black market is the best thing that happened for them. They don't want to work, and they don't want to become Austrians. Everything they do is secret and different, then they complain they aren't accepted. We should not show pity to the Jews. They are complaining about not getting their assets returned to them. Why should they get preferential treatment over others who lost their property? Besides, with the economic situation here in Austria so desperate, they should wait their turn like everyone else."

Elke replied, "I have been lectured to by British and American officers about the Jews. I am tired of it. The Americans no longer threaten us with bombs; now they chide us like a nanny, one who gets on your nerves with her boney index finger and her shrill old maid's voice. You feel you are sitting in a classroom and constantly told off in such a way that even the best-behaved pupil will soon become obstinate."

They laughed at this, then Ursula became quiet. "I don't want to hear about guilt of the past. I don't care about the judgement of history; I just want the suffering to cease. Have you read *Der Friede* (The Peace) written by Ernst Jünger? He wrote this early in the war. I understand the Allies hate it and will not license it to be printed. He says the blood of dead soldiers was the seed that would bring forth corn after the peace and that corn was for all to share, conquerors and conquered. It must be a peace in which all sides win. Hatred is a poor-quality corn. He says good corn that has been so finely ground should never be squandered, it must provide us with bread for a long time. Neither side can rid themselves of guilt."

Elke said, "I have no guilt. I never killed anyone. I didn't know about killings by Wehrmacht, and I couldn't have done anything about it, anyway."

"It is contrary to common sense that you can make a whole nation guilty of a crime. The criminal is always an individual," Ursula said. "Besides, most of us only learn about those things after the war. We are much more the victims than the perpetrator of these atrocities."

Elke became defiant. "We are being bombarded with film and pictures of these camps, with their dead bodies. The extermination camps, mass killings, and torture and atrocities are all lies, lies made up by enemies of Germany. The lies discredit the Fatherland, so that it will seem right and just to the rest of the world to heap humiliation on our country. The camps were built by the Allies after the war ended." She softened her voice. "The Jew is a curious creature. He either hogs everything for himself at the expense of others, or wallows in self-pity and degradation, mental and physical."

Ursula interrupted. "I don't know. I sometimes doubt Hitler. What was it all for? I mean the devastation of most of Europe, the people starving without jobs or hope."

Elke remained defiant. "He was a great man, a great man. One of the greatest the world will ever know. Unfortunately, history is written by the winners, or he would be a giant among men. Our enemies hate National Socialism because it exalts the superior qualities of the German people. One day the world will speak in a different way about the Third Reich and its goals and accomplishments than it does today. I promise you."

"I just remember our school days, I think they were the best days of my life," Ursula said. "How young we were. We had character and ideals and felt like we were the future of the world. The world today does not have character or ideals. There are no morals today, only survival." She said this with cold dispassion and deep conviction. Then, Ursula brightened. "Let's stop this depressing talk. Let's go to my place. Helga will meet us there soon."

*   *   *

Ursula's apartment was a short walk from the pastry shop, an area of Vienna which was once an attractive neighborhood. As the girls approached the building, Elke thought it looked representative of Vienna itself, a once-proud city now fallen on hard times. Ursula opened the door with her key and Elke was greeted by an unexpected sight. "Ursula, you have quite a place, and some really beautiful things. This furniture is lovely. Did it come from your parents?"

"*Nein, nein, nein!* I have worked hard and found some good bargains. The desk by the window is eighteenth-century Habsburg.

"I think someday I will find an American officer and get to the United States, but marriage is hardly in my current plans. I am having too much fun now, and I am not going to give that up."

"Be careful, Ursula, I have seen awful things since I got back: people begging for food or for anything, really. I have heard venereal disease is rampant so be sure and have protection with you."

"Oh, I am very careful who I go out with."

"Ursula, I am amazed at the beautiful things in your apartment. What do you do at the hospital?"

"My job is hard to define. Let's say I am a nurse who can quickly get things the head nurses and doctors need. I have many sources. However, enough talk of me. Helga will be here shortly. Let me show you my pride and joy."

Ursula walked triumphantly to an ornate, mahogany sliding wardrobe door and opened it with great fanfare, showing a closet full of beautiful clothes.

"*Grüss Gott!*" Elke cried. "I don't know when I have seen so many dresses. And look at all those shoes. I have not seen a pair of high heels since I have been back in Vienna. There must be dozens here."

"Well actually, several hundred. The ones I don't like I keep in a back room."

Elke looked down and frowned at her own flat, well-worn shoes. "Ursula, can you get me a job at the hospital?" she said.

"Helga will be here soon, and we can talk more about your future with her. She is very resourceful and has many contacts all over Vienna. It is fortunate that we ran into each other. But enough talk of business. Let us have a drink and talk of old times. Follow me to the parlor."

Elke followed Ursula into another sumptuous room, one with a well-stocked bar containing many fine whiskeys and cognac.

"Elke, how long were you a prisoner and how were you treated by the Americans?"

"It was a bit over two years. I was treated horribly at first. They tried to get me to admit to killing Jews. After a while they gave up and left me alone in my cell."

"Do you resent the Americans? Do you want to get revenge for the way you were treated?"

Elke said, "Right now I want to get that part of my life behind me, and to make some money. I want to know where my next meal is coming from."

Just then, the doorbell rang. Ursula said, "Ah, Helga is here! You will do better than your next meal, my dear."

Helga was wearing a heavy fur coat that covered a stunning dress and high heels. Her hair was done up immaculately. "Elke, it is so good to see you," she said. "You look remarkably well. I am sure these last few years have been quite awful."

The women moved to the parlor and Ursula poured a cognac for herself and Helga. Elke asked for vodka.

Helga sat in a deep leather chair. She pulled a pack of American cigarettes from her purse and lit one. "Elke, tell us what you have been doing since the war ended. Where are you living and do you need work? Remember we are your schoolmates, we have survived the war as you have and we want to help you."

Elke recounted the story she had told Ursula but was distracted by her friends' beautiful clothes. All the stunning things in Ursula's apartment could not have come from her hospital pay. Helga's high heels attracted her notice, because one does not walk in Vienna's cobble-stone streets in heels. Did she come by taxi? What intrigued Elke the most was the somewhat gaudy watch on Helga's left wrist. It looked like a gift from a gentleman with lots of money, but little knowledge of women's tastes. She now understood what her friends were doing and was obviously being given an opportunity to join. But would it be an opportunity or danger? She envied their lifestyle and the comfort the money gave them.

Ursula said, "Helga and I are attending a party tonight we think you would enjoy, and it could be beneficial to you. Would you like to join us?"

"But I have nothing to wear to a party."

"Nonsense, you have seen my wardrobe and I will help you. It will be fun."

"What kind of party is it?" Elke said.

"Look dear," Ursula said with some exasperation, "everyone will be friends of ours who can do a lot of good for you. People that, if you treat them right, will be very helpful to you. It is a dog-eat-dog world. The black market controls everything. The Americans, Russians, French, and Brits have all the money. You have an opportunity to get your share, or more than your share."

Helga said, "Elke, you have the natural beauty and intelligence to do very well for yourself. All you have to do is treat some very important men nicely and take care of them. You do what they want, and they will more than take care of you."

"I am not sure. I am a good Catholic girl."

"Hell, we were all good Catholic girls at one time," Ursula said.

Helga interrupted. Her words were harsh. "Look, you whiney little bitch. This is not about your God or your fucking religion. This is about power. Women having power over important men. You give them what they want sexually and you control them. Since the war ended you have had no power. Now you have the opportunity to be the one in control." She lowered her voice. "All you have to do is be nice to some American general and you will get your revenge for the way you were treated in that prison camp in Germany. The best revenge is to live well."

*   *   *

Elke declined the party invitation; she needed time to think. Her friends talked of the "syndicate" and that she would be an equal partner. They made it sound enticing. Maybe she owed it to herself after the dreadful last few years. However, she knew there was a downside. How much longer would she be attractive, and what would she do after her youth was gone?

She stayed in her apartment most of the following day, occasionally going down to talk with Walter, mostly because she knew he would have something to eat. Walter had come through on what he'd promised and provided her with a good supply of coal, so the apartment was finally relatively warm. She wanted to talk about the meeting with her friends the day before, but she was not comfortable talking to Walter about it. Oh, if she could just talk with her father or even her mother, though her father was more attuned to the world. What was she thinking? Her father would kill her rather than see his daughter become a prostitute. She had to do something. She knew the first step would be to see Ursula at General Hospital.

The next day, while she waited to see the matron, she saw more of the aftermath of the war, men lying in the cots in the hallways of the hospital. They were emaciated shadows of the soldiers who had almost conquered an entire continent. Sick, in pain, and groaning, they now looked pathetic to her in the tattered remnants of their Wehrmacht uniforms.

The interview with the matron went well, especially when Elke admitted she would do any kind of job.

"That is good, because it is 'any kind of job' we need here," said the matron, tapping her foot, seemingly in a hurry. "This 'Great Freeze' is creating havoc here. I cannot believe the number of people who have slipped on the ice and broken bones. Can you start tomorrow? The pay isn't much, but we will provide you with your uniform and we will feed you. Be here at eight tomorrow morning."

With that brief meeting, Elke had a job, food, and clothing for the first time since being released from the prison camp. She felt better about her life and her future than she had for years. She still hadn't decided about her friends' syndicate offer, but she was not going to rush into a decision she might regret. She decided to get a coffee and pastry and then take a walk in her favorite park, the Prater.

After having coffee and a muffin, she boarded the tram that would take her to the Second district and the Prater. This, however, was the Russian zone. She could see a vast difference between this and the American zone. The Russians apparently had no interest in rebuilding, likely as retribution for the war. Crossing the grey, flat, muddy Danube was depressing. She thought of Ursula's words, that no one can remain wholly clean in these times. It seemed to also apply to her beloved river.

As the tram rumbled on toward the Prater, Elke was ill prepared for what she saw when she got off near the Prater Wheel. The Prater lay desolate, full of frost-nipped weeds, the broken foundations of abandoned merry-go-rounds, and rusting iron tanks no one had cleared away. This park, her favorite spot in childhood, lay smashed as if a giant had stepped on it, its bones sticking crudely through the snow.

The place was nearly empty. At the one open food stall, children queued with their coupons to buy thin, flat cakes. It was a pleasure to see the Great Wheel operating, even if only a single car was in use, packed with a few courting couples and children. When the car reached the highest point of the Wheel as it revolved slowly above the city, it stopped for a couple of minutes and Elke could see tiny faces pressed against the glass.

As she walked on through the Prater, she was confronted with a sight like something from Dante's *Inferno*. Children seemed to be living in holes in the ground, camouflaged from head to foot in filth. Until they moved, it was impossible to tell they were there. With Elke's approach, they scattered like so many rabbits disappearing into holes. Once she passed them, they reemerged, sniffed and stared around them. They carried stones or sticks or iron bars, and their teeth were black and broken or they had no teeth. One had a single arm, another a crutch, and the only clean spots on their bodies were the whites of their eyes. She later learned that some had homes, but nonetheless went out and hunted in packs, stealing what they could from the conquerors.

The walk back to the tram stop was almost unbearable, with bleak thoughts once again unfolding in Elke's mind: fear for her future and the desolate city, the awful, unrelenting cold, and the thought of selling herself to survive. Maybe she was being a prude to not join her friends. Was she really being fair to herself by denying herself nice clothes and a comfortable place to live? True, she had a job, but one cleaning bedpans at General Hospital. She wanted the job only in order to eat properly. Once again, she thought about suicide. *What is the point of living?* she wondered.

She sat in a cold tram car and stared out the window at the once beautiful buildings along the "Ring"; buildings that no longer inspired awe in her. Now they reminded her of a shining past that would never return. The more she thought about her options, as the tram jerked along its path emitting loud screeches when the brakes were applied, she realized how trapped she really was. She had no money or papers that would allow her to travel out of Austria. Even if she had the necessary papers, the rest of Europe was as devastated as Vienna, some parts even more so. No, if she had a future at all, it was here. The tram was approaching her favorite building in the city. It had helped her before when she was thinking of killing herself. The tram screeched to a stop at the National Library. Why not go in? It would be a warm, comfortable place, and she could spend the rest of the day with a book.

She walked toward a room near the back, far from the activity of the main room. It was quiet with only one, older man bent over a book at a back table. He would not be a bother, she assured herself, and found a chair in a corner. At first, she busied herself by pulling out pen and paper from her bag, planning to write of her situation. Maybe writing out her options would make her feel better. She glanced over at the man and his book. He had curly hair and a curly beard, a bit longer than the present style. His expression was serious; she felt he had seen much of the world. Perhaps he had been someone of importance in the Hitler government. She turned back to her writing. However, the more she wrote the more despair she felt. She quietly broke down in tears.

"My dear, may I be of help?" said the man, who had stolen over to her silently. "I have helped many in the past with my writings, and I may be of help to you."

Maybe it was her desperation, or that there was no one else in the room, but this man had a kind face. His empathetic smile reminded Elke of how Father would look at her when she had been crying. Father always seemed able to understand her feelings, even when she could not understand them herself. Elke opened up to the man as she had never done with anyone else. She explained how she had lost her family, her financial future was dim, that the thought of cleaning bed pans or selling her body was revolting. There was something about this sympathetic old man that made Elke want to reveal her deepest fears to him.

"What do you mean your past writings may be of help to me?" she said through teary eyes.

"The world has gone through terrible times and those times are continuing in Europe. I have lived in Vienna for a long time. Have you ever read *Meditations*?

"I had a teacher in gymnasium, my last year. He admired Marcus Aurelius so much he made sure we all read and studied Aurelius and his writings. I understand the Emperor died near here in 180 A.D. Someone wrote that he was the last great Roman Emperor, I think it was Gibbon. How will this help me?"

"Remember my dear, God permits evil in order to allow us to appreciate beauty: Many ugly and ungraceful entities are placed in the universe by providence to enhance our aesthetic sense. So, dirt, mud, poison, earthquakes, and storms come from the same source as roses, seascapes, and the wonders of spring. Aurelius tells us that evil arises from false representations and false judgements that develop from ignorance. You take things you can't control and define them as "good" or "bad." So of course, when the "bad" things happen or the "good" ones don't, you blame the gods and feel hatred for the people responsible—or those you decide to make responsible.

The evil in the universe is caused by man's wickedness. Even wicked men, tyrants, and mass murderers believe that when they committed evil actions they were actually working for the greater good. I believe that is one more reason why we should be kind, noble, and forgiving. Man is free, which means free to do evil as well as good. Doing good not only benefits others, but also benefits the benefactor. Here my dear, take my copy of *Meditations*. I have others."

With that, the man moved toward the door. Before Elke could either thank him or ask his name, he seemed to have disappeared.

Her mind returned to her strange dream of a few days earlier. She had attributed that to the vodka she'd drunk, but now she was sober. Why was she having these visions/dreams of old men, presumably authors, visiting her from the past—but not her past? Could this have been Marcus Aurelius? What about the old man in her apartment? Could that have been Voltaire? What did they hope to accomplish with her? Probably, this was a dream, like the one she had about her parents a few nights earlier. With a shrug of her shoulders she convinced herself that these were all caused by the stress of her life and nothing more, until her hand fell on the book that the old man had given her. This book was not a dream, but a gift from an important man of the past to help her with her future, and maybe save her from her past.

"At break of day, when you are reluctant to get up, have this thought ready to mind: 'I am getting up for a man's work. Do I still then resent it, if I am going out to do what I was born for, the purpose for which I was brought into the world? Or was I created to wrap myself in blankets and keep warm?' 'But this is more pleasant.' Were you then born for pleasure—all for feeling, not for action? Can you not see plants, birds, ants, spiders, bees all doing their own work, each helping in their own way to order the world? And then you do not want to do the work of a human being—you do not hurry to the demands of your own nature. 'But one needs rest too.' One does indeed: I agree. But nature has set limits to this too, just as it has to eating and drinking, and yet you go beyond these limits, beyond what you need. Not in your actions, though, not any longer: here you stay below your capability. The point is that you do not love yourself—you love both your own nature and her purpose for you."

She was near the end of skimming the previous books when she began to read Book Twelve:

"All that you pray to reach at some point in the circuit of your life can be yours now—if you are generous to yourself. That is, if you leave all the past behind, entrust the future to Providence, and direct the present solely to reverence and justice. To reverence, so that you come to love your given lot: it was Nature that brought it to you and you to it. To justice, so that you are open and direct in word and action, speaking the truth, observing law and proportion in all you do. You should let nothing stand in your way—not the iniquity of others, not what anyone else thinks or says, still less any sensation of this poor flesh that has accreted around you: the afflicted part must see to its own concern."

Elke closed the book, laid her head on the table, and was soon fast asleep.

14

Fritz Baur

1936

Thomas Weyr wrote in his book, The Setting of the Pearl: Vienna Under Hitler, *the following: "The Nazis had been defeated, at least for now. Hitler dropped those responsible for the failed putsch and claimed the Reich had played no part in it—a blatant lie, but good enough to give Austria some temporary breathing room from Nazi intrigues. The Social-Democrats had been eliminated as an active political force. Red Vienna was gone. The corporative state rested on the twin pillars of a newly renascent Catholic Church, and the bayonets of the army and the* Heimwehr. *Kurt von Schuschnigg (the new Chancellor) was an ardent Catholic, and now the Church assumed a much more important role in political life than it had in the twenties.*

"But while political opposition had been outlawed, it seethed underground where social-democratic resentment grew and the illegal Nazi party flourished. As the economy worsened and unemployment skyrocketed, their party membership expanded dramatically, far more so than the Social-Democrats. The newly unemployed—dismissed bureaucrats, students who couldn't find

jobs, shopkeepers who lost their businesses, and other members
of the disgruntled lower middle class—all flocked to the NSDAP.
The Social-Democrats had reached their natural limits under
democracy and were hard put to add to their membership."

E lse had been rather hit and miss during the last few years of keeping up with her journal. Now that the family was preparing for their holiday leave in the Austrian resort of Bad Ischl, she was determined to renew the writing discipline she once had. Every year in August, Viktor was awarded with a month's leave from the bank, and the family had always gone to this resort spa in the Austrian Alps, where Viktor and Else could rub shoulders with the rich and famous of Vienna. All the great names of Austrian literature, journalism, and medicine, as well as the most famous actors and actresses, could be seen eating their breakfast eggs at the Café Zauner on the Esplanade. However, for twenty-two-year-old Fritz and seventeen-year-old Elke, the month took them away from their friends in Vienna. In fact, an argument had developed when Fritz announced that at his age, he had better things to do and would be staying in the city. This announcement had upset Viktor, but Else got him to calm down by saying, "Viktor, he has his own life now, after all he is a grown man."

"*Ja*, but what kind of life? He is always running off with his Nazi hoodlum friends."

"He will be all right. He has a good head on his shoulders."

Else's Journal
1 AUGUST 1936

I think I enjoy the travel preparations more than the actual
travel. The joy for me is in the preparation, being sure Viktor

doesn't forget something important. It is a six-hour train ride to Bad Ischl, but I had prepared a picnic hamper with cold chicken, ham, sausages, bread, butter, and cheese for the first hours of the trip. I knew the train would have fresh, hot coffee and freshly cooked frankfurters for the rest of the journey. I was excited when the train pulled into the station and a red cap helped us get our trunks and suitcases into a waiting taxi, which took us to the apartment we've rented for the month.

As soon as things were reasonably put away we were excited to go to Zauner's tea-room. Here you may see former princes or even Habsburg archdukes. I have always felt (maybe it is the altitude because rain clouds are always present) that the man who had stalked stag here, Emperor Franz Josef himself, is looking down benevolently on his people.

I have noticed many more German tourists here this year. Austro-German relations have improved a lot since Hitler ended the one thousand Reichsmark barrier which he imposed three years ago. It was keeping much-needed German tourists from Austrian resorts. The Germans have always seemed to have much more money to spend than we Austrians. This bothered Viktor more than me. What upset me more was how they would go on and on about the wonderful things happening in the Reich, lavishing praise on Hitler and the miracle he had performed in a few short years.

I am so proud of Elke. She has matured beyond her seventeen years. She seems to delight in Bad Ischl and has joined a group of young people. They go for long walks in the mountains, stroll along the Esplanade, and attend a dance every evening. She has done well in school, has a very nice figure and a wonderful personality. I think she has a bright future ahead of her. However, I worry about Fritz. He seems bitter and angry. Viktor is sure he is deeply involved with the Nazi party in Vienna. It seems like just the other day he was this rambunctious boy, playful and energetic. He loved to play the piano and was full of curiosity about things. I noticed a change in him during his last two years in gymnasium. He wasn't doing well in his studies. We didn't know why until the day he walked into the kitchen looking as though he had been crying and asked me an odd question: Are we Jews? I said we were not and whatever gave him that idea? He said one of his classmates called him a "dirty Jew" because our name is Baur.

I held him and said I believe it is all in the spelling. Some people get confused because Bauer, spelled with an e, can sometimes be a name for Jewish people.

He seemed to understand, but he must have been taunted again, because he sulked when frustrated and would talk about the unfairness of it. School kids can be very hurtful. It must have bothered him more than I thought because he became hostile, an unhappy loner. One time when we were having a small function at home, Fritz came into the living room and announced, "Nobody bothers themselves about me here!" and stomped out of the apartment. Some embarrassment ensued but the incident was soon forgotten.

Viktor and I realized he had had problems for years. We tried to discipline him with caning when he was younger, but that didn't seem to work. In fact, I think it was a challenge to him to withstand the pain. I have worried even more during the last few months as the Nazis seemed to be getting stronger and Fritz had spent more nights out doing what, we didn't know, but with his Nazi friends. It probably was not good.

I feel heartbroken for Fritz. At twenty-two, he should be still at university. But with his grades so low and so few jobs available there was little reason to stay in school. Since the banking crisis we have seen a third of the working population out of work. Even the employed are bringing back paychecks considerably smaller than before the war. I remember when Fritz first came to us and asked to join the Hitler Youth. Viktor and I laughed at the thought. We didn't think he was serious. I thought of them as mere boys, ones out to raise a ruckus, as boys will. Fritz responded that Hitler was one of the great thinkers of our time, right along with Karl Marx and Sigmund Freud. Viktor cut him off. "Hitler is not a thinker," he said. "Hitler is just a ranter and raver." This occurred a couple of years ago when Fritz was becoming more political. Maybe Viktor and I didn't take him seriously enough. Maybe we should have talked to him about his feelings. Some of his reasons for turning to Hitler and the Nazis were valid. He said it was high time someone brought the economic situation under control. He is right about that.

I almost wish our holiday were over. I lie awake nights worrying about Fritz.

*   *   *

Fritz Baur had been a secret member of the Hitler Youth for a year before his family's annual holiday. He wasn't really a secret member, because at twenty-one he could do as he pleased, but he kept the fact from his parents. Fritz had loved military uniforms since he had first seen his father wearing his Austrian Army uniform during the Great War. With the Nazis and Adolf Hitler growing in popularity across the border in Germany he had set his eyes on joining the SS. They were the elite and had the best-looking uniforms: all black with the stylized initials SS resembling twin lightning flashes. Fritz stood a hair over six feet tall. With his blond hair, long, narrow face, light blue eyes, pink-white skin, and cold, hard facial expression he looked the picture of a German soldier. Fritz enjoyed the weekly meetings of the Hitler Youth, usually held on Sunday evenings at a small meeting hall in Vienna. There, they ate sausages and potato salad and drank mugs of beer. Fritz liked the Nazi's New Order that projected an image of energy and determination. Even Hitler's murder of several political opponents, such as the Blood Purge of 1934, was widely interpreted to be a sign of his intention to guarantee stability.

Fritz was anxious for the meeting this Sunday because there was to be a speaker. "This should be good tonight," said Fritz's closest friend, Gerhard Rupp, sitting down beside him. The two had joined at about the same time. Although Gerhard had a cheerier personality than Fritz, they seemed to complement each other. Gerhard continued, "He's supposed to be an expert on the Jews. I hope he will convince me to go out and find some hot Jew girl I can screw right quick and get out."

"That is not funny and you know it. The thought sends cold chills down my spine."

"Your problem, Fritz, is your standards are way too high."

"I plan to join the SS where the standards are very high, and I know I can attain those standards."

A man appeared at the podium dressed in Austrian hunting attire. He thrust his right arm forward and a shouted strong, "*Heil* Hitler." This quickly brought the room to full attention, despite his odd attire. "The downfall of Germany is caused by the Jews," the unnamed speaker continued in a booming voice. "They entered our country as aliens intent on settlement, spoke a curious German, and sold shoddy merchandise and in a particularly persistent manner. We must fight them wherever we can—these capitalists, these bloodsuckers, who are concerned only with profit, who don't work but deal only in trade. We know the Jews committed ritual murder during the middle-ages—and they still do today. Do you all know Martin Luther portrayed Jews as miserable, demonic creatures, vermin and vampires? They enslaved Christians through usury along with poisoning the wells. They also drained the blood of Christian children for their secret rituals. Luther said Jewish schools, prayer books, and synagogues should be torched, homes destroyed, and Jews hounded from the land.

"You must believe in Germany as firmly, clearly, and truly as you believe in the sun, the moon, and the starlight. You must believe in Germany, as if Germany were yourself; and as you believe your soul strives toward eternity. You must believe in Germany—or your life is but death. And you must fight for Germany until the new dawn comes. You must be tough as leather, swift as a greyhound, and hard as Krupp steel. You must learn to be hard in bearing privations, frustration and pain."

The speaker's enthusiasm lit up the room. Boys leapt to their feet and shouted "*Heil* Hitler!" at the top of their lungs.

After the meeting, several of the young men assembled outside the hall in the diminishing daylight. One of them began to chant, *Juda Verrecke! Juda Verrecke!* (Perish Judah! Perish Judah!) over and over until they all took up the chant and walked down the street looking to cause trouble. Trouble soon appeared in the form of a small Jewish shoe store. The boys stood in front of the store's entrance and continued to shout *Juda Verrecke!* A crowd began to gather. Soon the owner of the shop appeared, hesitatingly, at the door in a vain attempt to convince the demonstrators he was harmless to them; merely a small businessman. Someone in the crowd had lettered a sign that read: "I am a dirty Jew. Don't buy at my store." The owner was grabbed by someone and held tightly while Fritz and Gerhard placed the sign around his neck to the amusement of the crowd of onlookers. The two brown shirt leaders marched the confused and bewildered store owner around in front of his store to the delight of the spectators. Probably because under the Schuschnigg regime it was still illegal to physically harm Jews, Fritz and Gerhard forcefully shoved the little man back into his store. However, the sign was removed from him and secured to the shop window while another man, with white paint, drew in large letters "JUD" on the window.

The crowd dispersed, and Gerhard and Fritz retired to their favorite Biergarten for some refreshment to celebrate their victory. On the walk there, Fritz sported a wide grin. "I feel really good about what we just did. Maybe that old Jew will shut down and leave Austria, then there would be one less Jew in a city full of them."

"Fritz, he was just a little old man."

"*Nein,* he is a symbol of the kind that needs to be removed from our greater Germany," Fritz said as they entered the establishment and took seats. "Brush away the old, weak, and decrepit, all those who no longer have the drive necessary to radically transform society. What we just did was to exercise our freedom, to give our instincts free reign. And that is all right if it is in the name of the Nazi cause. I believe a war of civilizations is coming and only Adolf Hitler can defend Europe against the Asiatic pestilence and Bolshevism."

As they raised their *bier* steins, Gerhard self-consciously glanced around the room to see if anyone else had heard his friend's explosive tirade of hate, but it went unremarked.

Fritz said, "Gerhard, I haven't talked with you since you went to Berlin for the Olympic Games. Did you see the *Führer?*"

"*Ja,* I saw him in his box in the Olympia Stadium, but the true star of the show was the city of Berlin. I was really impressed. It was clean, scrubbed down, with freshly painted house fronts, and clean streets on which you could not find even the smallest piece of paper. This cleanliness got the attention of the visitors. The main street, Unter den Linden, had a long row of flags and an ocean of lights came on at night—lanterns. There is such a great change since the hunger and unemployment of the early thirties. I give credit to Hitler. He promised work and he has created work. Remember, my father was not like your father, who had a good, steady bank job. My father was out of work more than he worked. We went hungry most of the time. My mother would cry because she couldn't give us enough food to eat. This is why I want Germany to take over Austria. What the *Führer* has done for Germany I want him to do for our country.

In Berlin I stayed for the week with my aunt who lives there, and we talked a lot about Hitler. She is part of the older generation and is beloved in her neighborhood for her volunteer work at the local kindergarten and a home for the poor and sick. She writes poems in a neat notebook she showed me. This gentle old woman wrote 'Heil Hitler' at the bottom of each page of her book of poems. She likes Hitler because he feeds the poor."

"Do you think we will ever see that in Vienna? The city is in such turmoil; there is no order. I don't see order being restored until an *Anschluss* with Germany happens. Schuschnigg is a weasel!" Fritz spat out the words.

"What can he do?"

"The people of Vienna crave stability; I would use the SS to sit on the communists and the Jews, even moving them all out of Austria. The penniless Jews are a drain on the public purse anyway," said Fritz.

"But where would they go?"

"I don't care, Poland. Or Russia. They must pack up and disappear from Europe."

"Poland and Russia don't want them. That is why there are so many Eastern Jews here in Vienna," Gerhard said.

"Maybe Poland and Russia won't have a choice."

Gerhard thought he detected a twinkle in his friend's eyes.

"What do you mean by that? Do you mean war—with us invading Poland and Russia? That will never happen, Napoleon tried, and you know how that turned out."

"Napoleon didn't have the kind of soldiers we can use against the weak Russians and Poles. This is why I want to be a part of the SS. Those soldiers are real men, capable of leading a German victory. Hitler needs tough, dedicated men to move the Jews out, and I want to be one of them. The Jews want to conquer the world, and we must conquer them before they conquer us."

"*Ja* Fritz, I believe what you say, but we are Austrian, not German. The SS belongs to Germany and I don't believe Schuschnigg will allow Germany to take over Austria, even though it is my wish that Germany do so."

Fritz retorted, "I disagree with you. I think *Anschluss* with Germany is inevitable and preferable. Look at what is happening in Germany since Hitler took over in 1932. He has generated jobs, confidence, and an affluence that is spreading rapidly among all classes of Germans. We Austrians really have only two choices: to try for a new beginning with the communists or join the National Socialists who are working to free Germany from the stranglehold of the Versailles Treaty. I, for one, choose to support Hitler and his movement to make a new start for our country."

"*Ja* Fritz, I suppose you could say that Hitler wants to do only what England and France have done for years with their worldwide colonies. Now Germany's historic hour has come, and the dream of her greatness will become a reality in our own lifetime in the Reich of the *Führer*. I feel we have been summoned to take part in a difficult and noble service by which we ourselves will be fulfilling our duty toward the Reich. All through our youth we lamented our defeat in the Great War, followed by the misery of the post-war years that have not ceased."

"We all believe world Jewry is among the enemies of Germany. Europe is divided into three blocks: The Western democracies, the National Socialist center, and the Bolshevik East. Nothing good comes out of the East, only evil things—like the plague. Austria has every reason to believe measures will soon be taken to restore the economy and solve the Jewish Question once and for all. Only Germany has the determination to defend European culture from Asiatic barbarism. World Jewry has corrupted the Western democracies."

The young men realized they'd had enough beer and talk. It was time to call an end to the day.

*   *   *

On a rainy Saturday in Vienna, Viktor was enjoying coffee and a pastry cake he had purchased from the excellent pastry cook's shop nearby, owned by *Herr* Beisiegl. The years at Länderbank had been good to him, not only with a secure job, but the girth of his stomach showed the mark of a successful banker. He was immersed in his newspaper, the *Neue Freie Presse*. He had read the front page and an article about the Austrian National team's upcoming football game, when a headline caught his eye: "The Pace of Industrialization is Upsetting Many." The article reported that many Austrians felt disoriented with the fast pace of industrialization and urbanization. The wartime defeat and the discredited Habsburg monarchy had left a vacuum that was being filled by industrialization and urbanization. The Jews seemed to personify the rise of the department store, theatre, advertising, and the stock exchange. These transformations were exciting, but also unnerving, as change often is.

They were certainly disconcerting to Viktor. A staunch Austrian, he was opposed to an *Anschluss* with Germany. The article started him thinking about Austria's 33 percent unemployment rate. If the journalist was correct, the other 67 percent were upset about where urbanization was taking Austria. Viktor was a supporter of Schuschnigg but recognized that he was an unlikable man with few friends. He lacked the popular touch; his speeches were often cold and stilted. Viktor felt Chancellor Schuschnigg had great personal courage but lacked vision beyond maintaining the authoritarian state he had inherited from Dollfuss.

Else entered the room and Viktor asked if Fritz was up yet.

"*Ja,* I think I heard him moving about in his room. Do you want to talk with him?"

"*Ja,* he worries me, and we haven't talked for some time because he is seldom home."

They heard a cheerful voice call out, "*Guten Morgan* Mother and Father! Is there coffee left? I am sure Father has eaten the pastry cake from *Herr* Beisiegl's?"

"You are in a good mood on a rainy day," Victor said as Fritz sat down opposite him. "Sorry, I didn't expect you up so soon, and those pastry cakes are too good to leave for long. Besides, it has been a difficult week at the bank. The unemployment numbers continue to grow."

"Austria's unemployment may be growing, but Germany's is going down. Father, we need the *Anschluss.* Hitler is stronger than Schsuchnigg; he can lead us out of all this."

Else indicated that she was going back to the kitchen.

"You may be right, son, but what can he do? Vienna is being overwhelmed by the *Ostjuden,* who are a major drain on the economy. They are poor, have no skills, and thus exacerbate the already acute shortage of food, housing, and fuel. You and I have fought over the years about Germany and Austria, but at my job I see these numbers come in and get more and more discouraged."

"Father, I never want to argue with you. I look up to you. I am proud of your service in the Austrian army and that you are a respected banker. I also understand losing your best friend in the war had to be devastating."

"*Ja.* Fritz, I'm proud of my service to my country. But after experiencing war, I can't believe any human being would want someone they love to go through it. And I saw how the failure of the Jewish bank, the Credit-Anstalt, ruined the Austrian banking system and led indirectly to the destruction of organized labor and our democratic republic. Our unemployment is higher than most other European countries.

"But I am worried that you seem 'hell bent' on joining Nazi groups like the SA and the SS. I want to see an Austria with jobs, peace in the streets, and freedom from the oppressive Treaty of Versailles, but I don't want to see a dead son."

"Isn't that the point, Father? In school we were taught France was our archenemy, the Italians were traitors, Jewish bankers and industrialists stabbed us in the back, and Germany must make up for the wrongs done to us during that time. Father, I am a realist. Austria is too small to get out of its twenty-year economic morass by itself. You must understand, young Austrians like me love Germany and all things German. Germany is the future of Austria."

Seeing Viktor's deep frown, Fritz paused. "But enough politics. Are you still upset about Austria losing to Italy in the Olympic finals?"

Viktor took a sip of coffee, relieved to have a calm conversation with Fritz. "*Ja,* we got into the finals by defeating Poland 3 to 1 in August. I really thought we could best Italy, even though they were the favorite. Still, losing to them 2 to 1 hurt. But you know I take my football seriously."

"My good friend, Gerhard Rupp, was at the game and enjoyed the spectacle of it all. He said the crowd was enormous. Newspapers reported one hundred and ninety-five thousand fans watched the two games, first for the bronze medal and then for the gold."

"That is why they are called the *Wunderteam.* Remember, if there is an *Anschluss* there will be no more *Wunderteam,*" Viktor teased.

"Well, that is something to consider, but I think the economy is more important than football."

"Are you still playing some football?"

"*Nein,* I don't have the time anymore."

"What do you do at those meetings you go to so often?"

"Well, I don't attend the Hitler Youth meetings—they are only for kids up to age 18. And the meetings are usually nothing more than singing, learning about heroic stories of past German and Austrian legends, and marching. But sports activities do play a large part."

"Fritz, I have heard children at age 10 can be a part of this *Jungvolk* (Young People) and they take an oath to Hitler. Is that true?"

"*Ja,* it's true. Swearing the first oath to *der Führer* is supposed to represent the holiest hour of their lives—a proud picture of solidarity of German youth to the entire world."

"That depresses me, Fritz. I hear stories of conflicts between the younger and older generations, disruptions in family life and divided loyalties. My generation is skeptical of this Nazi movement. What are *your* meetings like?"

"We play exciting games. We divide into two teams. The members of one team wear red armbands; the members of the other team wear blue ones. The aim is to conquer a tower, a bridge, or maybe even a village square in a small town defended by one of the teams. The other team plans tactics to outwit the defenders. Once an opponent captures you and tears off your armband you are considered 'dead' and can no longer participate. The game teaches teamwork and leadership. I have shown good leadership in this and am being considered for a commission in the SS, which I really want."

Viktor was stunned. "It sounds like war games to me," he said.

Fritz chose to ignore this comment. "Sorry, Father, I have to go," he said, striding from the room.

Viktor remained in his chair, holding his cup of now-cold coffee and stared, unseeing, at his many books. He was convinced that Austria was finished.

*   *   *

On a dark and surprisingly cold April night on the outskirts of
Vienna, a group of almost four hundred young Austrian men gathered
to participate in a solemn ceremony. It was 29 April, 1937, the birthday
of Adolf Hitler. The men, who were all dressed in black uniforms, had
come together for a rite of initiation. All had been carefully screened
to make certain their ancestry was free of any Jewish blood, even
going back as far as the eighteenth century. They had all proven to
be superior physical specimens, of sound morals and ideals, with the
mental toughness to execute certain distasteful assignments. They
were dedicating their lives to service in a mystical brotherhood, one
much like the order of Teutonic Knights of old. By torchlight, four
hundred voices repeated the oath in a prayer-like chorus:

> *"I swear to thee Adolf Hitler, as Führer and Chancellor of
> the German Reich. Loyalty and bravery, I vow to thee and to
> the superiors whom thou shalt appoint. Obedience unto death,
> so help me God!"*

Fritz Baur and Gerhard Rupp had worked hard to experience this
moment. Each had passed several tests, both mental and background
tests, to achieve their goal of joining the SS. Their enthusiasm had been
noticed by officials in the Austrian SS; they were soon recommended
to be promoted to *Sturmführer,* or lieutenants, in the burgeoning
number of Austria's SS recruits.

They were different in not only personality but background. While
Fritz came from a middle-class banking family, his friend Gerhard's
father was often-unemployed and drank what little earnings he made.
Gerhard remembered a pub on the corner and women with children
would attempt to keep their husbands from going in and drinking up
their pay. A year earlier he had attended a Nazi Party banquet where
they served rolls with butter. It was the first time Gerhard had tasted

butter. He knew it was because of Hitler and the Nazis and wanted that for Austria.

While Fritz was attracted by the SS uniforms, anti-Semitism, the idea of controlling others, being looked up to, and never again being bullied, Gerhard wanted to join the National Socialists because they were working to free Germany from the stranglehold of the Versailles Treaty. He had concluded that Adolf Hitler and his movement were his country's only hope. He had joined the SS when it was a small group in Vienna whose purpose was to protect the National Socialist Party, especially the party leadership. Gerhard wanted most to bring order to the streets, felt the SS would do just that, and wanted to be a part of this effort.

One day in May, the two SS lieutenants were summoned to the office of their superior, Maj. Otto Hoppe. It was a stark office, with no pictures of Hitler or Nazi flags, because the party and especially the SS were forbidden in Austria. However, as more and more young Austrians joined the party, this law became impossible to enforce. Maj. Hoppe began the conversation with no introduction and even less humor.

"Gentlemen, we have been seeing an increase in lawlessness and violence in the Jew quarter at Leopoldstadt. Each of you is to take your men in two lorries and patrol that area to try and prevent looting—if you can. It is full of Jew shops, so we don't care too much, but we still would prefer that no one is killed. We believe the presence alone of SS soldiers in uniform will be enough to keep the malcontents in line."

Fritz said, "What do we do if someone breaks a Jew's shop window, sir?"

"Nobody gets killed, Lieutenant. That is all we care about. Oh, one other thing. Some of these looters are taking some fairly valuable items from the Jews."

"Are we to give them back?" said Gerhard.

"Heavens no! Anything that looks as if it might have value you are to confiscate. Turn it into my office where we will properly dispose of it."

"I understand, sir," said Gerhard.

"That is all, gentlemen. Now, do your duty."

The brief meeting ended with a *Heil* Hitler salute. The lieutenants left the office and assembled their men and lorries. As they approached Leopoldstadt the SS men heard yelling, which grew louder the closer they came. The men quickly disembarked from the lorries and took their stations along the street, where they saw people totally out of control. The idea that these SS men, in their all-black uniforms, guns at the ready, and a no-nonsense look on their intense faces, would discourage the looting went for naught when people in the crowd began chanting *Juda verrecke! Juda verrecke!* Soon the glass fronts of store windows began to be shattered up and down the street.

"Sir, do you want me to put a stop to the looting?" It was Fritz's Technical Sergeant, Hulmut Schulze.

"*Nein,* let the boys have a bit of fun. I see even women and children are taking part today."

Fritz walked closer to the stores being attacked. He saw Jewish owners cowering in the backs of their shops. Walking further down the street, he came upon a young boy who had climbed into the broken window of a shoe store. His mother waited for him on the sidewalk. The boy emerged from the display window and proudly held up a pair of shoes. "Look, Mother! Look at these great shoes I just stole." She replied with some irritation, "Silly, you have shoes for two left feet. Go right back in there and get the right shoe."

Fritz smirked and walked back toward the lorry. Seeing Sgt. Schulze, he said, "I think they have done enough damage here. There is nothing more we can do. Let's go back to headquarters. His men returned to their lorry and drove back to headquarters, satisfied that all had gone well.

Maj. Hoppe was sitting at his desk, unsmiling. Fritz was not sure if he was to be praised or condemned for the afternoon's action.

"Did everything go all right, Lieutenant?"

"*Ja* sir! I think the action went very well. No one was hurt too badly."

"*Gut!* I have something here that may please you. *Reichsführer* Heinrich Himmler would like to meet you."

Fritz was taken aback. "How does the *Reichsführer* even know who I am, sir?"

Ignoring the question, Hoppe continued, "He is forming an elite corps with the special duty of protecting the Führer. I sent him your dossier and enclosed your photograph. The man is vain; it was your picture that created his interest. He sees you as the ideal German specimen, with your height and Nordic background. He has invited you to a Party Grand Ball in Munich on Saturday. You are scheduled to fly out of Aspern Airport Thursday at 6:00 a.m. Do you have a proper dress uniform for a fancy ball?"

"*Nein,* sir. I have never been to a Grand Ball."

"I will get you the proper uniform. There will be many important Party members at this Ball. I believe the *Anschluss* with Germany is coming, and this is a great opportunity for a young lieutenant. Don't screw it up."

Fritz noted a touch of sarcasm in Maj. Hoppe's tone. Perhaps Hoppe was jealous that he wasn't invited?

*   *   *

On the surface, the Grand Ball was impressive to the young Austrian SS lieutenant. All the officers in their black dress uniforms were young (even Himmler himself was only thirty-six) and eager for adventure. The music was grand, the food good, and the beer flowed abundantly. Fritz was soon approached by a man of average height and build (several inches shorter than himself) with mild eyes, slightly enlarged by spectacles, and a somewhat recessive chin. He looked out of place among the tall, chiseled SS officers in the room. He introduced himself as Heinrich Himmler, then proceeded to talk about the value of herbs as opposed to orthodox medical treatment. The *Reichsführer* seemed to Fritz almost a crank, a little man with little obsessions. Himmler then moved on to speak with others, leaving Fritz to wonder why he had been invited to this ball.

Almost immediately, a tall blond officer of the SS mold came up to Fritz. "I know he doesn't impress," he said, "but keep this in mind: Himmler's SS is Hitler's private guard and he himself has demonstrated unswerving loyalty to him. The Führer knows the value of the SS. We are his favorite and most valuable organization because we have never let him down."

"But he didn't even seem to know who I am," stammered Fritz.

"Don't underestimate him. If you are here, he knows exactly who you are."

As the officer moved off, a young woman walked by and gave Fritz a sly smile. He watched her join her friends. She held a glass of wine in her hand. As she glanced back at him, his thoughts raced: Would she turn him down for a dance and make him look a fool? Well, he was here by himself and no one else seemed interested in him, so what the hell. He walked over to her. Up close, he saw a pretty girl with long, honey blond hair, cute dimples, and a fetching smile. Her sleek gown shimmered in the light. She was smiling as Fritz introduced himself as SS *Strumführer* Fritz Baur from Vienna.

"Nice to meet you, Lt. Fritz Baur from Vienna. I am Krista von Rehm, from here in Munich."

"Would you care to dance, Krista von Rehm?"

"That would be very nice," she said, still smiling.

On the dance floor, Krista said, "Have you been to Munich before, Lt. Baur?"

"*Nein*, it is my first time," replied Fritz, trying to talk above the music.

"How long will you be here?"

"Only a couple of days. I fly back to Vienna tomorrow. Have you been to Vienna, Krista?" Fritz said.

"When I was young our parents took us on a Danube cruise, and we stopped briefly in Vienna. A beautiful city and I love the Strauss music. I think I could dance to it all night long."

"You seem to know a lot of people here. Do you work for the SS?"

"You mean, how can a woman be working for the SS? For some time, I have shown an interest and ability in statistics. A friend of my father's knew the SS needed someone with my skills. My job is to keep track of money, especially Jew money, but really all money. Who has it and where is it?"

This sounded boring to Fritz. But a spark had been lit between the two, and they continued to dance well into the evening. When the music ended, too soon, Fritz promised to write, and Krista promised to come to Vienna to see him. On the flight back to Aspern Airport, Fritz had forgotten about his brief conversation with Himmler, the head of the SS. His only thought was: How could he see Krista von Rehm again?

15

Anschluss – Part I

1938

At 7:47 p.m. on 11 March, 1938, the Austrian Chancellor, Kurt von Schuschnigg, gave the following radio address to the nation:

"Austrian men and Austrian women: This day has placed us in a tragic and decisive situation. I have to give my Austrian fellow countrymen the details of the events of the day. The German government today handed to President Miklas an ultimatum with a time-limit attached, ordering him to nominate as Chancellor a person to be designated by the German government and to appoint members of a Cabinet on the orders of the German government; otherwise, German troops would invade Austria.

"I declare before the world that the reports put into circulation concerning disorders by the workers, the shedding of streams of blood and the allegation that the situation had got out of control of the government, are lies from A to Z. President Miklas has asked me to tell the people of Austria that we have yielded to force, since we are not prepared even in this terrible situation to shed blood. We decided to order the troops to offer no serious—(pause) to offer no resistance.

"So I take my leave of the Austrian people with the German word of farewell uttered from the depths of my heart—'God protect Austria.' "

Else's Journal
SATURDAY, 12 MARCH 1938

Dear Journal, These last twenty-four hours have been heartbreaking. First, we thought there would be a plebiscite for the Austrian people on whether we were for a "free, independent, social, Christian and united Austria—Ja oder Nein?" The plebiscite was to be held tomorrow, Sunday. Viktor was thrilled and could not wait. I have always leaned toward Anschluss *with Germany, because I feel it will bring law and order back to Vienna. Viktor feels we should be independent, as he doesn't trust the Hitler government.*

At first, we felt our Austria would remain independent when early this morning aero-planes circled lazily, dropping hundreds of thousands of propaganda leaflets, calling on Austrians to say "Ja." Viktor and I hired a taxi and had the driver take us to the Ringstrasse, the Kärntnerstrasse, and the Graben shopping street. We observed long columns of motor-lorries filled with enthusiastic men and women wearing the red-white-red ribbons of Austria. They displayed banners with patriotic slogans and scattered enormous quantities of leaflets. The motor columns were greeted everywhere with waving handkerchiefs, cheers, and shouts of encouragement. However, by the time we returned to our apartment, the mood of the city seemed to change. I made coffee and Viktor turned on the radio. We sat down in the living room, looking forward to enjoying our coffee and listening to gay, patriotic music.

Suddenly, the music was interrupted by a voice announcing: "All unmarried reservists of the 1915 class will report immediately for duty." Viktor looked despondent. "It is all over, my dear. Austria is done," he said.

A little after 7:00 p.m., Chancellor Schuschnigg came on the radio with the news we had been dreading since the rumor started that the plebiscite had been called off. The announcement ended with words which will live with us forever: "God Protect Austria!" I thought the Chancellor's voice would break and he would begin to sob, but he managed to control himself to the end. There was a moment of silence when his voice fell away. I could hear Viktor's muffled sobs. I will try to talk Viktor into going to Mass at St. Stephen's downtown tomorrow. He prefers our local church, but with everything going on, I know he will want to see the central city for himself.

*   *   *

Sunday, 13 March was cold. There was a light dusting of snow on the ground but it was a bright, sunny day with a slight smell of spring in the air. When their taxi pulled up to St. Stephen's Cathedral for early Mass, Else was thinking of Elke, concerned that she was all right. They were both hoping the family would be together on this momentous day. She knew Fritz was busy with his army work but hoped Elke would join them.

St. Stephen's was crowded, even for the early Mass. Most worshipers had their heads bowed, praying for themselves and their country. The sanctity of the church was a blessing. Here they could honor their God, pray for a good outcome, and hear beautiful music. However, after Mass, they had walked only a few steps from the church when they heard the thunderous drone of German bombers. Flying very low in exact formation, they looked big and black against the blue sky, their engines throbbing menacingly. Squadron after squadron of Luftwaffe planes appeared until there were hundreds of them circling over the city.

"Viktor, let's go home, I'm frightened!" Else pulled on his arm and they began hurrying toward a taxi.

Viktor stopped and turned to his wife. "Dear, we need to eat, and I will not allow these Nazis to ruin my Sunday."

The restaurant was strangely quiet and only about half occupied when a waiter showed them to a table near a window facing the bustling street.

"Not very busy today?" said Viktor.

"Everyone is out in the street. There have been a lot of SA and SS men rounding up the Jews to clean the streets." The waiter said this with a satisfied smile.

"What do you mean, 'cleaning up the streets?' " Else asked.

"The Jews are being forced to clean Schuschnigg slogans off the sidewalks with water and acid. I bet that hurts. Serves the Jews right for supporting Schuschnigg," he chortled.

Neither Viktor nor Else responded to the waiter's comments.

As the meal progressed, things seemed to calm down outside the restaurant. They began to enjoy their meal and their wine. The enjoyment ended when their waiter pointed to their window and said, "Look, they've got a bunch of Jews now."

A crowd of jostling, jeering, laughing men and women were watching as a mob dragged Jews from shops, offices, and homes, and put them to work with scrubbing-brushes splashed with acid. They were made to go down on their knees to remove Schuschnigg propaganda. From time to time a roar of delight went up from the onlookers. They were especially amused when a man urinated on the head of a well-dressed woman who was stooped over, scrubbing, her face contorted with anguish. The crowd chanted, "Work for the Jews, at last, work for the Jews! We thank our Führer for finding work for the Jews." Storm-troopers dragged an elderly Jewish workingman and his wife through the assembly. Tears rolled down the woman's cheeks. She looked straight ahead and through her tormentors, holding her husband's arm. Else and Viktor could see her trying to pat his hand.

With tears in *her* eyes, Else looked at Viktor. "Let's go home."

Inside their apartment, the two held each other close. They sat down next to each other. "I guess what bothers me most," Viktor said, "is that those appalling acts were committed by Austrians. I saw no German soldiers, but we probably will tomorrow. I don't know that they will be any more brutal than what we saw today. We saw the underworld vomiting forth its lowest, filthiest, nastiest demons."

Else struggled to control her sobs. She said through her tears, "The last twenty years have been a nightmare, but this may be the worst of all."

Viktor smiled grimly. "I have to be in the office tomorrow. I can't imagine what that will be like."

*   *   *

Viktor was at work early the next day, Monday, but not as early as he had hoped. His train had been packed with cheering people, many carrying swastika flags. Rumors were flying among the men on the tram that Hitler, who had spent the night in Linz, would be in Vienna in the early afternoon. One man said his daughter, a telephone operator in Linz, had told him the German Eighth Army crossed the Austro-Bavarian frontier at border towns including Mittenwald and Burghausen. Someone else said he'd heard that enormous cheering crowds had slowed the caravan so much that no one knew when Hitler would reach Vienna, and that excited workers had walked off their jobs to greet the Germans. Viktor could hardly believe what he was hearing. It was as though these people were discussing an Austrian football victory, not the takeover of their country.

Viktor was greeted at work by his secretary, Horst, and his fellow bankers. All were excited about the Führer's impending arrival. Horst brought Viktor his coffee but really wanted to talk.

"Our office in Linz says the German Army has been bombarded by swastika flags, flowers, and cheering crowds while they make their way to Vienna."

"What time is Hitler expected?" said Viktor.

"Originally around 1:00 p.m., but the crowds are so large the motorcade has been slowed to a crawl." Horst showed the same excitement Viktor had seen on the tram. He soon realized that very little work was going to be accomplished in the Economics Department of the Länderbank on this day.

At about three in the afternoon, Horst burst into Viktor's office and asked for the rest of the day off so he could get a good place to view Hitler when he finally arrived.

"I suppose so, nothing is being done anyway," was Viktor's glum reply.

"I almost forgot," said Horst, a bit embarrassed, "Hans Reinhardt telephoned for you. He said to call him as soon as possible."

Victor hadn't heard much from Hans since his recovery from his concussion. He knew Hans was still in economics with the Schuschnigg government, but events had moved too quickly for any social time.

"Hans, good to hear from you. How are you doing?"

"Viktor, I can't say much now but I must meet with you."

"Sure, Hans, but can we make it tomorrow, after this Hitler celebration is over? How about Cafe Central at noon?"

"*Nein,* too public. Meet me at the National Library as soon as possible. Back room, go to the right as you enter. See you soon."

The phone clicked off. Hans's pleading tone startled Viktor. He glanced at his watch; it was a little after 4:00 p.m. Hitler was now due at the Habsburg Palace at around 5:30. Viktor knew the mobs at the Heldenplatz would only grow larger. He knew a back way to the library and was there quickly, going to the back room as Hans had directed. This was certainly the right place for a secret meeting. Despite the noise of the crowds outside, there was virtual quiet here. Viktor found Hans sitting alone near the back.

"Hans, what is wrong? This is not like you." The fear on Hans's face scared Viktor.

"Viktor, we are in awful trouble."

"*Ja*, Austria is in trouble, but what more are you thinking?"

Hans said, "The Nazis will soon be coming for us."

"They won't be looking for you, you weren't a head of the government. What makes you say that?"

"Inga is Jewish, Viktor!"

"What! *Nein*, she is not."

"She told me before we were married that her great-grandmother on her mother's side was Jewish."

"That was four generations ago. That won't count."

"It does to the Nazis. Besides, my working for both Schuschnigg and Dollfuss makes me a target also."

"Can you get out of Austria?"

"We tried. Inga has a brother in Prague who begged us to come there. We thought we were getting ahead of the mob. On Saturday we got tickets on the 11:15 p.m. to Prague at Eastbohnhoff.

"Viktor, the train was packed with Jews desperate to get out, and also Army officers, government officials, communists, Catholic priests, civil servants, and journalists. Not only was every seat filled, but there was barely any standing room left. Before the train could leave, stormtroopers boarded. They were half-uniformed but all wore the Swastika brassard (armband). They were hoarse from shouting and eager for vengeance.

The troopers went through the train cracking dog-whips. Men, women, and children were dragged out and herded off to prison. Those who remained were plundered openly of everything in their possession—money, jewelry, watches, and furs. Finally, after hours of agony for us trembling survivors still aboard, the train began slowly moving off to Breclav. But after twenty minutes, the train stopped again in open country. Out of the darkness came more stormtroopers, carrying torches and lanterns. They searched us all again, and more people were removed. The train started up again.

At the Czech border came the Czech examinations. Everyone with an Austrian passport was moved to a waiting room. After what seemed like an eternity, the Chief of Police came in and announced that, without exception, all Austrians were to be turned back. I asked to call Inga's brother and was denied. That is our story."

Hans folded his arms across his chest. "For now, we will be free until they discover my connection to the previous government and Inga's great-grandmother's background, but we are talking a matter of time."

"You didn't say if you lost anything in the search," said Viktor.

"Inga lost her fur because she insisted on wearing it, but we hid jewelry and my watch. The troopers were more interested in grabbing whatever was visible."

"I am not sure you would be safe in Czechoslovakia; Hitler may move in that direction soon. I have some connections with our correspondent bank in Paris; you would both be safe in France."

"I hope so, but I am scared, not for myself as much as for Inga. She doesn't deserve this. Even if I can't get out, I want her safe. She is the best thing in my life."

"We will get you both to Paris." The friends stood and hugged. Viktor tried to maintain a positive expression, but he feared the future.

*   *   *

Else's Journal
Saturday, 26 March 1938

Dear Journal, It has been two weeks under the Nazis and things are finally beginning to calm down. The past two weeks have been a period of great turmoil. Viktor says many people at his bank have lost their jobs because they were supporters of Schuschnigg and have been replaced with supporters of National Socialism. He says the few Jews at Länderbank are gone. He doesn't know where they are, but Jews are being replaced all over Vienna in all forms of employment.

Viktor said the only Jew in the Economics Department was Heinrich Weinstein, who had worked there for several years, but was let go suddenly. Viktor always feared Hitler would overstep with the Anschluss, but I think now he has seen the advantage of belonging to a big national state for the first time in our history. After only two weeks, the changes are overwhelming. The Austrian schilling is 10 to 15 percent higher, workers' wages have grown, and unemployment has declined. Austria has not seen such relief since before the Great War. We are on our way with work and bread for everyone.

Since the Fuhrer's arrival in Vienna on March 14, only now do I have time to write about it. About 5:30 p.m., his Mercedes drove onto the Ringstrasse to the sound of cheers and peeling bells. The Imperial boulevard was so full of spectators, the police and SA had a difficult time keeping the crowds back. There was someone at every window and cheering people sitting on rooftops. Hitler was staying at the Hotel Imperial. Initially it was reported he was too tired to speak, but the crowds refused to disburse, chanting, "We want to see our Führer."

Finally, he appeared at a balcony and delivered a brief address that concluded with "no one will ever again divide the German Reich as it exists today." The next day, Vienna saw thousands of men, women, and children stream into the city from the surrounding countryside to glimpse our native son, who had come home. By midmorning, it was said a quarter of a million people packed the Inner City. The police had to be three-deep to hold back the mass of humanity.

Shortly before 11:00 a.m., Hitler ascended to the terrace of the Hoffburg Palace and delivered a spellbinding address. He proclaimed a 'new mission' for Austria, then stood at attention, stared into space, and saluted. A roar of applause was punctuated by endless shouts and chants. After lunch, Hitler reviewed a military parade. I couldn't count the number of airplanes, tanks, guns, and soldiers that paraded on the Ringstrasse. After that military display, Austria can rest assured no other country will attack us. I was very pleased to see, for once, workers and bourgeois standing side by side with undivided enthusiasm. My impression was of young faces, but not reactionaries, to greet this triumph.

* * *

While Else Baur believed in the *Anschluss*, her husband was struggling with it. The brutal treatment of helpless Jews he and Else had seen from the restaurant was a scene he could not shake. The sudden disappearance of the Jew, Heinrich Weinstein, from the bank had also unsettled him. He could not help but think how little he knew about Weinstein, whose office was down the hall from his own. Other than department meetings, they had shared little interaction. Heinrich was a quiet man, but could Viktor have done more to get to know him?

And Hans! Viktor was haunted by the look on Hans's face when they parted. Viktor feared that this goodbye was real. His mind raced back to when they worked together at the Länderbank and how surprised and saddened he was when Hans quit to work at Credit-Anstalt. However, Viktor and Hans had remained close even after Hans left. Viktor had few close friends; maybe this was by unconscious design after he lost Christian. Viktor's worst fear was coming to pass—the fear of being helpless. He glanced out the window of his fourth-floor office. Nazi flags were flying everywhere in central Vienna.

Viktor stood up, grabbed his briefcase, walked out of his office, and told Horst he was taking the rest of the day off and would not be available to anyone. He hailed a taxi and gave the driver the address of Hans and Inga's apartment. He had never been there and had no idea what he was going to say, because his contact in Paris had sounded less than confident about getting them to France.

The taxi drove him to a quiet brownstone in an area in the north part of the city, somewhat south of where he and Else lived. Viktor walked up to the second floor. He just wanted to see them; he hoped they were all right. He rang the bell, waited, and rang again. No one answered. Viktor rang a third time, this time with dread. He looked for a window so he could see inside, but there wasn't one on the door side. "Maybe they are out this afternoon," he told himself, walking back down to the main floor. At the landing he noticed a man's face appear at the window of the first-floor apartment.

"*Wie bitte?*" Viktor said, hoping the man would come out. After long seconds, the door opened slowly and the face appeared at the crack in the door.

"*Bitte,* can you tell me the whereabouts of Hans and Inga Reinhardt?"

"Are you a friend?"

"*Ja,* a good friend of both. I have some news for them."

"I am afraid you are too late. The SS took them away yesterday."

"Any idea where they may have been taken?"

"Dachau is the most logical," the man said with a shrug and shut the door.

Victor couldn't seem to catch his breath. Instead of looking for a taxi, he began to walk. *Could I have done anything?* he thought. *Is there any chance they could be released?* He found himself in front of a bar, walked in, and ordered a scotch whiskey. As he took his first sip, he considered what had befallen his beloved country in barely three weeks. As Viktor saw things, government leaders had dithered while waiting for history to overtake them, leaving their president politically isolated. He believed there could be no leading member of the Austrian government, with the exception of President Miklas, who could be unreservedly proud of his conduct. He thought about the realization that the SS could knock on a door and take away the inhabitants—no defense lawyer, no court, no judge or jury, just an SS officer looking to arrest someone the Nazis didn't like.

And his son was an SS officer.

16

Anschluss – Part II

1938

George Clare wrote a moving history of the Klaar family in his book, Last Waltz in Vienna, The Rise and Destruction of a Family, 1842–1942. *"The first top Nazi to arrive in Vienna from the Reich, Heinrich Himmler, landed with his cohorts at Aspern Airport at 4:30 in the morning. The abject surrender of Schuschnigg and his government made Himmler's task only too easy. The Austrian police files were now in Himmler's hands."*

As the Luftwaffe plane touched down in Vienna on 12 March, among those on hand to meet Reichsführer Heinrich Himmler that early morning were several members of the Austrian SS, among them *OberSturmführer* Fritz Baur.

Himmler had no time for lengthy greetings on a windy March morning. He told everyone to reconvene at the Hotel Imperial as soon as possible. The hotel had been cleared of all guests and would be used by Hitler and his entourage during their stay in Vienna. In a meeting room off the main floor lobby, Himmler called everyone to order. The officers sat and faced the *Reichsführer.*

"There are approximately three hundred thousand Jews in Austria, and we must make our newest member of the Reich *Judenrein* (free of Jews) in keeping with the wishes of the Führer. We must establish a central bureau whose function will be to assemble all parties concerned in one office and streamline the plan for Jewish emigration. The receiver nations will not accept penniless Jews who would be a burden on the public purse, and the majority of Austrian Jews are destitute. Our answer is to extract a certain amount of money from the rich Jews who want to emigrate. The problem is not to make the rich Jews leave but to get rid of the Jew mob. The Jew is a form of bacillus which poisons the German body politic. Thus, they constitute a medical rather than a political problem. To combat it means major surgery. The Jews are our misfortune." Himmler clicked his heals and gave the Hitler salute, as did everyone in the room.

Fritz took all this in eagerly. He saw this as a way to move up the ranks of the SS. His motives were power-related; he refused to be out-distanced by others in the competitive struggle for higher rank. Hitler needed tough, dedicated men to implement his plans to eliminate European Jewry, and toughness was a quality Fritz was determined to show he possessed. He now did something totally out of character. Instead of waiting for events to overtake him, he walked up to the *Reichsführer,* put out his hand, and introduced himself.

"I know who you are, young man. You were at the Grand Ball in Munich. We only talked briefly but I have heard good things about you."

"*Danke, Mein Herr,* but I would like to tell you of an idea I have. I agree with you that the total emigration of the Jews needs to be a central-ized operation. An operation, I believe, that belongs entirely to the SS. The only way to make Germany *Judenrein* is to keep the Party and other Nazi organizations who want to deal with the Jews out of the picture."

"I am assuming you would like this job, *Herr Obersturmführer?*"

"I can do the job, *Reichsführer.*"

"Hmm! Put together a plan for me while I am in Vienna. I will get back to you, Lt. Baur."

"What was that all about?" It was Gerhard. "Looking for a job?"

"Rupp, I am convinced the Nazis themselves don't know what to do with the Jews. Do they simply quarantine them from Aryans and ship them off to some distant part of the globe, like Palestine? Or do they take on a more radical solution, such as eliminating them?"

"Elimination would not be tolerated in a civilized country. Can't we just send them to Poland or Russia?"

"Most are destitute, who would want them? Gerhard, *Judenrein* is not about technocratic efficiency, it is about power within the Third Reich. Because Austria is new to the Reich and I am Austrian, I believe helping with *Judenrein* will allow me to advance in the SS."

Fritz went back to his apartment to write out his thoughts on setting up a plan. He began with "Security is just as important as espionage." He meant to start a new SS department of security and intelligence service. It would be a counterintelligence corps consisting of a small network of spies and informers. Young Lt. Baur took for granted that he could do anything Himmler required of him. He thought Himmler was a weak man who was happy to have others make decisions for him. Fritz believed he could use this to gain favor with Himmler to enable him to get the only thing he really wanted: power.

* * *

Things moved swiftly following the German annexation. An orgy of plundering and brutality began against the Jews. Hitler Youth members pulled Orthodox Jews around by their beards. Jews in the shadow of Vienna's enormous Ferris wheel in the Prater were compelled to do calisthenics, then lie down and eat grass. Gangs of Austrian Nazis invaded Jewish department stores, then the homes of Jewish bankers where they stole money, art treasures, furs, jewelry, even furniture. Some Jews were robbed of their money on the street. All automobiles owned by Jews were confiscated. Jews who complained to the police about the thefts were lucky if they escaped arrest or physical violence. The violence began to subside about a week later when people realized they could buy Jewish possessions at nominal prices; word would get around that this or that Jewish family was desperate for money.

Things were also moving quickly for Fritz. His proposal for the SS to control Jewish emigration was accepted by Himmler with enthusiasm. Fritz was rewarded with promotion to *Hauptstrumführer* (captain), which also came with a small office. His first important task was the takeover of all Austrian police forces. This turned out to be easy; the police were a tight-knit organization staffed with the type of tough professional officers who would be loyal followers; they fell in line with little resistance.

Capt. Baur now found himself with the power to propagate rules that excluded Jews from most areas of public entertainment—and to some extent, public transportation. All public baths and swimming pools were closed to Jews. The words *Juden verboten* were stenciled on park benches across the city. Jews were not admitted to theater performances, concerts, or the opera.

As Fritz sat and looked out of his office window on a beautiful day in mid-April, he thought again, as he had so often, about Krista von Rehm. They had corresponded by letter several times since the Grand Ball in March. With his help she had secured military air transport to Vienna on this day. She was scheduled to arrive about noon. Fritz kept checking his watch in happy anticipation of leaving for the short drive to the airport. His driver greeted him with the Hitler salute and held out the door of Frtiz's car. As an SS captain he had access to a driver and a large black Mercedes-Benz. Fritz knew both would impress Krista. She had been to Vienna only once, as a child. Fritz was anxious to show her his beautiful city. His rank gave him the privilege of attaining two tickets in a box overlooking the stage at the *Staatsoper* (the Vienna State Opera). He planned to take her shopping on *Kartnerstrasse* in the afternoon.

Getting out of the car, Fritz looked up to see a large twin-engine transport with swastikas on the wings and tail fin coming in for a landing. As the plane taxied up to the group standing outside the airdrome, Capt. Baur checked his black uniform, his best, and tried to look as professional as possible, even though his heart was pounding with anticipation.

She was as lovely as he remembered. She ran toward him and fell into his arms. Fritz was not sure he could maintain his composure when he smelled her hair and perfume. They shared a long kiss. Fritz picked up her suitcase and walked her toward the waiting Mercedes.

"My, you have done well for yourself," she said as the driver held open the back door.

Fritz settled in, put his arm around her, kissed her again, and said, "I am so happy you are here. *Ja*, things are going well for me. Himmler has given me additional responsibility—mostly things he prefers not to do. We will take you to the Hotel Imperial where you can freshen-up. Then I thought we would walk down *Kartnerstrasse*, our famous shopping street. I have two excellent seats for the opera tonight and a quiet dinner before we go to the theatre."

"I wish I could stay longer than overnight," she said. "But I am busy, and I know you are also. Hopefully we can do this again soon."

"Driver, let's drive along the Ringstrasse so she can see the Imperial buildings."

"*Jawohl*." The driver slowed the car so Fritz could point out the splendid buildings around the Imperial Boulevard. They held hands and sat close. Fritz casually put his arm around her shoulder. He pointed out the Parliament Building and the Habsburg Palace. Mostly he just wished to look at her. He had never been in love before. Perhaps he wasn't this time, but he couldn't take his eyes off of her.

The driver pulled in front of the Hotel Imperial. They were greeted warmly by the staff and escorted to her room by the bellhop. Krista's eyes opened wide when they entered the magnificent room. Red velvet drapes and a matching bedspread dominated the space. A gold chandelier hung from the ceiling. Ornate furniture and a lush painting of flowers set in a gold frame sat over the headboard.

"Fritz you have some pull to get us such an impressive room."

Fritz smiled at the "us" and said, "The party has taken over this hotel because it is the finest in town. Hitler stayed here during the *Anschluss*. But it happens there are few high-ranking officers in town, so a lowly captain was able to get this room."

They explored Vienna's shops after first stopping to sample its famous coffee and pastries. However, the *Kartnerstrasse* was not the same. Every Jewish shop was closed, and not only had their windows been broken, but none had been repaired, or even boarded up. Almost all the open shops displayed signs in their front windows that read: "Only Aryan guests desired." They stepped into a lady's shoe store. Its window displayed a swastika flag, a picture of Hitler, and a sign that read: "Aryan German business." None of this seemed to disturb Krista. She made Fritz wait while she tried on seemingly endless pairs of shoes.

The afternoon went quickly. The opera didn't start until eight and Krista needed time to change into the gown she had brought. They enjoyed a pleasant dinner at the Hotel Sacher and Krista exclaimed over everything she had seen in the city. Fritz lit a cigarette for her. She exhaled and said, "Shopping will improve when Aryan businesses takes over for the Jew businesses. It will be better anyway, because the Jews always cheat us. I have been impressed by you Austrians."

"How do you mean?"

"Well, you have rid yourselves of the Jews almost overnight, something we Germans have failed to do. In Germany, organizing a boycott of Jewish stores must be authorized by some bureaucrat. Here in Vienna, I understand, the people just do it. In Germany the Jews still control their assets. We Germans need to work together to get those assets." She leaned back in her chair and blew smoke into the air.

Her words impressed Fritz. She had said them with no emotion, just a matter-of-fact statement. What he heard planted a seed in his mind. Perhaps Austria could be the model to the rest of the Third Reich for the elimination of the Jews.

But this was a night for memories, not politics. Fritz waited patiently while Krista changed for the opera, occasionally looking at his watch each time she said she was almost ready. It was worth the wait. Krista looked luminous in a stunning blue gown trimmed with a sliver of white. Their driver had them at the theatre entrance in plenty of time. A beaming Fritz escorted Krista up the marble staircase to their seats, she in her blue gown and he in his black SS uniform.

During the overture, Fritz whispered to Krista, "I played the piano for years, and my parents thought I had a future in music. I loved to play works like the ones we will hear tonight, like Beethoven's *Fidelio*."

"What happened?"

"My interests became more political. I wanted to join the SS and poured my energy into that. How about you? Did you play music?"

"My parents tried to get me interested in music, but I love to read novels. I enjoy keeping myself entertained."

As the opera began, Fritz moved his hand to gently hold Krista's. They were quiet during the performance, turning to each other with an occasional smile. Little was said in the car back to the hotel. When they got to the door of the room, Fritz said, "Krista, I want you to know that I am a gentleman. I have loved being with you and will hate when you have to leave tomorrow. But as far as tonight . . ." She put her finger to his lips and said, "Pour us a brandy."

The trip back from the airport was long for Fritz. He thought only of the feel of Krista's body, the smell of her skin, the way her eyes shone as they made love. There were many tears when they parted and vows to see each other again soon. Now there was work to be done. Krista's words about Germany came back to him. He was eager to get to work; he had a report to write for Himmler.

Back in the office he became again the dedicated bureaucrat striving for a higher position. Fritz realized two things had to happen in the next few months: First, the random looting and destruction of Jewish property by hoodlums on the street had to be stopped. Austrian and German insurance companies were having to pick up the tab on the destruction. Second, Austria needed to establish procedures for the expropriation of Jewish wealth, which in Vienna alone was estimated at three million Reichmarks. He recommended setting up a Central Office for Jewish Emigration, an agency designed to expel Austrian Jews via a system that robbed them of their assets. This would require an order requiring the registration of all property in excess of five thousand Reichmarks. He estimated if this were done in a "business-like" way, by the year 1942 the Jewish element in Vienna would be wiped out. No shop, no business would be permitted by that time to be under Jewish management; no Jew would find an opportunity anywhere to earn a living. The Jew must go—and his assets must remain in Austria.

*   *   *

Early November in Germany is cold, with considerable snow that turns the surrounding mountains into a tourist delight. Fritz was in a car with three other SS officers amid a caravan of black Mercedes-Benz limousines following the lead car to a secret rendezvous in the mountains of Westphalia. They were on their way to the Castle of

Wewelsburg, near the village of Paderborn. The castle, built on a triangular layout with three round towers connected by massive walls, had been built in the early seventeenth century. It had been purchased by Himmler several years earlier and turned into a combination monastery and "knightly" playground. Himmler often had his favorite officers there to dine at a great round table like the one in the King Arthur legend. The dining room itself measured 145 feet by 100 feet and functioned as an SS shrine. Himmler wanted his castle to be an SS leadership school, where the men engaged in proper pursuits like fencing and chess. Each officer had his own study room with a title. Fritz's room was *König Artus* (King Arthur).

At the end of dinner on the first night, an officer spoke up: "Why do we believe in Germany and the Führer?" followed by every voice in the room: "Because we believe in God, we believe in Germany, which He created in His world, and in the Führer Adolf Hitler, whom He has sent to us."

Fritz spent a restless first night in the castle, partly because of the environment but also because he had decided he wanted to marry Krista. For that he knew he needed permission from Himmler and felt this was a good opportunity to ask for it. The second day, Himmler seemed relaxed and in a jovial mood. Fritz decided this would be a good time. He didn't think there would be problems, since Krista worked for the SS.

"I know her," said Himmler. "Fine girl, you will have lots of children. Get the form from my secretary and send it with a photograph, preferably wearing a bathing suit, to the SS Race and Resettlement Office. They will do a background check to be sure she is of unadulterated Germanic background. If approved, they will send it to me along with the photograph, where I will have final say. Then a marriage license can be issued." Himmler gave Fritz no indication he would receive special treatment.

Lunch was served at the Great Round Table to cheers and merriment. But soon, Himmler called for order. "Unfortunately, I have
grave news, and your help is needed quickly. I have just received word
from Propaganda Minister Joseph Goebbels that our secretary at the
German Embassy in Paris, Ernst vom Rath, has been shot and is near
death. This shameful deed was committed by a Polish Jew and shows
once again the global Jewish conspiracy. All Jews will pay the price
for this outrage."

The room erupted with cries for revenge. Himmler interrupted
them. "Go back to your cities," he said. "Organize your men, as well
as the SA and the Hitler Youth. Let us make the year 1938 a year not
only of a greater Germany, but of a solution to the Jewish problem.
Goebbels is ordering a nationwide pogrom, not just against the Jews
but their symbol of depravity, their synagogues. We shall have our
revenge. The Jews are our misfortune."

The "Knights of the Round Table" hurried to pack their things
and make arrangements to return to their units. In two days it would
be November 9, the anniversary of the failed Great Putsch of 1923.
The men were anxious to use this date to avenge the shooting of the
German secretary by this Jew. On the Luftwaffe flight back to Vienna,
Fritz found himself wondering if Himmler would remember his request
to marry Krista. Another thought intruded: He had not asked Krista
if she would marry him.

17

Kristallnacht

1938

On 9 November, 1938, "The Night of Broken Glass," every-
thing changed for Germany's Jews. On 7 November, Herschel
Grynszpan, a seventeen-year-old German-Polish Jew living in
Paris, shot Ernst vom Rath, a third secretary at the German
Embassy in Paris. The Nazis used this act to further demonize
the Jews and stoke the fires of anti-Semitism.

On 9 November, when news of Rath's death reached Hitler, he
held a brief, intense conversation with his Minister of Propaganda,
Joseph Goebbels. Moments later, Goebbels delivered a vitriolic
anti-Semitic speech that laid out a program of violence against
Jews throughout Germany.

Hand grenades were thrown into synagogues and prayer
houses. Some forty to fifty houses of worship in Vienna alone were
destroyed. Squads of stormtroopers shattered shop windows and
emptied stores of merchandise. Jews were outed from their homes
and herded into cellars. This night saw the slow transition from
innocence to guilt and then to shame, from the Nazi thugs to the

confused citizens unsure of what was going on in front of them.
Underlying all these acts was the shift to war and the Holocaust.

In a bar in the Floridsdorf District north of the central city, Kurt Hoffmann was enjoying a beer with some SA friends. These were the famous—or infamous, depending on your politics—"Brown Shirts," an undisciplined group that wreaked havoc on those who opposed the Nazis: Social-Democrats, the Catholic Church, and the Jews. Kurt was twenty-one, a bright young man with a good education in European literature, not someone one would expect to find in a group of Brown Shirts. However, like many of his educated classmates, he needed to make a choice: either to resist the Nazis, likely be beaten up and end his days in a concentration camp, or to join them.

Kurt had another problem; he was in love with young Elke Baur, a leader in the Hitler Youth for girls. He had known her since their days in gymnasium, when they would sit in the Stadtpark and discuss Russian literature. Elke had been in the BdM for almost three years and looked to have a good future with them. She wrote for their local newspaper and seemed to know everything going on in the city. Kurt admired Elke and her work with the BdM; she devoted all her energy to uniting youth both inwardly and outwardly to the Hitler image. She believed that anybody who disagreed with Hitler threatened the future of the Reich.

But this afternoon was for laughter and drinking. Kurt was looking forward to being with his Brown Shirt friends until his friend Werner burst into the bar, excited about what he had just heard on the radio. "Big news, my friends! Some Jew in Paris has just shot and killed our ambassador there."

The bartender turned on the bar's radio, and they heard the unmistakable voice of Joseph Goebbels. "Are Germans to be sitting ducks all over the world for Jew murderers? Are the German people to stand helpless while the Führer's representatives are shot down by the Jew swine? Are the *Schweinehunde* to get off scot free? Is the wrath of the German people against the Israelite scum to be restrained any longer? If vom Rath dies, the Jews of Germany will answer to the German people, not tomorrow, but today. The German people have suffered long enough from the parasite assassins."

The Brown Shirts' reaction was rage. Most stood up, ready to swarm into the street and direct their vengeance on the first Jew they met. Someone had to be the adult; Kurt decided he was the one.

"Wait, *Bitte,* we don't know enough yet, and nobody has died. We don't even know who this vom Rath is. Let us wait like good soldiers for orders." There was desperation in Kurt's voice.

"Why wait, let's get the Jew scum now," yelled a Brown Shirt.

"You don't know that this isn't a Jew trick. I say we wait for orders. Besides, vom Rath is alive, he might not die." Kurt had to yell this over all the noise.

Others ran into the bar, some with questions about the situation, others with wild rumors. One man yelled, "We must do something. In two days it will be the fifteenth anniversary of the greatest day in the history of the German people, the day the liberators of the German homeland shed their blood for liberty in Munich."

"Kurt says we are to wait for orders," someone else shouted.

"We haven't heard from Headquarters, they may have plans for us," said Kurt, although with scant confidence. On the pretense of calling Headquarters, he went next door to a small hotel to use a public telephone. Instead of Headquarters, he called Elke at home, not sure he would reach her.

"*Guten Tag! Hallo!*"

Kurt was happy to hear her voice.

"Elke, it is Kurt. Are you all right?"

"*Ja,* I am fine. What about you?"

"*Ja,* trying to keep my friends from doing something stupid. Do you know what is going on?"

"*Ja,* but don't do anything now. Tomorrow in the *Völkischer Beobachter* paper there will be instructions for everyone. I must go, but I promise we will get together after this is over. It won't be long."

Kurt got the impression she knew exactly what was happening, and he and his men had best wait to see what developed. Back at the bar, he convinced the others he had talked with Headquarters and they had been instructed to wait.

*   *   *

The next morning, the Vienna edition of *Völkischer Beobachter,* the voice of the Nazi Party throughout all Germany, carried an article describing the precise location of every temple and synagogue in the city. It even printed a picture of two rabbis. Kurt's brown-shirted SA waited patiently for orders, which didn't arrive until much later. The men were quiet with no talk of either vom Rath or Jewish depravity. They sensed something big was going to happen, but no one knew what. At almost midnight, *Standartenführer* Pfrimer entered the bar and drew all eyes. "No more drinking!" he barked. "Those who want to help, come into the private room with me."

Kurt and about half the men followed him into the room.

"I need to send two of us to reconnoiter the church. Hoffmann, how about you and I go?"

"*Jawohl!*" said Kurt.

"The rest of you remain here until you get orders."

The two men crossed the street to a synagogue, pushed open the iron gate, then tried the side and back doors. The furnace-room door was unlocked. After entering and looking around, they returned to the bar.

"All right men, the building is empty and so are the streets. Let's grab those cans of oil and get this done!" Pfrimer pointed to canisters of oil standing against a wall at the back of the bar.

"But it is floor oil," said the bartender.

"I don't care," said Pfrimer. "This is oil. This is your duty."

The men carried four three-gallon canisters into the furnace room and emptied the oil onto the floor. Pfrimer lit a match and threw it into the oil. The men took off running back to the bar. Once inside they waited, silent, until the city's church bells struck 1:00 a.m. and someone outside yelled, "The synagogue is on fire, everyone out of the bar."

The men now screamed orders at each other: "Close off the street." "Shall we call the fire department?"

Heavy black smoke had begun to pour through the broken synagogue windows.

As the first fire company pulled up there was an immense whoosh—an updraft caused the rose-colored windows in the synagogue's dome to shatter. Sparks flew into the sky. Firemen broke in the front doors of the building but there was no dousing the updraft; the dome itself was glowing now. A sector of it fell onto the pews with a roar and a column of fire shot into the air. It was too dangerous to enter the prayer hall.

Kurt saw plenty of SA men and firemen, but none of them were attempting to control the fire. He overheard a short conversation between two bystanders, an elderly lady and a young man, perhaps her grandson.

"A church, a church, a church," she repeated, looking distraught.

"A Jew church," the young man responded with contempt.

"A church, a church, a church," she chanted.

The young man yelled at her: "It's a synagogue; *Juda verreche!*" as e stared with satisfaction at the burning building.

*   *   *

That evening at his office, Fritz received a call from Headquarters in Munich: He and his men were to take all Jews into protective custody. When he complained that he had too few men to carry out this order, they said to round up professional Jews—lawyers, doctors, business owners. Fritz had one man in mind, the owner of the *Stadt-Kino* movie theatre. He and two of his men drove to the owner's apartment in a large green car. These cars, when seen in predominately Jewish neighborhoods, inspired terror. The SS soldiers banged hard on the door of the large apartment belonging to Leon Weizmann, as if they resented the door even being there. The fearful woman who answered the door said her husband was ill and in bed.

"You are lying! Take us to him," yelled one of the soldiers. Mrs. Weizman produced a medical certificate and gave it to Cpt. Baur, who looked it over carefully. It was signed by a Dr. Schoenberg and possessed the legal seal bearing the swastika. Capt. Baur nodded to one of his soldiers, who kicked open the door to the bedroom where *Herr* Weizmann was lying in bed, his two young daughters at his side; all were frozen with fear. The men proceeded to open and ransack every drawer in the room, and then the apartment. Once again Baur nodded to his men, and the three men left the apartment.

But once outside Fritz said, "I should have taken him regardless of that medical certificate; forced him out of bed and shot him on the spot. However, there is a Jew house next door, let's go there."

After forcing their way in, the men took their rage out on this family. Drawers were pulled open and their contents tossed on the floor. Furniture was smashed, dinnerware was thrown against walls. The soldiers stole all they could carry—fur coats, money, securities, cameras, radios, suits, dresses, and jewelry. They grabbed the occupant and threw him down the stairs leading to the street and roughly shoved him into the car while the woman and her children screamed and cried inside the apartment.

*   *   *

Elke Baur had been writing mundane articles for her local BdM weekly newsletter. She felt constrained writing about what Hitler Youth maidens should wear and what exercises to do to stay in physical shape. The evening of 9 November changed everything. Like most of her fellow BdM members, she patiently waited at the Reich Youth Leadership Office to see what was going to happen.

At about 1:00 a.m., the first word of a burning synagogue reached her group. She grabbed her writing pads and raced out of the office.

It didn't take long to discover that Jewish synagogues across the city were burning. She spent the night going from one burning house of worship to another. As dawn approached, the crowds of spectators grew larger. During the night, the residents who had ventured out were quiet, even respectful, seeing holy structures being burned. But when the light of day showed the true immensity of the spectacle, the crowd became more vocal—and more violent. Jewish shops now felt the wrath of bystanders shouting *Ju-da verr-rreckta!* They broke storefront windows and looted or destroyed everything in each store so completely that police closed and sealed the shops. Next, the crowd turned on Jewish apartments in the first district. Furniture and mattresses were destroyed while the looters searched for silver, jewelry, and other valuables. Some of the men who tried to defend their homes were beaten to death.

About midday, Elke found herself in the Döbling area, where she watched SA men loaded Jews of all ages—children, women young and old, elderly men and teenagers—onto a truck. An SA man scowled at Elke and asked her business there. Her BdM journalist card satisfied 'im. Elke asked where they were taking the Jews. To the Spanish riding 'ol near the Habsburg Palace, he said. She hailed a taxi and told the driver to drive fast. Again using her press card, Elke convinced the guards at the riding school to let her in.

The sandy floor was about a hundred yards long with windows that reached close to the ceiling. Floor-length swastika flags framed a picture of Hitler. Everywhere Elke looked she saw bruised and beaten men with broken arms and legs and split lips. She figured about two thousand people were in the hall, with more arriving every minute. Old men collapsed and the SS left them lying in the sand where they had fallen. At 2:30 p.m., men under sixty and over eighteen were called up front. An hour later, the gates opened and they were told to run as fast as they could.

Elke had seen enough. She wanted only to go home, hug her parents, and get some sleep.

*   *   *

After a few hours of sleep, Elke lazed in bed, appreciating the familiarity of her bedroom knowing her mother was in the kitchen and her father at work at the bank. She began to realize what a stable life she had—a good home, a job she enjoyed, and parents who loved her. As her mind cleared, she realized that today was her twentieth birthday. This thought got the best of her laziness. She put on a bathrobe and went to the kitchen to greet her mother,

"*Guten Morgen, mein Mutter!*"

"*Guten Morgen, mein Tochter!* Your father is taking the rest of Friday off. He will be home soon and take us to dinner tonight. It is hard to believe you are twenty. By the way, what was it like last night? Your father and I assumed you were in the middle of it."

"There was a lot of violence and destruction of property. And the burning of their churches was quite a sight. I hate to see all this," she said, shaking off her discomfort at the attacks of the day before, "but the Jews don't belong here. Now maybe they will get the idea and leave Austria, actually Germany, now," she said, correcting herself.

Elke's words made Else uncomfortable, and she quickly changed the subject. "We are looking forward to dinner tonight to celebrate this event. Would you like to invite your friend Kurt? He might like to be with you on this day."

"*Ja* I will call him."

She was pleased when Kurt sounded happy to be invited to this special occasion. After hanging up, she poured herself a cup of coffee, settled into Father's oversized chair, and began to put her thoughts together for her weekly newspaper column. She was busy writing when her father arrived.

"How is my favorite daughter on her birthday?"

"I am your only daughter, Father, and I am fine, *danke!*"

Viktor was never sure Elke saw the humor in this greeting, but he enjoyed teasing her with it.

"I see you survived last night. Terrible thing about the churches. Maybe these hoodlums got it out of their system. Someone starts something like this and it gets out of control." Elke could hear the sadness in her father's words. She didn't want to add politics to this happy occasion. Obviously, her parents didn't know that the events of the day before had been planned beforehand.

At about 5:00 p.m. Kurt arrived with a bouquet of flowers for Elke. Her parents then surprised her with a leather attaché case, monogramed with her initials.

"We want you to look like a professional journalist," said her mother, giving Elke a big hug. Her father also hugged her and said, "We are so proud of you, honey!" Elke noticed a trace of emotion in his voice and thought some of this was worry about what brother Fritz was doing in the SS.

At dinner, the events of the previous night hung over the patrons in the small neighborhood restaurant. The talk varied from questioning the burning of the houses of worship to speculating that the Jews might get the message and leave. But the evening ended well. Elke's parents stayed a respectful distance away to give her and Kurt some privacy. They held each other, kissed goodnight, and promised to go to dinner again soon.

"He really likes you, Elke," said her mother, standing in the darkened living room.

"Oh Mother, I am not ready for love from anyone. Kurt and I have been good friends for a long time." Elke paused. "I am not going to let a romantic relationship stand in the way of my career. There will always be another Kurt around the next corner. I have plenty of time for love."

*　*　*

BdM Zeittung
MONDAY, 14 NOVEMBER 1938
BY ELKE BAUR

The events of 9 and 10 November will stay with us and our city for a long time. It is a time when our national soul boiled over. We have all seen the destruction resulting from "The Night of Broken Glass," a night which has caused an inconvenience to shoppers in our city and created a mess that has to be cleaned up.

In the interest of their own security, a number of male Jews have been taken into custody. People who take pity on the Jews still don't understand what the Jew is. To allow Jews to continue living in the German body politic and to take pity on them is like taking pity on germs. Pity is the greatest danger facing the German people.

In every country there are really two kinds of people: those who dissent or associate with dissenters, and those who mistrust the dissenters and are suspicious of their motives. In Austria, one man dreads the policeman on the beat and another waves "hello" to him. The laws are hateful to those who hate them, but who hates them? It is dangerous to go to a Communist meeting or to read the Manchester Guardian, but who wants to go to a Communist meeting or read the Manchester Guardian?

Report after report has noted how happy the population is that at last authorities are showing a firm hand with the Jews. We have a new hope of a good life after so many years of hopelessness, a new belief after so many years of disillusion.

The Jews are the enemies of the new Germany. At Kristalnacht they got a taste of what this means. Let us hope that World Jewry, which has resolved to hinder Germany's path toward greatness, will take the events of these past days as a warning. If the Jews sow hatred against us all over the world, they must learn that we have hostages of them in our own hands. The Jewish problem is no longer just an issue for the German people, but for the whole world."

18
War

1939

William L. Shirer, American journalist and war correspondent, wrote in his 20th Century Journey, The Nightmare Years 1930-1940, *"How often in this very Reichstag I had heard Hitler spew out one grotesque lie after another and sometimes I would marvel at how completely the gullible German people swallowed them. But on this morning he seemed to be outdoing himself:*

'In my talks with Polish statesmen I formulated at last the German proposals . . . these proposals have been rejected. But I am wrongly judged if my love of peace and my patience are mistaken for weakness or even cowardice. I have therefore resolved to speak to Poland in the same language that Poland for months past has used toward us. This past night, soldiers fired on our territory. Since 5:45 a.m. we have been returning the fire, and from now on bombs will be met with bombs.' "

Shirer continued, "Neither regular Polish troops nor any other kind fired on German territory, nor did Polish war planes drop a single bomb on Germany."

C apt. Fritz Baur had begun to make his mark and establish methods of operation in Vienna. His lynx-like eyes stared aggressively at both foe and presumed friend alike. No one felt safe in his presence, and all were certain, with considerable justification, that the Vienna Gestapo, which Baur headed, possessed files on everybody.

Baur assumed everyone was his enemy. He reversed the concept that a man was innocent until proven guilty. Furthermore, current proof of innocence in no way guaranteed future invulnerability. His work habits were legendary. He regularly worked fourteen-hour days, at the end of which his exhausted colleagues would be dragooned into accompanying him on tours of the Vienna nightclubs. Capt. Baur wanted more; his ambition to rise in the SS was unquenchable.

One evening in one of those Vienna nightclubs, the talk turned to Poland with Fritz's friend Gerhard. "Do you think there will be war with Poland, Gerhard?"

"I doubt it; an attack on Poland would bring in England and France, and Hitler wouldn't want to risk a major war."

With a smile, Fritz replied, "I don't think the English or the French have the balls to go against us. In fact, the Polish government officials should all be shot to even think about fighting against our superiority. However, if the Poles do attack us and we hit back at them immediately, Britain and France will be too afraid to attack us."

"My friend, you are forgetting about the small problem of Russia, because they will want to protect Poland."

"The main problem for the German people that our Führer faces, is the need for *Lebensraum*. Russia is a large country with plenty of room for its people. Taking over Poland will give us the *Lebensraum* we need. It will benefit both Poland and Germany. Poland is a poor, backward country which will profit from the German work ethic."

Gerhard interrupted. "I doubt if England and France will see the need for Germany to have more *Lebensraum*."

"That is the genius of our Führer. He understands that the encirclement of Germany by England, France, and Russia is designed to crush us and keep us a small, poor nation. After our experience in the Great War, Hitler is right in his attempt to break the encirclement before it is completed."

"I see your point, but couldn't this be accomplished without war?" asked Gerhard.

Fritz smiled. "Hitler will get what he wants even if he has to provoke Poland into starting it or maybe stage a Polish attack on Germany. See what he did in Austria and Czechoslovakia? He will outsmart the foreign tyrants trying to keep Germany down. He has restored Germany to its proper place in the world and done it without a shot being fired, nor the life of one German soldier sacrificed."

"The German people want peace, Fritz."

"*Ja*, but a German peace, one ensured by the German army. The army is for us the shield that will provide for a powerful people its necessary rights."

Gerhard sighed. "On a lighter note, how are you doing with Krista? The last I knew you wanted to marry the girl."

"I am glad you asked. We talked last Saturday by telephone and she agreed to marry me. But we need to wait and see if there is a war."

"Did you get your permission from Himmler?"

"*Ja*, that came pretty quickly. I understand she is highly praised at headquarters."

The two said goodnight, and Fritz stepped out into the warm August evening. The streets of Vienna were alive with tension at the threat of possible war with Russia, Poland, France, England—or all of them together.

* * *

Viktor Baur was getting ready for bed at about 11:00 p.m. on a hot August evening. He was retiring later than usual; Else had turned in an hour earlier. However, Viktor had several meetings the next day with bank clients concerned about the threat of looming war. They wanted Viktor to advise them on what to do with their bank deposit accounts. He was quietly listening to a musical program on the German radio station when the music was interrupted. An excited voice cut in and announced: "The Reich government and the Soviet government have agreed to conclude a pact of nonaggression. The Reich minister for foreign affairs will arrive in Moscow on Wednesday, 23 August, for the conclusion of negotiations."

Viktor could scarcely believe it. He had not heard this deal was being discussed. He quickly awoke Else to tell her the news.

"What do you mean?" a sleepy Else asked.

"I am at a loss, but my first thought is we will attack Poland."

"You mean war?"

"*Ja*, but we should be able to overwhelm them. My concern is what will England and France do. I understand they have agreed to declare war if we attack Poland."

"Why would we want to attack Poland?"

"I have heard the Poles are creating trouble at the border. But Hitler feels we need the seaport of Danzig as well as more living space."

"Seems a silly reason to go to war. Hopefully it will be short." Else rolled over and went back to sleep.

At the office the next morning, everyone was consumed with the news of the Nonaggression Pact. Viktor sat at his desk thinking about what it might mean. Had Hitler maneuvered the Soviet Union out of the Allied camp, which would leave him free to go into Poland? Or would the pact frighten France and England into fulfilling their guarantees to Poland? Maybe the Poles themselves would see the light and give Danzig back to Germany. Although most citizens of Danzig were German, the Treaty of Versailles had made it a free city under the control of the League of Nations.

According to the morning paper, the German press was fully behind the agreement. "The world stands before a towering fact: Two peoples have placed themselves on the basis of a common foreign policy which during a long and traditional friendship produced a foundation for a common understanding. There exist no real conflicts between the interests of Germany and Russia. It has gone well with both countries previously when they were friends and badly when they were enemies."

Viktor was not sure which depressed him more—the prospect of another French/British betrayal of a country whose destruction Hitler was bent on, which had allowed him to gobble up Austria with not one word of support; or the prospect of war, which might destroy what was left of Western Civilization, slaughtering millions of people, obliterating their cities.

To get a better feel for the mood in Vienna, Viktor left his office and walked around the area near his building. The headlines in the newspapers only added to his fears: "COMPLETE CHAOS IN POLAND —GERMAN FAMILIES FLEE—POLISH SOLDIERS PUSH TO EDGE OF GERMAN BORDER!" screamed the *Bösen Zeitung.* The Nazi newspaper, the *Völkische Beobachter,* splashed the front page with this headline: WHOLE OF POLAND IN WAR FEVER! 1,500,000 MEN MOBILIZED! UNINTERRUPTED TROOP TRANSPORT TOWARD THE FRONTIER! CHAOS IN UPPER SILESIA!

For Viktor, seeing so much hysteria and war fever, it was almost impossible to cling to some shred of reality. He felt he was floundering in a turbulent sea, one which was about to engulf him.

*   *   *

Ever since Fritz's conversation with Gerhard, and Fritz's off-hand remark about staging a Polish attack on the German border, he had been unable to get the idea out of his mind. Astonishingly, when Fritz mentioned it to his superior, it had gone up the chain of command to the very top, and now he found himself in charge of the attack.

On a moonless night near the German/Polish border on the final day of August in 1939, SS-Hauptsturmführer Baur was leading a squad of two trucks. Each carried thirteen soldiers, all wearing Polish army uniforms. However, the thirteen soldiers in the second truck were condemned concentration camp criminals. Having been heavily drugged, they now lay quietly on the truck bed. The purpose of this charade was to convince the world that the Polish army had attacked an innocent Germany.

Assuming they were not spotted, the soldiers in the first truck would change back into their SS uniforms to show the newspapers and local authorities Germany had everything under control. The world would be alerted because one of the soldiers, who spoke Polish, would make an inflammatory broadcast from the transmitter at the radio station at the small German border town of Gleiwitz.

About an hour before dawn, the two trucks arrived in Gleiwitz. The plan was to stage a fake attack on the station, then broadcast an inflammatory speech announcing that Poland's attack on Germany had begun. This should bring the press and local authorities, thus allowing Fritz and his SS soldiers to show reporters "proof" of the Polish attack. The key to success hung on whether his soldiers could change back into their SS uniforms before the press arrived at the radio station. There was even a code name for this operation: "Canned Goods."

When the trucks pulled up to the station, the SS first assured themselves that the building and surrounding area were deserted. They then carefully pulled the Polish prisoners from the truck and strategically placed their bodies around the station, as if they had been attacking it. Capt. Baur surveyed each of the thirteen and was satisfied with their location.

"*Das ist gut*! Now, shoot each one as if he had been shot in the attack, head and chest only," he ordered his sergeant.

"Jawohl mein Herr!" was the quick reply with a Nazi salute.

The SS soldiers now fired their guns in the air and yelled the Polish words they had been taught. At the same time, the sergeant and another soldier shot each Pole in the face and stomach, and made sure they were lying on their backs as if they had been charging into a battle. In the meantime, Fritz accompanied another Polish-speaking Nazi agent into the darkened station. He found the light switch and the SS soldier began setting up the transmitter. The soldier then began to broadcast an inflammatory speech, announcing in Polish and German that the attack on Germany had begun, and calling all Poles to come to the colors. He ended with the words "Long live Poland!" Fritz sat nervously beside him, staring out the window. He knew the authorities in Gleiwitz, alerted by the broadcast, would arrive soon.

Running out of the station ahead of the speaker, Fritz called for his sergeant. "Sergeant, shoot the man doing the broadcast—now! I want his body found with the microphone. This operation must be kept secret."

"Jawohl mein Herr!" Seconds later, gunshots were heard inside. The sergeant emerged and nodded to Fritz that he had another dead Polish soldier to show the press.

Dawn was beginning to break when Fritz ordered the remaining men to change back into their SS uniforms. They had barely done so when autos carrying local press and government officials arrived at the station.

"I am the mayor! Who is in charge here?"

Capt. Baur assured the officials that his SS soldiers had everything under control and no German soldier had been injured or killed. Fritz now felt he could calm these small town officials down and assure everyone he and his men were in charge and they were merely in the way of good order.

"I am Capt. Baur of SS Battalion 101. Because of the tension on the Polish border and the vulnerably of the radio station, my men were assigned to this region. Just before daybreak we discovered activity at the radio station. Unfortunately, one man had gotten into the station before we noticed him and was able to make his broadcast. My men attacked the others quickly and as you can see (pointing to the dead bodies) handled the situation professionally."

There were voices of approval while the press and authorities moved closer to the dead Polish soldiers. Fritz felt the group was satisfied, although the local press reporter seemed to have some doubt. He asked Fritz where the Poles had come from, since the actual border was five miles away. Fritz brushed that aside and focused his attention on the authorities, who seemed satisfied with the scene.

The SS men were packing up and placing the dead Poles into the back of the second truck when the newspaper man asked, "If there was a real attack, wouldn't you leave some of your men here?"

"My orders are to bring the bodies back to headquarters so they can be examined. I don't see any other threat," Fritz replied, with undisguised impatience.

Everything broke up. The local authorities returned to Gleiwitz and the SS soldiers to headquarters. Fritz could now call his commander and tell him "Canned Goods" had been a success. About ten minutes later, the sky filled with Luftwaffe bombers heading toward Poland.

*   *   *

War or no war, on Friday, 1 September, 1939, the banks were open. When Viktor got off the tram near his office, it was a grey, sultry morning with low clouds hovering over the city. He thought the low clouds would be good protection against Polish bombers. Walking to the office he saw the newsboys loudly hawking their Extras, but the

Viennese people were going about their morning business as usual, walking swiftly from the bus or tram stations on their way to work. Nobody stopped to buy an Extra. No doubt they had heard the news on the radio before leaving for work. Most had been sure that Hitler would humble Poland as he had Austria and Czechoslovakia, without resorting to war. They could not quite believe it had come to this.

Viktor remembered the joyous crowds that welcomed the start of the war in 1914. Then, there had been wild enthusiasm for the war. The streets had filled with delirious crowds. They even tossed flowers at the marching troops and shouted their support. Today was nothing but gray apathy. No soldiers paraded by, and the streets were mostly deserted except for the trams. How could people cope with a war with no enthusiasm whatsoever? The population seemed to be collectively holding its breath.

Viktor worked at his desk, but his heart wasn't in it. He called some of his clients. Predictably, they were concerned with how the situation would affect their investments. Viktor had no answers; he was as confused and shocked as they were. The longer he stayed in the office the more frustrated he became. He did not know how to answer his clients that were frightened about their financial future.

A few minutes after three o'clock, he had had enough. He left the office to be with his wife. There was talk the Poles might bomb Vienna at dusk. This had everyone on edge. On the tram, one man said he had heard that Polish bombers had been seen over both Germany and Austria. Viktor didn't believe the rumors, but to be safe he wanted to be home with Else.

The rest of the afternoon they spent together with no talk of war, until Else asked, "If there is an air raid where do we go?"

"I don't know, but I can't believe the Poles have the ability to attack Vienna. We are a lot farther away from the Polish airfields than is Berlin."

At about 7:00 p.m., when it was still light, the war's first air raid alarm sounded.

"Viktor, what do we do?"

"Well, we are far from the central city. I am sure this is a false alarm. Let's go outside and watch the fireworks that probably are not coming. But it will be good practice for everyone."

After they had waited about ten minutes, Viktor's patience ran out. "Come, let's get a beer."

The neighborhood pub was the perfect place. All the talk was, as expected, about the war. The biggest question was whether France and England would come in. One man said if they did, Hitler would turn tail and run right back to Germany. The bar went quiet at this, and folks began quietly moving away from the man.

Viktor had talked with people on Vienna's streets and concluded there was little enthusiasm for war. Its coming seemed to surprise most everyone. At about nine o'clock, Viktor and Else left and walked out into the dark night. The earlier air raid warning, though a false alarm, reminded everyone to be cautious; the first blackout had begun. The Baurs quickly discovered that the blackout of a great city was eerie. Initially, in the darkness, one could make out nothing. Gradually, their eyes adjusted and they could vaguely see a few objects: a building looming behind the sidewalk, the whitewashed curbs along the streets, even a darkened lamppost.

They walked arm in arm back to their building. Else's voice trembled. "Viktor, I don't know how my nerves can stand this night after night, wandering around in darkness and with the long, cold winter nights coming. I fear the air raid sirens; they're so shrill, and being herded like sheep into the shelters, especially after the bombs begin to fall. How could Hitler have led us into war?"

*   *   *

Kurt Hoffmann had avoided the army for as long as he could. Finally, in June, he succumbed to the lure of the Wehrmacht. He found he didn't have to belong to the Nazi Party and was relieved to discover that most of his comrades gave the Party no thought whatsoever. He was also surprised that he was, for the most part, around respectable people, people who were as interested in literature and music as he was. He would have much rathered to continue his studies at university, but the threat of war interrupted that. After the freedom of student life, boot camp—which he found to be monotonous, intellectually dead, and filled with ridiculous drills—was hell. It was only now, with the start of war, that he realized the drills had been far from silly. Rather, they had conditioned the men to throw themselves under cover in a tenth of a second.

Kurt determined to make the best of things. He had no interest in talking politics. Neither did his comrades. They felt their job was to protect their homes, their people, and their country.

Kurt was a part of the 26th Infantry Regiment. It crossed the German/Polish border at 5:00 a.m. on 3 September. They were part of Army Group South. Its goal was to get to the Vistula River as quickly as possible. They were then to turn north and meet up with Army Group North in Warsaw. While his regiment poured across the border on that early September morning, Kurt and his fellow soldiers saw the awesome power of the German forces for the first time. The sky filled with Stuka dive bombers that flew low, just above the treetops, and thousands of tanks, armored cars, and troop-carrying vehicles roared along the roads. One soldier yelled out it was great to be a German.

Each soldier carried a Mauser rifle, two grenades, sixty rounds of ammunition, a gas mask, canteen, trenching tool, mess kit, and rucksack. All this for one man to carry on forced marches that could be as much as forty miles a day. They had to maintain this pace in order to keep up with the tank divisions. Everyone complained of the

September heat and terrible thirst. However, everywhere on their route to the Vistula, the evidence of the army's might lifted their spirits, especially when they saw the bodies of dead Poles that lay piled among a chaotic litter of baggage wagons, motor vehicles, and teams of horses lying dead in their harnesses. Heaps of munitions lay next to countless hurriedly discarded rifles, bayonets, gas masks, and other equipment.

With the regiment marching deeper into Poland, Kurt had a strong sense of entering a very un-German world. He was struck by the poverty of the towns, the unbelievable filth in the streets, and the misery of the Polish civilians fleeing toward them with bedding, bicycles, and small children all piled on small farm-carts pulled by a single horse. Their houses were worse than German pigsties. Most Poles walked around barefoot. Kurt did not want to touch any of them.

After three days of constant marching, Kurt and the men of the 26th were getting close to the Vistula River when word came down that they were going to rest for several hours. The exhausted men threw down their rucksacks, which instantly became pillows. Many fell right to sleep. Ernst Schmidt lay next to Kurt, awake and curious about their surroundings. Having been raised on a farm in Eastern Austria, Ernst felt the soil. "See how poor the earth is? It doesn't smell good here. The land is poor and so everyone is poor."

Kurt, who knew little of farming, said, "What can they grow here?"

"They might grow wheat, but only one crop a year." Ernst lay his head on his rucksack and said, "Kurt, do you think this invasion of Poland is justified?"

"I don't know, but I don't think it is worth risking war with Britain and France."

The night went too quickly. At the crack of dawn on 7 September, Kurt's world and that of his fellow soldiers turned upside down. Trees flew like birds, and birds flew to earth like leaves. The air was grey with smoke, dust, and flying earth. The sound of large artillery guns surrounded them and did not diminish. Fortunately, the Polish artillery gunmen were not accurate, and many German soldiers found cover in a long drainage ditch alongside the road. Officers quickly assembled the men and marched them out of the area and toward a small village. As they approached it, they were met by sniper fire from villagers defending their homes. From a primitive peasant hut a woman fired a machine gun. Kurt's unit surrounded the house and set it afire. When she tried to escape, the soldiers fired toward her to keep her inside. Her cries rang in Kurt's ears for a long time.

They were ordered to burn the village. Soon, burning houses lined the street through the small settlement, and from the flames resounded the cries of those who had hidden inside and could not save themselves. Kurt couldn't get out of his mind the sounds of fires crackling, cattle lowing, and a dog howling. He told this to Ernst that evening. "But the worst," he said, "was the screaming of the people."

Ernst replied, "It was cruel. But they shot at us, so what else could we have done?"

By the next morning, the entire village was in flames and the German soldiers had to walk down the middle of the street, so great was the heat of the burning houses on both sides. When night fell, they saw the eastern horizon was red with the blaze of other villages.

Early the next day, the 26th turned north toward Warsaw. Now they came under fire from an old factory building that had already seen bombing; it was little more than a shell. The men took cover and returned fire with rifles and a machine gun. But it took an artillery piece to knock out the Polish machine gun. German soldiers herded a dozen Polish civilians out of the building. Kurt did not see what happened to them.

19

Resettlement

1940

John Toland wrote in his book, Adolf Hitler: *"Hitler's hatred of Poles was of relatively recent origin. He was convinced that during the past few years numerous atrocities had been inflicted on the German minority in Poland. By mid-autumn (1939) 3,500 intelligentsia (whom Hitler considered carriers of Polish nationalism) were liquidated. 'It is only in this manner,' he explained, 'that we can acquire the vital territory which we need.' This terror was accompanied by the ruthless expulsion of 1,200,000 ordinary Poles from their ancestral homes so that Germans from the Baltic and outlying portions of Poland could be properly housed. In the ensuing bitter months more Poles lost their lives in the resettlement from exposure to zero degree weather than those on the execution list."*

It was mid-February. A bitter cold, snowy landscape greeted Elke as her train headed east in southern Poland. It had just left Krakow on the Vistula River and was still a long distance from her destination—the small town of Lviv.

The war with Poland had ended in October. Since then there had been little fighting, because both England and France were acting more like spectators than participants. To Elke, the "East" evoked violence, but also romance. It had a "Cowboy and Indian" stereotype in German literature and film. The popular culture of the Third Reich projected this area as the "Wild East," a land where Teutonic bounty hunters and pioneers tamed the land and its savages. Hitler was among those fascinated with the American West. He proclaimed it his duty to "Germanize" the East with an immigration of Germans, and for his countrymen to view the natives as "Redskins."

Elke had two reasons for her trip to eastern Poland: First, she would write reports on how Germany was setting up schools for the newly resettled German children (and future children) as part of Hitler's *Lebensraum* in Poland. Second, she wanted to become an editor of a large newspaper or magazine, and thought her current position would someday provide that experience. Also, she was convinced something new and important was being built here and wanted to be part of it. Yet as much as she believed Poland was Germany's future Garden of Eden, a place of opportunity, she realized it was currently hostile terrain. She also knew it contained inferior, threatening races and political opponents. As a woman this worried her, but she knew proper security measures would be inaugurated.

Elke's other job was to acquire and train German teachers who would educate German youth in the service of nationhood and the National Socialist spirit. These teachers had to be trained to become conduits of that spirit, one which would burn the racial sense and racial feeling into the instinct and the intellect, as well as the heart and brain of the youths entrusted to her.

* * *

Elke's Journal
WEDNESDAY, 14 FEBRUARY 1940

I am looking forward to my adventure in Lviv, but the beginning has been difficult. It was cold, dark, and snowy when I got off the train. I had the address of the Hitler Youth Office but no idea how to find it. I asked a young woman for directions to a certain street, but she gave me a hostile look and turned her back in silence. After this I had no desire to ask my way again. I climbed into one of the horse-drawn cabs waiting in a long line at the station. Unfortunately, I had chosen an old, dilapidated cab, with stinking shavings coming out of the torn upholstery. Snow fell onto my lap from the leaky roof. The clatter of hooves on the cobblestones reminded me of American western films I had seen, but that was the only positive moment in this experience.

After inquiring at the office of the Hitler Youth, I was taken by a taciturn man to a house where a room had been requisitioned for me. When I rang the bell, the front door opened at once, as if I had been expected. An elderly, bent-over woman with yellowing grey hair and a cane took me to my room on the third floor. A bed had been made up for me there. Although the room gave an impression of cleanliness, it also gave off a strong musty smell. The lady had clearly given me her best room, which obviously was rarely used or aired. The room was like other lower-middle-class rooms I had seen in Vienna. It consisted of the small bed and two chairs. The bathroom was down the hall.

I slept little the first night in the unheated room. I had opened all the windows because the musty smell made it hard to breathe. I could hear men and women talking softly next door, and often, the cry of a child. I had the feeling a great many people were sheltering in the house. I was half asleep when a burst of gunfire woke me. I groped my way, shivering, to the window, and looked down onto the street into total darkness. A feeling came over me that I was shut away in a tower, my escape barred by enemies. I pushed a chair against the door, which had no lock.

Elke's Journal
SATURDAY, 14 FEBRUARY 1940

I've gradually gained the impression that the other rooms in the house are occupied by Polish refugees who probably live in painfully cramped conditions. When I ring, the woman who opened the door for me always answers. She often asks anxiously, in broken German, if I am satisfied with my quarters. When I threatened to move out a few days ago because I didn't feel safe, she begged me with tears in her eyes to stay, and said she would fix the lock. She was clearly afraid of the next compulsory lodger. The thought occurs to me that the refugees I have never seen, but whom I have heard, must be hiding in the house. Lviv is a small town, I don't yet know where else to go, and I've decided it is easier to stay for now.

*   *   *

It wasn't long before young German women began arriving in the East on the heels of the German army. The German government and Nazi organizations had deployed colonizing agents whose job was to replace Jews and Slavic Poles with Aryan Germans in jobs and homes. Elke soon found that many of those wanting to be teachers were unqualified. Many turned out to be carpetbaggers, entrepreneurs, dilettantes, social climbers, or former convicts. Elke would take the applicants and set up a training school where they were subjected to ideology training. In history class, ideological lessons focused on German military prowess, past empires, and heroic pioneers. Hitler was placed within a pantheon of heroes including Charlemagne, Frederick the Great, and Bismarck.

Elke had learned in school how England had conquered a world empire for itself, also how the French had acquired colony after colony. She believed that Germany's historic hour had at last come, and the dream of greatness would become a reality in the Reich of the Führer during her lifetime. In math class, students calculated government welfare costs for the disabled living in state asylums, with the purpose of implanting in young minds an economic justification for the mass-murder program of the patients, who were called "useless eaters," that is, useless mouths. Language instruction explained speech patterns not as regional dialects, but as racial variants.

All of this went through her head as she prepared to meet a new set of teachers for the area. German families were moving in and their children needed to be educated. "Welcome, everyone," she began, "I am Elke Baur, the head of the BdM for this area. The first thing to understand is you are not in Germany anymore. Although, with your efforts and energy, and with time, we are confident this area will become civilized. For now, you will find only workers, peasants, farmers, and lower-class tradespeople.

"Obviously, these Poles are not a responsible people and thus they are incapable of forming a ruling class. They have misery written on their faces; they smell of stale bread and dirty clothes, and children with rags on their feet are visibly starving. This town of run-down tenement houses is swarming with unwashed, begging children, old people, and cripples who hold out their hands to us. Give them nothing. Walk past them. If I see anyone here helping these people you will be on the next train back to Germany. You must have no sympathy for these pathetic people."

An innocent hand was raised. "Will there be any Jew students?" This brought stifled laughter.

Elke ignored the question. "You will all be given a textbook on how to observe the Jew, because this country is filled with them. They have a special way of walking, even their bearing, gestures, and movements when talking are obscene. The Jew is ugly, not only on the outside but on the inside too. You will emphasize the superiority of the German race and that the Jews are subhuman and should be treated as such."

Elke finished her talk with an appeal to the teachers' patriotism: "You are in a fight for Germany's existence, the ultimate showdown between the Aryan and the Slav, between German fascism and Judeo-Bolshevism. We are part of a great adventure. As young Germans, we have been summoned to take part in a noble service and are fulfilling our duty for the Reich. Throughout our childhood we heard of the German defeat in the World War and the misery of the post-war years. We are now allowed to perform colonization work, work that has begun to heal the wounds we suffered in childhood and early youth. We are finished being ashamed of our fatherland. We now want to honor, admire, and love it."

* * *

Elke's Journal
FRIDAY, 22 MARCH 1940

I have been in Lviv for over a month and need a break. This weekend, my fellow teacher, Jutta Landau, and I will use our weekend pass to travel to Krakow for some relaxation. I enjoy Jutta. She has a good sense of humor and is a dedicated teacher.

Lviv has been difficult. The Poles I must deal with despise us. Whenever I find myself showing pity toward these people, I am reminded of the colored map of Europe Herr Klinghöfer showed us in gymnasium, *with small children "sitting" on each country. I especially remember the little boy representing Poland crawling toward the girl representing Germany.* Herr Klinghöfer *meant to convey that since Polish families are so much larger than German families, one day Poland would overrun Germany.*

I see these Poles using every means possible not to lose the Eastern province which the German nation requires for Lebensraum. *They are our enemies, and it is my duty to suppress my private feelings when I see people who are going hungry if they conflict with political necessity. That* Lebensraum *can be secured at the expense of the neighboring nations causes me no moral discomfort. A country that believes itself to be called and chosen to lead, as we are, has no inhibitions when it comes to taking territory from inferior elements. It is an honor to be allowed to help in conquering this area for our own nation and for German culture. I feel like a "cultural missionary."*

*   *   *

Elke looked forward to the trip to Krakow with Jutta, a tall girl with strawberry blond hair that came almost to her shoulders. Elke loved that Jutta could make her laugh, especially when Elke was stressed from work.

Jutta was from a small village near Salzburg and had done her teacher's training in Vienna. While she was not a member of the Party and was no fan of the Nazis, she was a proud German with a sense of duty. She believed it was her calling to educate German children.

It was a long train ride to Krakow. Elke had been deep in thought for some time when Jutta said, "I have heard of a great bar with good beer at the Metropolitan Hotel in central Krakow. I hope there will be soldiers there. I could use some male companionship."

Elke smiled and replied, "Now you be a good girl this week-end, Jutta."

"I am always a good girl, especially in the arms of a strong German soldier," Jutta said, lighting a cigarette.

"I am not going to be your mother, so if you get into trouble it will be your fault."

"Oh, I know how to take care of myself. But I am looking forward to male conversation," Jutta said expectantly.

"Don't expect much conversation except about sex and women. I think this is all men think about, though I agree it will be nice for some male companionship."

"God, Poland is dreary," Jutta said. "I miss Salzburg! Oh, I need a new perfume. Do you think there is a quality store in Krakow that would sell such a thing?"

"I could use a nice perfume too. Probably our best chance is at our hotel. Funny, I have never been to Salzburg despite its short distance from Vienna. My parents always vacationed in Bad Ishl, they enjoyed seeing the famous people at Café Zauner. I loved the mountains there, but I am a city girl. I miss Vienna and hope Krakow is a real city."

The women stared out the window of the half-filled train. There was not much to see, just gray plains interspersed by occasional patches of bare birch trees. They saw no people, hardly even a bird. The incessant turning and screeching of the train wheels added to the monotony.

To break the silence, Elke said, "How is everything at your school, Jutta?"

"I like most of the children, and most seem eager to learn. But I have several new children recently who are unruly, difficult to man-age, and create trouble for the others."

"Are these the children the SS are bringing you?"

"*Ja,* and I don't know anything about their parents. It is almost as if they have no parents."

"That will continue, and you must do the best you can. These are racially valuable children with Aryan features who need to be brought up and educated as good Germans, to learn German, sing German songs, and to memorize proper behavior and the superiority of the German race."

"But what about their parents?" Jutta persisted.

The question surprised Elke, who had never considered the parents.

"Don't worry about them, they are probably dead. We will find good German parents for these children who can bring them up properly. This is the job of the Race and Resettlement Office. The SS are looking for nice-looking blond-haired, blue-eyed children. They can grab the child and examiners then determine if the child has enough German blood. If so, the child will be put up for adoption to infertile German women desperate to prove their racial merit by being mothers."

"Where are their original parents?" asked Jutta, with growing impatience.

"Jutta, these are orphaned children who will be better off growing up with a German mother and father." Now Elke was getting impatient and she wanted to end the conversation.

Jutta suddenly realized Elke was her superior and she wouldn't jeopardize a job she mostly enjoyed.

The Metropolitan Hotel was as the girls had anticipated: old and tired. But their room was clean, and the door had a lock. It may have been elegant at one time, but wars have a tendency to abuse people and buildings. On this Friday night the hotel's large bar was filled with soldiers. To Jutta and Elke's surprise, several women of all ages and sizes were also there. There was no music, thus no dancing, so conversation was the only interaction between the sexes. Shortly, two soldiers introduced themselves to Elke and Jutta. Neither woman was overly impressed with the men, and it wasn't long before the beer and the train trip caught up with them. At a nod from Elke, she and Jutta made their excuses and went up to their room.

The girls slept in on Saturday. Refreshed, they went downstairs for a late breakfast at the hotel. They had an unspoken agreement to stay near the hotel. They felt it was safer than the city, especially because of the hotel's large contingent of Wehrmacht soldiers. They were soon joined at breakfast by Heinrich and Bruno; no one seemed interested in last names. The men were pleasant enough and decent looking, if a bit rough around the edges.

Bruno asked, "Have you ladies been to Krakow before?"

"*Nein*, and we have no interest in leaving the hotel," said Elke condescendingly.

"I don't want to push you, but I do know a nice little cafe with really good goulash," said Bruno, unperturbed by Elke's attitude.

Jutta spoke up. "My mother used to make goulash. Elke, I would love to go. We need to get out a little while we are here."

Heinrich said, "At one time this was a beautiful city. A walk later will give you a chance to explore some of it."

Elke agreed, but first she wanted to learn more about the soldiers. It turned out both were from Germany, near Munich. Both had started college, but the lack of potential jobs drove them to the Wehrmacht. Neither had seen much action in Poland and seemed convinced that neither England nor France wanted to fight Germany. Having heard the term *Sitzkrieg* (sit-down war), the men were convinced this was the only war they would see.

The four walked to the restaurant in the late afternoon. They found the goulash as good as Bruno had claimed. During dinner, Elke and Bruno learned they had more in common than did Jutta and Heinrich. After dinner the two couples split up. Elke and Bruno returned to the hotel and were drawn to the sound of an improvised band playing German music in the bar.

As the evening wore on, Elke became bored with Bruno, but she didn't want to be rude. Her thoughts were of her work back in Lviv and wondering if Jutta was all right. Elke knew Jutta could take care of herself, but felt responsible for her, since Jutta worked for her.

Her thoughts were interrupted by a soldier who stopped at their table.

"I don't believe my eyes! Elke Baur, what are you doing here, of all places?"

"Oh, my God, Kurt Hoffmann. I could ask you the same thing."

"I am here to supposedly fight a war, but I guess they called it off."

"Ahem!" Bruno cleared his throat.

"Oh Bruno, I am so sorry. This is an old friend from school, Kurt Hoffmann."

"Good to meet you, Bruno. Take care of this girl, she is special. By the way Elke, what are the BdM doing here?"

"I am training teachers to educate German children emigrating to Poland, and writing articles on the resettlement and schooling. A fellow teacher and I are in Krakow on a break. We are stationed in Lviv, and head back tomorrow. How about you?"

"My regiment is encamped nearby. We spend most weekends here at the Metropolitan, it's the only decent place to stay. Look, I am sorry I interrupted you two. I really only meant to say hello."

Bruno understood when three was a crowd. "I am interrupting you two. Elke, it has been a pleasure to meet you. Good luck and keep writing," he said, somewhat downcast, as he took his leave.

"I really didn't mean to intrude on you two. I was just so surprised to see you here." Kurt said.

"Don't be sorry. I was trying to come up with an excuse to move on, but I didn't want to be rude."

"Well, I am thrilled to see you again. How is your writing coming along?"

Elke explained that she had managed to send several articles to the Hitler Youth newsletter, that there had been inquiries about her articles from larger German newspapers, and she planned to work for one in the future. Kurt enthusiastically urged her to follow her dreams, went over to the bar and returned with two beers.

He was pleased to see Elke again and anxious to know if she had softened her attitude about a serious romance. "You look really good, Elke." As soon as he said this, he regretted it. He thought the words sounded juvenile.

"*Danke Kurt*, you look fit in your uniform."

"How is your work going in Lviv?"

"Overworked. I can't get enough qualified teachers. The children are coming faster than I can find someone to teach them."

"How is your social life? Anybody special?" he said, finally getting up the courage to ask.

"Social life, are you kidding? I work with young women all day, and Lviv is not a town for social life. Mostly a lot of Jews are being moved out, resettled further east to make room for the German families moving in."

Kurt didn't respond to this. Elke continued, "No, there is no one in my life. I have no time for it. I am not sure I am the romantic type anyway. How about you?"

"I am still available, Elke. If I survive this war I will come looking for you."

"Don't you have a girl back home?" she said, hoping to change the subject.

"*Nein*, I am afraid you stole my heart back during those walks in Stadtpark."

"First things first. I want us both to survive the war. Assuming there will be one."

"Oh, there will be a war. England and France are testing each other and building up their forces. The real war will begin as soon as the weather improves. Besides, there has been too much bloodshed already." Kurt said this to see her reaction, but she was unfazed.

"What do you mean, bloodshed? We defeated Poland easily."

"Oh Elke, I have seen things you would not believe."

"Well, things happen in a backward country. The Poles have misery and dejection written on their faces, but one can tell by looking at the proud Germans that we are the conquerors." She said this offhandedly.

"Elke, I mean what we are doing to the Jews."

"The wretchedness of their children does upset me, but gradually I have learned to switch off my private feelings in such situations. This is terrible, I say to myself, but driving the Jews out of Poland is one of the unfortunate things we must do if this is to become a German country."

Kurt listened intently. "Elke, I am not talking about moving the Jews out. I am talking about brutal killings."

"Just a few hundred Jews, a nasty bunch," she said with disdain. "They are the most dangerous enemies of Germany. Their wretchedness is merely a spectacle which might, for all we know, be our own someday if we lose this war. I have seen the sufferings of the German community. I have learned that one must harden oneself against the sight of human suffering."

"Elke, I have a story to tell you about something I saw myself. If you want to hear it, that is."

"Go ahead." She folded her arms in front of her.

Kurt knew she didn't want to hear the truth, but felt he had to get through to her.

"Elke, let's go outside. I don't want to be overheard."

The two walked out into the cold March evening. Kurt didn't think he could tell his story against the music inside. He was also concerned about how Elke would react.

"This occurred in mid-December. Our regiment was encamped near the town of Lublin. Three or four of us went into the town one evening with the intention of getting drunk. I had a little too much to drink and I went home with a woman. Her apartment was across the street from a cinema that I later learned was used by the SS as a gathering place for Jews for their relocation.

"About 3:00 or 4:00 a.m. in the morning, I was awakened by the sound of voices and people banging on tin cups. I got up and went to the window. On the street a crowd of people was leaving the cinema. They were under SS guard, being led away. I recognized men, women, children, and the elderly. On their clothing I could see clearly the yellow star. At first, I did not understand what was happening. Why were they throwing pots and pans on the pavement with such rage? Then it came to me. They were trying to draw attention to themselves: 'See what is happening to us! Do not allow this! Help us!'

"I stood behind the window and wanted to cry out: *Do something! Arm yourselves! You are the majority! A few of you could save yourselves*! I guess there were about three hundred Jews being led by a handful of soldiers. But aside from hurling pots and pans, the Jews dragged their feet, muttered with their heads down, capitulated without a further fight. I watched until the entire column disappeared, then I lay down again. My companion asked what the commotion was about. When I explained, she merely said, 'only Jews' and went back to sleep. I lay there thinking these people would be killed. I knew it. I thought I could hear screaming and gunfire in the distance.

"In the morning I again told my companion what I had seen. I said I was surprised the Jews didn't put up a fight. She said if the Jews wouldn't put up a fight for themselves, that surely absolved her of any responsibility to get involved."

Kurt looked at Elke. "What do you think about all this?"

In a calm voice, Elke said, "You jump to conclusions quicker than a rabbit looking for a carrot. First, you see a bunch of Jews being herded off into the darkness. Do you think they just might be getting resettled somewhere? I deal with this every day in my work. Second, you heard a few gunshots and decide Jews are being killed. It was almost dawn; this is when farmers hunt rabbits for their dinner."

Her voice rose higher, her eyes narrowed, and she began to visibly shake. "You have always been against National Socialism, and you were always negative about Austria's future. You are little more than a traitor, and I should turn you in. You are a disgrace to the uniform." Elke began to walk away.

Suddenly, she turned and with clenched fists began to beat on Kurt's chest, yelling, "You bastard! I don't want to hear your crap again. I swear I will turn you in as a traitor. I never want to see you again." Her voice was choked with anger and tears. Kurt called her name hoping she would come back, but she had already turned and run off into the dark.

20

Fritz Baur

1941

Daniel Jonah Goldhagen wrote in his book, Hitler's Willing Executioners, Ordinary Germans and the Holocaust: *"In explaining the perpetrator's actions . . . We must attempt the difficult enterprise of imagining ourselves in their places, performing their deeds, acting as they did, viewing what they beheld. To do so we must always bear in mind the essential nature of their actions as perpetrators: They were killing defenseless men, women, and children, people who were obviously of no martial threat to them, often emaciated and weak, in unmistakable physical and emotional agony, and sometimes begging for their lives or the lives of their children.*

"The Germans' persecution of the Jews culminating in the Holocaust is thus the central feature of Germany during the Nazi period. It is so not because we are retrospectively shocked by the most shocking event of the century, but because of what it meant to Germans at the time and why so many of them contributed to it. It marked their departure from the community of 'civilized peoples'. Explaining the Holocaust is the central intellectual

problem for understanding Germany during the Nazi period . . .
There is no comparable event in the twentieth century, indeed
in modern European history."

On 9 April, Fritz Baur, now promoted to *Standartenführer* (colonel), was back at Himmler's castle at Wewelsberg. Fritz and
Krista had now been married for a little over a year. It had turned
out to be a difficult marriage, because the beginning of the fighting
on 10 May, 1940, and the German army plunging into Holland and
Belgium meant that Fritz was almost constantly in meetings, mostly
concerning how to make Germany *Judenrein*.

Fritz hated attending these meetings at Wewelsberg. He thought
them a colossal waste of time. Himmler would act out a twentieth-
century version of the Knights of the Round Table with his officers
seated at the large round oak table in the vast dining room. Each
colonel sat in a high-backed chair made of pigskin while Himmler
saw himself as Henry I, the king who had protected Germany from
invasions from the east. Here Himmler would either commune in
silence with the great king, or the officers would sit patiently while
he delivered lectures on the Goths and Visigoths.

None of this had any meaning or relevance for Fritz, or indeed
for most of the others seated at the table. They had little or no interest
in mystical groping into an obscure Teutonic past. Fritz had a job
to do. His office desk was piled high with inter-office memoranda
prepared by his underlings at his Vienna headquarters. With his
job, a high-ranking uniform, and considerable social status, Col.
Baur felt the important thing was to consolidate his empire and
his personal standing within the Third Reich. He saw no reason
to let himself be bogged down with Himmler or the bureaucratic
gobbledygook which emanated from his staff in Vienna or his

superiors in Berlin. He saw his job as dealing with what Hitler had called "the reservoir of Bolshevism" in the east. It was up to him to direct this important security operation. The prime targets were the Jews, and it was to them *Standartenführer* Baur now addressed himself.

The problem was a man he had known briefly back in Vienna, Adolf Eichmann. Eichmann had been put in charge of Jewish affairs. He and his associates seemed bent on isolating the Jews in a locality sufficiently removed from Germany, to protect the Aryan race from contamination. He had the mad idea, with the defeat of France in 1940, that the Foreign Office would add a provision to the peace treaty that the French-owned island of Madagascar be ceded to the Reich. After that, the French who resided there would be evacuated, and the island used as a colony for at least four million Jews who would be productively employed there. Production and trade would be managed by German-run organizations. There would be purely German and purely Jewish businesses. Eichmann also considered relocating the Jews to Palestine. However, both ideas were quickly abandoned because of the strain each location would place on shipping and transport already earmarked to carry on the war.

However, Col. Baur had been told—to make Germany *Judenrein.* To help him with this task, the SS were being set up with *Einsatzgruppen* (assault squads) to deal with "housecleaning" in Poland. "Housecleaning" meant the elimination of Polish Jews, intelligentsia, clergy, and nobility.

When the meeting came to its close, the officers moved down a flight of steps from the dining room into a crypt which contained twelve stone pedestals. From this strange place Himmler told the gathering SS colonels of Germany's coming mission in the east. He told them this campaign in Russia would be the most barbaric of all time. He shouted, "Bolshevism is a sociological crime. We must abandon any thought of soldierly comradeship. They are all criminals and must be treated as such."

To end this strange meeting, the officers gathered in a circle to honor the death of a lieutenant general who had recently died of a heart attack. An urn containing his ashes was placed on a pedestal in the center of the circle and the smoke from his ashes was directed upward into the vents of the ceiling so those assembled could watch his spirit ascend into Valhalla.

At the end of this charade, Fritz and his driver were on their way to the airfield and his flight back to Vienna. He felt he was prepared for the task he had been assigned: to make all of Europe *Judenrein.*

* * *

At dawn on 22 June, 1941 everything changed for Col. Baur and all of Europe when the German invasion of Russia began. Hitler sent 121 divisions by ground, and three thousand airplanes filled the morning sky. Fritz was at last freed from the bureaucratic paperwork he hated, and was now in charge of an *Einsatzgruppen*. He knew his duty was to secure the conquered rear areas behind the ever-advancing army. This required him to identify and kill leading representatives of the communist regime, anyone who might foment and organize resistance against the German occupation.

In this region lived many Jews who had to be exterminated through liquidation. He understood that Eastern Jewry was a breeding ground of World Jewry and was to be annihilated—all Jews, without regard to age or sex.

Fritz commanded one of four *Einsatzgruppen* that would spearhead the wholesale slaughter. Each was then subdivided into several smaller units, called *Ordnungspolizei* (order police). Fritz and the other *Einsatzgruppen* officers were instructed to ease these men into their new vocation as genocidal executioners through a stepwise escalation of killing. First, by shooting primarily teenage and adult Jewish males, they would acclimatize themselves to mass executions without the shock of killing women, young children, and the infirm. Once the men became used to slaughtering Jews on this sex-select and smaller scale, the officers could more easily expand the scope and size of the killing operations.

Himmler's own inspection trip to the area provided him with evidence that the initial genocidal forays had been successful insofar as they demonstrated the men could bring themselves to kill Jews *en masse.* The program of utter annihilation was a novel enterprise that required the Germans learn through experimentation how to organize the killing operations logistically, and what the most effective techniques were. After all, no models existed for this unprecedented undertaking. Hitler and his subordinates had crossed a psychological and moral Rubicon to genocide—the die was cast for all European Jewry. All that was left was for the Germans to devise the operational plan, organize the resources, and implement the mass murder strategy on a full scale.

Most important to Fritz and the *Einsatzgruppen* were the Order Police. They were the ones most intimately involved in the mission. These were not well trained eighteen-year-olds easily molded into diehard Nazis and killers. In fact, the men were often chosen in a haphazard manner and were frequently the least desirable in the manpower pool. They received little training in weapons and procedures; even ideological training was minimal. Also, they were not Nazified in any significant sense.

The men in Police Battalion 309 led relatively easy lives. They were off duty much of the time and, like most soldiers, they went to church and to movies, had sports competitions, enjoyed furloughs, and wrote letters home. They went to night spots and bars, drank, sang, had sex, and conversations. Like all people, they had opinions about the character of their lives and what they were doing. Most of the men in Police Battalion 309 were older, married with children, and had a lot of life experience.

*   *   *

In just a few days, while the German army moved into Russia, Police Battalion 309 entered the Polish city of Bialystok, an area north east of Warsaw. The German army had captured the city without a fight. It now moved deeper into Russian territory, leaving the city to the tender mercies of Col. Baur and his Police Battalion to do the "housecleaning."

On 27 June, Col. Baur met with the battalion commander, Maj. Beck, just outside the city. Beck was a bureaucrat, short of stature, balding, with round, frameless glasses. Baur addressed the major coldly and laid out the plans. "Major, I want this done quickly and with any amount of brutality your men see fit against every Jew in the city."

"Including women and children, colonel?"

"Especially women and children. I want these Jews, and every Jew in Russia, to fear us and your Battalion."

Maj. Beck seemed to relish the assignment; it would be his opportunity to show what he could do for Germany and the Führer.

Fritz continued, "Let's enter the city with guns blazing. Then go house to house to be sure every Jew is rounded up. Anyone who resists is to be shot immediately. Also, send squads to the forest outside the city and make sure no one gets away."

Maj. Beck gave a crisp Nazi salute and went off to address his lieutenants. The men then quickly but orderly piled into the waiting trucks and sped into the unsuspecting town.

Col. Baur had been ordered to consolidate the Jews in the central city before killing them; he had received no instructions about the manner in which the Germans should extinguish their lives. His thought was to round them up first, then decide the best way to kill them. These Germans could finally unleash themselves upon the Jews without restraint.

The unit had barely driven into the city when the soldiers swarmed out of their trucks and started shooting to announce their arrival and spread fear. For an entire day, they shot blindly into homes and windows, with no regard for whether they hit anyone. The battalion broke into people's homes, dragged them out, kicked them, beat them with rifle butts, and shot them. The streets were strewn with corpses.

During the roundup, a lieutenant noticed a door slightly ajar. Thinking someone behind the door was peeking out to assess the scene, the officer fired into the small opening—and a lifeless body fell out of the door. Elderly Jewish men were forced to dance before the soldiers while they mocked and denigrated the Jews, asserting their mastery over them. If a Jew failed to dance to a sufficiently brisk and pleasing tempo, the soldiers would set his beard on fire.

Col. Baur observed the entire proceedings. His face betrayed no emotion whatsoever, not approval or disapproval of the events unfolding before his eyes. Suddenly, two desperate Jews, recognizing a high-ranking officer, fell on their knees begging the German colonel for protection. A member of Police Battalion 309 decided to intervene with what he thought a fitting response: He unzipped his pants and urinated on the two Jews to the laughter of those around him. The anti-Semitic atmosphere among these Germans was such that this man had brazenly exposed himself in front of a colonel to perform an act of unspeakable disdain. Indeed, the soldier had nothing to fear for his breach of military discipline. Neither Col. Baur nor anyone else sought to stop him.

The day continued to worsen for the Jews; even those in the Bialystok Hospital. Soldiers combed through the hospital in search of Jewish patients to kill. They were not out to kill any enemy of Germany, just the Jewish enemy. They showed no interest in the Soviet soldiers lying wounded in the hospital. They thirsted only for the blood of Jews.

The soldiers used the marketplace near the Jewish districts to assemble their victims. During the afternoon they took hundreds of Jews from the marketplace to nearby sites, where they shot them. Yet the killing was proceeding too slowly for the Germans. The men were bringing more Jews to the assembly points in the marketplace and the area in front of the main synagogue faster than they could kill them. Since Col. Baur did not have precise orders about the method to be used to attain their ends, he took it upon himself to devise a new course of action.

Bialystok's main synagogue was a towering symbol of Jewish life. An impressive squarish stone structure crowned with a dome, it was also the largest synagogue in Poland. Col. Baur now thought of a way to dispose of the mass of assembled Jews under the shadow of this looming testament to the life of the Jewish enemy. He would destroy both simultaneously—the Jews as well as their spiritual and symbolic home. This seemed a natural solution to his inflamed anti-Semitic mind.

The men of Police Battalion 309 drove their victims into the synagogue. Any resistance was met with liberal blows of "encouragement." The Germans packed the large synagogue full while the Jews began to chant and pray loudly. After spreading gasoline around the building, the Germans lit it ablaze, and one of the men tossed a grenade through a window to ignite the holocaust. The Jews' prayers turned into screams. One hundred and fifty police encircled the building to shoot anyone who attempted to escape. They now watched as over seven hundred people died a hideous, painful death, listening to their screams of agony. Most of the victims were men, though there were some women and children among them. At least six Jews came running out of the synagogue, their clothes and bodies aflame. The Germans shot each one down, then watched these human torches burn themselves out. One soldier said to another, "Let it burn, it's a nice little fire, it's great fun."

* * *

Fritz didn't sleep well for several nights after the action at Bialystok. His sleep deprivation had nothing to do with the killing of several thousand Jews; he was more concerned that his superiors might criticize him for the destruction of the synagogue. He hadn't disobeyed anyone, but perhaps he had overstepped his bounds . . . if indeed, there were any to be overstepped.

As the year wore on, Col. Baur was not reprimanded in any way. Thus, he continued the "house cleaning" even more aggressively. Each day brought so many Jews that killing them with guns took too long. Also, killing the elderly and children was taking a toll on some of the men. Additionally, there was a constant search for clean uniforms because after a "house cleaning" many uniforms were covered in blood, pieces of bone, and human skin. Getting them cleaned was proving difficult.

Fritz now had gas vans transported to the woods northwest of Lodz, and large numbers of Jews were taken there and told to strip for a shower. They were then led into hermetically sealed vans, and gas was forced into the enclosures. The Germans hoped death would only take fifteen minutes, but the process often took hours. The victims were buried in mass graves.

Summer seemed to end quickly in this part of Poland. The weather virtually forgot about autumn, with the first snow falling in October. However, in early December Fritz was greeted with a grand surprise— he was promoted to *Oberführer* (Brigadier-General), quite an honor at only twenty-seven. His reputation for innovation was well known in the Reich and SS leadership wanted to reward him.

Fritz was anxious to tell Krista the news, and a week's leave was included in his promotion. He wanted her to meet him in Vienna for the week. This would also give him a chance to see his parents.

Although the young marrieds had talked several times during the year, the separation was difficult for Krista. Many times a phone call ended with tears on her end. However, this conversation went well. Krista loved Vienna and enjoyed his parents. Fritz got a suite in the Hotel Imperial. This was no problem now that he was a Brigadier-General.

Christmastime in Vienna was always special to Fritz. Even with a war on, the city was in a festive mood. The war was going well; the Viennese hoped it would be over soon. Being with Krista again after the long separation made everything better. Seeing and holding her made Fritz wish he didn't have to go back to war.

The hotel staff went out of their way to make the couple comfortable. Krista appeared very pleased with her husband's promotion, and obviously relished the attention he received at the hotel. The second night they were to have dinner with Viktor and Else. Krista didn't know them well, but the brief times she had met them she had really liked them both. Viktor seemed a bit aloof, but Else had greeted Krista warmly, almost like a daughter. Else was pleased that Fritz and the hotel were going all out to entertain them, and she and Viktor were happy to see that their son had done so well for himself.

"A brigadier general. Hell, I didn't get past captain," Viktor said, laughing. "We are proud of you, son." He shook Fritz's hand and patted him on the back as they entered the dining room. Fritz was beaming. He turned to his parents and hugged them both. The evening was delightful—until they began to talk of the war.

"How is the fighting going?" Viktor said. "I am worried we didn't capture Stalingrad before the hard winter set in."

"We will, it is just a matter of time. We are fighting crazy people that need to be subdued. Their equipment is old, so we may be in Stalingrad by Christmas."

"Where are you stationed, my boy? Your mother and I worry about you."

"*Nein* Mother," Fritz said shaking his head, "I oversee a district.

"What is your job there? I have heard some stories of mass killing," Viktor said with concern.

Fritz replied, "There is a lot of resistance to the resettlement; the area is full of resistance fighters. They have to be controlled for the protection of the German families who are moving into the area."

"Women and children are not resistance fighters," Viktor said. "I have heard about the killing of whole populations, including women and children."

"Don't believe everything you hear, Father," Fritz said with a light-hearted laugh. "It is a difficult job, and sometimes innocents suffer. We try to do everything we can to control an area by harming as few as possible, but sometimes it is unavoidable."

"I have lots of friends, Fritz, some inside the government with intimate knowledge. They have told me the temperature in Russia has dropped to minus forty degrees centigrade. It is so cold that neither side's rifles and machine guns will fire. But what disturbs me is our troops don't have winter clothes, only a thin coat and nothing else. It's unforgivable that our soldiers don't have felt boots."

Fritz replied with an air of superiority, "It is only December. *Ja*, there has been a supply mix-up, but the war has only begun. There will be mistakes made. But I assure you, our soldiers will be taken care of. The Führer will see to it, he loves his troops. As we speak, the Red Army is on the point of collapse, and we will soon be in Moscow and Stalingrad."

Krista noticed doubt in Viktor's expression. She glanced at Else and saw fear and worry in hers. When the evening ended, Krista could feel the tension that had built during the visit. Near the busy street in front of the hotel, the four stood looking at each other, not sure how to end the night. Else, near tears, realized she might never see her son again. Viktor was proud of Fritz. He believed Fritz was a good officer but thought this was the wrong war for him. Krista could feel her mother-in-law and Viktor's concern. Fritz loved his parents and wanted to get away with as few hurt feelings as possible. The two couples hugged and said their goodbyes.

Viktor turned away and hailed a taxi. He was quiet on the ride home. Else said, "You didn't believe him, did you?"

"*Nein*, not at all! In terms of Russia, our army is not prepared for the Russian winter. I understand the highway from Tula to Orel is a sheet of ice, covered in places by drifting snow. Our vehicles won't start and must be abandoned. As for Poland, I have heard too many stories of horrors going on there. Not just Jews, but the upper crust of Poland. Germany wants to kill the entire leadership of the country."

"Why would Fritz know anything about that?"

"He is a brigadier general in the SS, for God's sake. He is probably in charge of much of what is going on. Well, the one good thing about the Russian winter—it affects both sides. I assume there won't be much fighting until spring." Viktor sighed, looked at Else, and reached for her hand.

At that moment, the Russian army had been increased by over a million men who manned eight thousand guns and mortars, 720 tanks, and 1,370 aircraft, all poised to counterattack.

*   *   *

As the world entered the uncertain year 1942, for Brig. Gen. Fritz Baur it was the beginning of a great year. His immediate supervisor was Adolf Eichmann, a weak character. Fritz had discovered early that Eichmann could be easily manipulated. The one thing Eichmann did for Fritz was to bring him to the attention of Reinhard Heydrich, the head of RSHA (the Reich Security Main Office). Both men were impressed with Gen. Baur's innovation and resourcefulness at Bialystok. Heydrich knew that to make all Europe *Judenrein*, new methods of extermination were needed. He wanted generals like Baur working for him. However, with all the recognition Fritz had received in the past few months, nothing surpassed a surprise invitation he got in the mail in early January from Heydrich himself:

> *You are invited to a meeting on Tuesday morning, 20 January, 1942, at the villa 56-58 Am Grossen Wannsee. I wish the assistance of all central authorities to make all necessary organizational and technical reparations for a comprehensive solution of the Jewish question and present a comprehensive proposal at an early opportunity. I propose to hold a meeting on these issues. This is all the more important because since 15 October, 1941, transports of Jews from the Reich territory, including the Protectorate of Bohemia and Moravia, have been regularly evacuated to the East. I therefore invite you to the above meeting in order to discuss a solution. The residence has been completely refurbished with guest rooms, a music room, a billiard room, a large meeting room, and a terrace looking out onto the Wannsee. Central heating, hot and cold running water, and all comforts. The house offers good food, including lunch and dinner. Wine, beer, and cigarettes are available.*

Fritz was stunned. Wannsee was a beautiful suburb to the southwest of Berlin. The villa lay on the western shore with marvelous views of the larger of the two Wannsee lakes. He was surprised at this invitation not only because he was so junior, but also because he wondered what kind of clarification was needed on the Jewish question. What kind of preparation needed still to be made?

It was a snowy morning on January 20 when some fifteen senior officials gathered at the Gestapo villa by the Wannsee lake. Fritz was disappointed that neither Hitler nor Himmler would be attending. He knew Eichmann well from his days in Vienna, but none of the government department officials. The SS was represented by officials with a special interest in race questions, men he had worked with. Men like Gerhard Klopfer (Party Chancellery) and Otto Hofmann (SS Main Office for Race and Settlement). The largest group around the table were the representatives of ministries with responsibilities for the Jewish question. Wilhelm Stuckart (Interior), Roland Freisler (Justice), Erich Neumann (Four Year Plan), Fredrich-Wilhelm Kritzinger (Reich Chancellery), and Martin Luther (Foreign Office). These were all educated and distinguished men and Fritz was once again concerned as to why he was included. He decided to be inconspicuous and had started to move to a quiet area of the room when Eichmann came over to put the young general at ease.

"Well Baur, are you settling in?"

"Not really, sir. These are some important people. I know many are lawyers, and I didn't finish college."

"Not important, Baur. You showed initiative on the battlefield and Reinhardt Heydrich wants to show you off as the kind of leader he is looking for."

At that moment Heydrich himself walked up, introduced himself, and asked if Fritz was comfortable. A tall man with a Nordic face and blond hair combed straight back, his eyes seemed to look right through one.

"I am becoming more comfortable, sir."

"No reason for you not to be. These men are here to receive instructions from Göring, through me, to provide a coherent plan for the solution to the Jewish problem. Our goal is to cleanse German living space from Jews in a legal manner. Of necessity, this means a close liaison between the various ministries. The Foreign Office and the Ministry of Justice transports must also be coordinated so that Jews arrive at the correct destinations. You are invited as a battlefield hero, Baur. So, enjoy the meeting."

With a strange smile, Heydrich went to the podium. The attendees, standing in groups chatting among themselves, quieted. "I want to begin this meeting by letting you know that Reich Marshal Göring has entrusted me with preparing the final solution for the European Jewish question. The purpose of this meeting is to establish clarity on fundamental concerns. Göring's desire is to be provided with an outline of the organization, policy, and technical prerequisites for this solution. It is necessary to ensure in advance that the central organizations involved are brought together and their policies properly coordinated. Overall control of the final solution lies with the Reichsfürer (Hitler), the SS Chief of the German police (Himmler), and specifically with myself as Hitler's representative.

"Our principal goal thus far has been to remove Jews from different sectors of German society and from German soil. The only solution available at the time was to accelerate Jewish emigration. This led to the Reich Central Office for Jewish Emigration. The disadvantages of a policy of emigration are clear, but in the absence of alternatives the policy had to be tolerated, at least initially.

"Instead of immigration, the Führer has given his approval for a new kind of solution—the evacuation of Jews to the East. This includes not only those countries under German occupation or control but also Germany's European allies, neutral countries, and those with whom we are still at war. In the course of the final solution, the Jews should be put to work in the East. Jews fit to work will work their way eastward, constructing roads. Doubtless, the large majority will be eliminated by natural causes. Any final remnant that survives will consist of the most resistant elements. They will have to be dealt with appropriately because otherwise, they would form the germ cell of a new Jewish revival."

Heydrich ended his presentation and asked for questions. Somewhat fortified by brandy, the participants turned what had been a monologue by Heydrich into a bit of a free-for-all. Joseph Bühler, head of security police, asked that the final solution begin in Poland. He added, "As quickly as possible because of the danger of epidemics being brought on by Jews. Jewish black-market activities are destabilizing the region's economy and should be eliminated immediately, though without alarming the populace."

As Fritz walked to his room, he played over in his mind what this meant. Wannsee was simply an occasion for the murderous rhetoric surrounding the deportations that now were to be ratcheted up. It was clear that all Jews were to die. The reference to killing Jewish workers who survived the working conditions could scarcely have been more explicit. Brig. Gen. Fritz Baur was ready to play his part.

21
Krista Baur

1942

To quote Daniel Goldhagen again from his book, Hitler's Willing Executioners, Ordinary Germans and the Holocaust: *"The most important group of people responsible for the slaughter of European Jewry, excepting the Nazi leadership itself, have received little concerted attention in the literature that describes the events and purports to explain them. Surprisingly, the vast literature on the Holocaust contains little on the people who were its executors. Little is known of who the perpetrators were, the details of their actions, the circumstances of many of their deeds, let alone their motivations. A decent estimate of how many people contributed to the genocide, of how many perpetrators there were, has never been made."*

It had been six years since Krista and Fritz met at the Grand Ball in Munich in 1936. Her blond hair was shorter now, but she had kept her figure. As 1942 progressed, her life and her marriage improved immensely. Brig. Gen. Fritz Baur oversaw all SS actions in Poland,

and since the fighting had moved into Russia and north toward Moscow, he was also in charge of "housecleaning" in this area. The couple enjoyed relative freedom, the riches of this fertile land, a sense of adventure, and the plunder of items confiscated from the Jews.

Their elegant mansion was outside Lviv. Called Grzenda, it once had been the manor house of a Polish noble. It was set amid rolling hills and meadows and overlooked the surrounding villages. Visitors passed through an ornamental wrought-iron gate onto a road leading to a circular drive, passing an array of chicken coops and servants' quarters. Inside the great door, visitors walked across small, carefully laid black-and-white terra cotta tiles on the floors of the north portico and vestibule. Ornate balustrades decorated the staircase and the veranda.

The Grzenda estate comprised lovely gardens and places to stroll on Sunday afternoons. Many high-ranking officials from the nearby towns had been hinting at seeing the mansion, but the "housecleaning" Fritz was in charge of precluded this, even though Krista was eager to show off their home.

It was a lovely summer day when Fritz came home from work in mid-afternoon. He called out for Krista and she answered, "I am out on the balcony. Come join me and bring us a drink."

Fritz smiled in anticipation. While a drink sounded good, he visualized his comely wife in her bathing suit, enjoying the warm sun on her long legs.

"I am so glad to be home," he said, handing Krista her drink and kissing her on the forehead. "Berlin is putting more pressure on me to eliminate more Jews. My men are exhausted, but they are doing their job. God, you look good!"

Fritz embraced her, then began to lower the shoulder straps of her swimsuit, kissing her deeply. She wrapped her arms around his back, pulling him closer. "Let's get to the bed," she said breathlessly.

They moved to the spacious bedroom near the balcony and practically tore off their clothes. The two clawed at each other like the love-starved people they were; they hadn't seen each other in several days. Afterward, as they lay naked in bed, Krista reached for the little bell on her nightstand to summon her Jew maid. With no hint of embarrassment by the couple (and no hint of awareness from the maid), Krista told the woman to bring them champagne and caviar.

"I don't like her!" Fritz said after the maid left the room. "She is arrogant, and I hate that in a Jew. Turn her over to me and I will end her."

"Not now, she is knitting a sweater for me. I can't believe how good these Jews are at knitting. Besides, she thinks that bowing to my every wish will keep her alive. She is staying alive at my pleasure."

Soon the maid brought the champagne and caviar with the lovers still naked, lying provocatively in bed. Krista was more passionate in lovemaking than ever before. Her husband's newfound power created a euphoria in her which was expressed in sex and violence.

Krista ran her fingernails down her husband's chest and said, "Fritz, we need to throw a party to show off our villa."

"Darling, I don't have the time to arrange one."

"Please Fritz, I will do all the work and besides, I will really thank you afterward," Krista said, running her fingers lower down his bare stomach.

Fritz considered this. "You are right. It is a good idea!" he decided. "Friday would be the best day; there will be several high-ranking officers in town for the weekend. They have asked me about doing a little rabbit hunting, and I told them this would be the perfect place. Get your Jew slaves to make everything look great."

Krista's eyes lit up with excitement. At last, she would be able to show off her home. She could already imagine the envy of the guests as they strolled through her beautiful mansion. She could hardly wait for Friday.

* * *

The party began early; the guests sensed the day would be exceptionally interesting. The plan was for the partygoers to go rabbit hunting in the nearby forest. Everyone, officers and ladies, gathered at the Baur villa to get to know each other, but mainly to partake in the plentiful alcohol. By mid-morning the alcohol had taken effect, and everyone was driven by horse and carriage to the nearby forest. These were senior officers with their ladies, who wore beautiful, stolen fur coats. During the ride to the forest there was much hugging, kissing and shouting. Peals of laughter echoed off the trees. There now appeared a group of about a hundred Jews, middle-aged and old men, women and young children. The partygoers mocked the Jews, laughed at them, and struck those nearby with whips. The Jews were made to walk a long plank which had been placed over a mass grave. Then the shooting began. The men took careful aim and everyone else watched as the victims were hit and fell into the pit. Soon everyone was taking their turns at "rabbit hunting."

Back at the mansion, the laughter and the drinking continued. Many of the officers proudly showed off drops of blood on boots or uniforms as if they were medals. As the evening progressed, more alcohol was consumed, and slowly, couples began to disappear into various bedrooms.

*   *   *

On a cold, dark December night in 1942, two young Polish men parachuted into a forest area well north of Lviv. They promptly buried their parachutes and began the long walk to a contact who was expecting them. Stas Czreslaw and Tomas Sobieski were both in their late twenties and members of the Polish resistance. They had been training in England since they'd managed to flee Poland when Germany attacked in 1939. They were with Free Polish units who trained and waited, driven men who would sacrifice themselves in any way that would help their country. These resistance groups in England were growing as new members arrived and brought stories of merciless atrocities in Poland. The name of Gen. Fritz Baur seemed always to be at the center of these atrocities. With the growth of the group, the assassination of Gen. Baur became a prime topic. Of course he would be replaced, possibly by someone more ruthless, and of course Gestapo reprisals were terrifying to contemplate. But these Free Poles felt they had to do something, or they would have no influence in a government of Poland after the war.

It was clear that getting these men into Poland by airdrop would be infinitely easier than getting them out. Thus, unless they were extremely lucky, they were essentially on a suicide mission. However, both Czreslaw and Sobieski had been well trained in England. They had attended special intelligence classes, received training in sabotage in Scotland, and were given their final sessions in Surrey in southern England.

On the night of 28 December 1942, a Halifax bomber of the Royal Air Force took off from an English base with the men aboard. Arrangements had been made by radio for them to link up with resistance units in the area. But the RAF pilot lost his bearings and the drop was made about twelve miles off the target.

Thankfully, luck was with them. They were first seen by a game-keeper connected to the Polish resistance who got them to the local resistance group. These people were in a position to know Baur's movements. After several brief meetings, however, it became apparent that killing this general would not be quick and easy. Especially not at this time of year, because of the bitter cold and heavy snow cover. Killing him in his office was out of the question as all his office work was done in his villa, Grzenda, which was well guarded by elite SS troops. The men decided to await warmer weather when Baur would do most of his traveling. This seemed to offer the best chance of success.

When the weather improved in April, the assassins had a clearer picture of how to accomplish their task. Baur had a special train he sometimes used to commute to Berlin. The small railway station at Lviv offered an opportunity since Baur's train always waited there for a minute or two until clearance came that the main track to Berlin was clear. A line of trees some three hundred yards from the station would provide cover. Czreslaw and Sobieski decided a portable anti-tank gun could be mounted on the thick branches of one of the trees and, given correct timing and sighting, Baur's train would suffer a direct hit. But this plan was soon abandoned because there was no assurance Baur would be killed. They might eliminate members of his entourage, but there was a possibility the main target would escape.

Czreslaw and Sobieski became restless, fearful that the thing was too difficult, too risky. However, Sobieski continued to follow Baur's movements as closely as he could without raising suspicions. He made small changes in his appearance, wearing eyeglasses, fake beards, or mustaches in case anyone would notice one man who, curiously, was always around. One day Tomas noticed an inconsistency in Baur's movements. Whenever Baur made his way between his villa and his private train he was accompanied by a unit of tough security men. But when he went from his villa to the airport (he loved to fly), he traveled with only his six-foot-seven driver, Klein. In good weather, the top of the Mercedes was lowered so the two could enjoy the sunshine. The route to the airport seemed to offer the best possibility for an attack. The conspirators spent considerable time inspecting the route and noticed the road entered a hairpin bend before crossing a small bridge. Here the car would be forced to reduce speed. Finally, on 27 May 1943, the plotters heard Baur would be flying out of the airfield that very morning. Even better, the forecast called for a warm, sunny day, meaning the car's top would be open. A third man was assigned to signal the approach of Baur's car. Czreslaw had a Luger pistol hidden under his raincoat and Sobieski carried a hand grenade he could lob into the car if Czreslaw failed in shooting Baur and his driver. The two men stationed themselves at the agreed-upon points shortly after 9:00 a.m. The minutes slowly ticked by with no sign from the third member of the group that the car was approaching. Time seemed interminable as 10:00 a.m. neared. Finally, at about 10:15 the signal came from the lookout. Everything seemed in order; Klein was Baur's only protection and the top of the Mercedes was down.

Baur sat in the front passenger seat. Klein slowed the car to change gears in order to negotiate the bend in the road. This was their chance. Czreslaw opened his raincoat, drew his Luger and took aim, but the gun didn't fire. In his nervousness he had forgotten to release the safety catch.

Czreslaw and his luger were now in full view of the men in the Mercedes. Baur quickly rose from his seat, drew his revolver, and fired at Czreslaw. Klein braked in order to assist, but this threw off Baur's aim. At that moment, Sobieski lobbed his hand grenade into the stationary car. It exploded on contact, wounding Baur badly. Despite his wounds, Baur leaped from the car and emptied his gun at the fleeing Czreslaw.

The Poles got away and Baur was transported to the nearest hospital in the back of a baker's van; he was in considerable pain. The incident was kept quiet. Only a few in the SS were aware that a brigadier general had been shot in broad daylight by two Poles who had gotten away. Almost worst of all, an SS general had been driven to the hospital in a baker's van.

Krista was told that afternoon that her husband had been injured. He would be fine but must be left alone in order to recover properly. She was told Fritz was a hero, emptying his gun at the fleeing assassins until he collapsed of his wounds. She was given pills to help her sleep and a 'round-the-clock nurse was assigned to her.

* * *

When Krista woke, she felt drugged. She had forgotten what she had been told, but the presence of the nurse convinced her something was very wrong.

"Who are you and why are you here? What day is this? *Where is my husband?*"

"Now my dear, you have been through a lot and need rest. My job is to see that you get your rest. Your husband is fine and should be home in the next day or two. Here is a pill to help you sleep. You will feel better when he gets home." This was clearly an order.

"My husband is a brigadier general and very respected," Krista said as she became drowsy.

"I am sure he is being taken care of properly," the nurse replied, as if speaking to a child.

When Krista next awoke it looked like mid-morning. She was not sure how long she had been asleep.

Her nurse greeted her with a joyful, "My dear, glad to see you awake. Good news, you have a letter from your husband."

Krista grabbed the letter but wondered why Fritz had not called. The date stamp on the envelope had been cut out. This didn't seem right, but she was glad to see her husband's handwriting. His letter read:

My Darling Krista,

As you may know by now, some foolish resistance fighters have tried to kill me. The doctors thought at first I would recover, but infection has set in and now it is not looking as good. If I don't make it, I want you to know I love you very much. I am sorry my responsibilities have kept me away from you so often. But you are always in my thoughts. The outside world thinks we are savages but when this war is over it will see what we have done is for the greater good of all Europe. We are political soldiers of a secret front who must perform our work silently. Any soldier can display bravery in battle, get his Iron Cross, and come home to universal applause. My men must operate in secret because of the larger issues involved. Even when they have demonstrated their courage they cannot rely on public recognition.

Carry on without me, my darling. Our task is noble, great, and long.

Your loving husband, Fritz

As if they had seen her put down the letter, two unfamiliar SS officers entered the room and offered Krista their condolences. For his services to the Führer, they presented her with her husband's dagger, a prized possession. Before she knew it, she was alone in the villa. Even her nurse, the jailer, had disappeared.

At first, she was too stunned to react. She went to the bar and poured herself a brandy. With the first sip, reality overtook her. Fritz was dead. And not only had she lost her husband, but now she would have to leave Grzenda. She felt it was hers, even though she had known that someday she and Fritz would have to leave. Her anger began to build at the way she had been treated by the SS. Why had they kept her from seeing Fritz? Why had she been held like a prisoner and not told the truth of his injuries?

The more brandy she consumed, the more her mind whirled. Suddenly, no longer was Grzenda her villa to show off to other officers and their wives. It had become a prison, and she wanted to break out. Krista grabbed the remainder of the brandy bottle and went outside. Her coachman was sitting in her coach, ready if she needed to go shopping. He obediently brought the carriage around at her order: "Take me shopping, pig!"

It was a sunny day. Krista reclined in the carriage while the coachman handled the reins. As the carriage drove over the familiar road to the town, she saw something in the distance. As the carriage drew closer, she could see four children crouching along the side of the road, dressed in tattered clothing. It occurred to her these children had escaped from a train car while it was stopped at the station. The children were terrified and hungry. She beckoned to them. Cautiously, they climbed into the carriage seats. Krista instructed the driver to take them back to Grzenda. Once there, she sent the coachman home and instructed him to leave her the carriage. She took the children inside, calmed them down, and gained their trust by bringing them food from the kitchen. After she had cleaned them up a bit and they had eagerly consumed the food, she said she would take them for a ride. The children gleefully shouted their approval and ran to the carriage.

Taking the reins, she drove to the pit in the woods where other Jews had been shot and buried. She brought a pistol her father had kept from the first war as a parting gift to protect her in the "wild east" of Poland. She told the children to line up facing away from her in front of the ditch. She held the pistol about ten centimeters from the first child's neck and pulled the trigger, then did the same with the second. The other two were shocked and began to cry, not loudly, more of a whimper. Exhausted, they did not try to run away. After Krista shot the fourth child, she stepped back to take in what she had done. Suddenly, she threw the pistol into the ditch, turned and ran to the carriage. Whipping the two horses to a gallop, she drove away from Grzenda . . . as if trying to shed herself of this life.

22

Viktor & Else Baur

1944

As a city that had not seen Allied bombs during the war, Vienna was able to celebrate important dates. For more than a month, a dozen Richard Strauss operas were performed on various Viennese stages. On 11 June, his birthday, the eighty-year-old composer attended and rose to acknowledge the cheers of the audience. However, Thomas Weyr wrote in his book, The Setting of the Pearl, Vienna under Hitler: "With the Allies already ashore in Normandy and in possession of Rome, it was too late for substantive reforms, nor could music soothe Vienna's jitters. The war was going badly. The mood of the city kept darkening and not because the population had suddenly turned against the regime. The Viennese liked the Nazis just fine—better when they were winning, of course, but well enough. The darkness was fueled by fear, by the memories of 1918, by the near certainty they would be on the losing end of another war. And no amount of bread and circuses could alleviate that foreboding."

On an early September day, Viktor gazed out of his office window at the trees in the park below. They had not yet begun to turn colors. He decided it would be awhile because the weather was still summer warm.

Viktor followed the progress of the war in Europe intently. He had posted a large map on his office wall to mark updates and developments. He still wished he were in the war, but the bank needed him. Besides, he could not leave Else a second time. He knew the war in Russia was going badly but believed the Luftwaffe was winning in the West, despite the Allied landings in northern France in June. There were rumors Germany had developed a miracle weapon that could win the war, but Viktor distrusted virtually everything he heard.

Mostly, Viktor was lonely. The Länderbank's younger employees had been let go so they could serve in the military. The bank had brought back some recently retired former employees. This meant the bank was being run by a skeleton crew of mostly older men. Viktor was now fifty-three. He was beginning to have dreams of retirement but knew that would not happen as long as the war dragged on. His only true friend at the Länderbank was Herbert Stadler, one of those recent retirees. The two had much in common. Herbert had two sons in the Wehrmacht and another son in the navy.

Viktor looked at his watch, it was just past 3:30 p.m. and he desperately wanted a beer. Things were quiet at the bank, so he closed his office and walked over to Herbert's. "I am ready for a beer. How about you?"

"God, I thought you would never ask."

Herbert was about Viktor's age. He was balding, with a stomach that represented his love of food and beer. People were attracted to his friendly attitude and sense of humor. Like Viktor, he worried about his sons in the military.

Their local bar was busy; the economists had to search for a quiet table. But their beers were cold and tasted good on a warm September day.

"Have you heard from any of your sons?" asked Viktor.

"I do hear from my two in the army occasionally, but nothing from Erich in the navy. Their letters are heavily censored, so I don't learn much. Have you heard from Fritz or Elke?"

"Elke writes quite often but we hear nothing from Fritz. I think his work has him very busy and I am sure it is all very secretive."

"Still no bombing here in Vienna, Viktor. No Allied planes since the attack in July. I think it may have been a mistake; maybe it was a rogue pilot or maybe Churchill *does* have a favorite aunt in Vienna," Herbert said with a laugh.

"I wish I could believe you, but clients in Munich tell me about the bombing there. I think it is just a matter of time until the Allies get their airfields built so they can reach Vienna. I think everything changed when they landed in France. They are close enough now to create the same havoc here as they have in Germany."

"Ah Viktor, you are too pessimistic. The Führer knows what he is doing. Besides, I keep hearing about rocket bombs which are supposed to give us the upper hand."

Viktor looked at his beer and said, "I don't know, I have given some thought to moving to a quiet town with no military production facilities the Allies want to destroy."

"Is there such a place?"

"I have considered Dresden. It is an exceptionally beautiful city with no military whatsoever. No factories, no supply buildings, no military of any kind, just a wonderful, old German city."

"Would you quit your job?"

"I have thought about it but Else would never allow me to do something so drastic."

"What if the war were to last another five years or more, the bank wouldn't hold your job. History has shown some European wars can last that long."

"Maybe I will get a job with a Dresden bank. Oh well, it is all talk anyway. I need to get home. See you tomorrow."

*   *   *

Else and Viktor got out of a taxi in front of St. Stephen's Cathedral on 10 September, a beautiful Sunday morning. Else looked up at the ornately patterned, richly colored roof and exclaimed, "I love this church so much and on such a lovely day."

They found seats near the High Altar. It had been built in 1641 and represented the stoning of St. Stephen. They enjoyed the music and the church service, but when they stepped outside their world took a deadly turn. Air raid sirens began to screech. At first, those outside thought this was a drill. But when they looked up they saw American bombers unloading deadly cargo. All was confusion at first as people scrambled for safety. Women screamed and children cried.

Viktor knew the area well. He grabbed Else's hand and they ran to the nearest shelter. Inside was no better, with the boom of exploding bombs. Some people screamed. Some prayed. Some sobbed. Else crossed herself and said a short prayer. Vienna was unprepared for this. No officials entered the shelter to offer comfort or water. The bombing seemed to stop after about twenty minutes, but no one moved or ventured outside. Soon the air became so stuffy that someone had to open the door. A man near the entrance cautiously walked out. After looking around, he motioned for the rest to follow. Else and Viktor were among the last to leave and survey the damage. People seemed more astonished than dismayed. A few cursed the Americans; a few broke into tears. Most were amazed that the capital of Austria had been subjected to a "terrorist strike."

Viktor looked up and saw a gray-green wall of smoke so dense that the corner houses on nearby *Mariahilferstrasse* were hidden. It was obvious no street cars or taxis would be running, so the couple began to walk home. The noise of police, military, and fire equipment rushing about with sirens blaring was frightening in itself. They were relieved that the Hofburg Palace had not been hit but noticed a Baroque archangel had toppled from the entrance to St. Michael's Church on the Michaelerplatz. At Café Central, where Viktor had enjoyed countless coffees and Trotsky had once played chess, Wehrmacht soldiers were busily nailing wooden planks across shattered windows.

"Dear," Viktor said, turning to Else as they slowly walked away from the destruction, "I have been thinking of leaving Vienna."

"Leave? Where would we go?"

"I think this bombing will get worse and I am afraid for us. I have worked for the bank a long time. I am hoping they will grant me time off."

"Viktor, where would we go? What about our apartment?"

"We could lock up the apartment and hope the war doesn't last much longer. We'll return when it is over. As to where to go, I have been looking at Dresden. It has never been attacked because there are no military facilities there. Why would the Allies even care about it? We could move there and wait out the rest of the war."

"Viktor, I don't want to leave my home. Besides, what if Elke or Fritz gets leave to come home and we are gone?"

"We would write them to let them know what we are doing," he said gently. "I think Elke would be in favor of our moving to a safer situation."

"*Nein*, I am against this idea. Today is the first day Vienna has seen an attack and it was in the central area. Our apartment is a long way from there. There is no military in the north part of the city. I think we are safer here than in some strange place where we know no one. It will be new and unfamiliar to us. Where will we live? Where will I shop? What about my friends? You are only thinking of yourself! It is a bad idea and I don't want to talk about it anymore."

They were silent during the rest of the walk to Daringergasse. Viktor was sorry he had brought up the subject. Experiencing air attacks on the city he loved so much had shaken his confidence in their future.

That evening as they relaxed at home, Viktor could feel Else's tension. He again said they would not move and Else seemed satisfied. As he slowly drank a whisky, his mind drifted back to his early banking days. He remembered a bank meeting he and Hans Reinhard had attended in the late '20s. The speaker was now a famous economist, Dr. Friedrich Hayek. Viktor remembered Hayek talking about socialism and the danger of it producing a dictator. He had kept notes on the presentation and sat down to see what he had written so long ago. His note was dated July 1927. He remembered he and Hans having coffee with the then unknown economist.

Viktor began to read: "Instead of freedom and prosperity, bondage and misery stare us in the face. We are the victims of some evil power which must be conquered before we can resume the road to better things . . . Democracy attaches all possible value to each man; Socialism makes each man a mere agent, a mere number." The words were beginning to come back to Viktor. "The control of the production of wealth is the control of human life itself. Economic control is not merely control of a sector of human life—it is control of the means for all our lives." At the end of his notes he had underlined a quote from Voltaire: "Man is free if he needs to obey no person but solely the laws."

Viktor leaned back in his chair and stared at Voltaire's words. When he wrote those words, they had meant a lot to him. He remembered being impressed with Hayek and believing his words explicitly. *What happened to me over those seventeen years? How did I get so caught up with Hitler and Nazism?* Victor thought. It all flew directly in the face of Hayek's words.

Else broke into his reverie. "Viktor, I am going to bed now. Are you coming?"

"*Nein,* I would like to read a bit longer. I apologize again and am deeply sorry I upset you."

Else didn't respond. She turned away to prepare for bed and Viktor turned back to his thoughts. He continued to stare into the distance, then got up to pour himself another whiskey. Returning to his chair, he looked at his scotch and water and thought: *I am an economist so, of course, it was the awful economy after the war. No one was working, the krone was worthless. We were looking for a savior. The Jews? I never gave them much thought. There were few at the bank. I never knew them well, never socialized with them. They were just different, not my kind of people.*

I bought sausages from Mr. Weiss until one day the Nazis closed his shop and he was gone. I assumed he just moved out of Vienna. Our doctor was Jewish, I remember we were not allowed to go to him anymore. He came to me one day and said if we ever needed him he would still come to see us and we would not even need to pay him. Soon, the whole family had disappeared. Naturally, we asked ourselves where they could be, but where could we have gone to find out? I believed they were in a protective custody camp.

I have heard stories about what happens in these concentration camps and about some of the things that have taken place in Poland, but I don't believe any of it. We are a civilized country; those stories are made up by the Allies. Things happen in war we may not approve of in normal times, but these are not normal times. You tend to pretty much go along with the crowd. You believe certain things because you want to believe them, you want to be able to sleep at night.

Viktor went to join Else in bed, but sleep did not come easily for either of them.

*   *   *

September turned into October. Vienna had seen only sporadic raids, mainly to its oil facilities. But after the raid of 10 September, the population knew it could happen again. Business went on as usual for the economists at the Länderbank. At least, they kept up a pretense of work. By mid-October, the mood in the city was apathetic and resigned. There were constant air-raid alerts. Most were false alarms, but the lack of bombs did not stop a deterioration of basic services of every imaginable kind. There were also changes in dress and behavior: Fashionable women abandoned frocks and gowns for informal clothes. Men began carrying shaving gear, tobacco, and a change of underwear in their briefcases. Goods began to disappear from store shelves, and a thriving black market developed in the carnival district of the Prater.

One day, an excited Herbert entered Viktor's office carrying a copy of the newspaper *Dresdener Zeitung*. Had Viktor seen a certain article? Viktor had not, and Herbert began to read: "The air murderers had killed with the same mechanical ice-cold cruelty they had done over Germany. But if they had hoped to split the population they were sadly mistaken. The only result was a growing deep-seated, silent hatred that thinks only about one thing: revenge and retribution."

"Sorry Herbert," replied Viktor, folding his arms across his chest. "I have heard the authorities have confiscated even more apartments, and demanded those with an extra room or two take in people who have lost their homes. We are united, but we have no ability for revenge. I am afraid the only revenge and retribution will come in the form of bombs from Allied planes."

*   *   *

In October, alarms were frequent but raids were few. The people had begun to live with the fact that most streetcar lines were down. Major thoroughfares were filled with people walking home from work. The gas had been turned off and most restaurants had nothing to sell. The two-toned air-raid sound, named the cuckoo, was nerve-racking. Most were false alarms. There were no bombs dropped in the 19th District, so most residents ignored them and didn't run to a shelter. Else knew this could change at any time. Viktor, with his office in the central city, was in more danger. He saw death and destruction every time bombs were dropped, which was becoming more frequent. He thought the bombers were making up for all the months Vienna was spared.

On 5 November, everything changed. The American Air Force sent 500 bombers against Vienna. The planes dropped 1,100 tons of bombs, mostly on oil refinery targets, but many did heavy damage to the central city. This was the first time the Americans had used firebombs; the result was massive fires everywhere. The smell of phosphorus engulfed the city. Fire trucks roared up and down main traffic arteries. The Americans usually attacked between 11:00 a.m. and 2:00 p.m. When that occurred, Else used a shelter near the Baur home when Viktor was at work. She began to believe fear was the emotion which dominates all others. She wrote in her diary, "We are afraid when we get up in the morning and when we go to bed at night. Fear when we leave the house, fear when thinking about people close to us. Fear in every hour and minute of our existence."

The next day, Herbert came into Viktor's office even more upset than Viktor at the damage the American bombers had caused. "Why would they do this to us? They are supposed to be liberating us from the Germans."

Viktor was becoming more frustrated with this world he was condemned to live in. He barked at Herbert, "God dammit! Have you forgotten we voted to join Germany; 99 percent of us voted for the *Anschluss* in 1938. We *are* Germany! We stopped being Austria with that vote. The damn Americans couldn't care less about Austria. Vienna will be bombed regularly now and see the same destruction the German cities have endured. They just want to kick the shit out of anyone who speaks German, including you and me."

Viktor stormed out of his office and the building, not sure where he was going. On the streets he saw burned houses virtually everywhere. People were picking through the ruins, hoping to find something familiar. He stepped over debris of all kinds until he spotted St. Stephen's Cathedral. It seemed to have some power, which drew him inside. A crowd of people, including many soldiers, was gathered around the altar where a priest was conducting afternoon services. It had been only two months since he and Else had been here on 10 September. Viktor looked around this holy place, with which he was so familiar. He had found comfort here as a young boy in school and especially when he was at the University. He remembered praying he would survive the first war and later praying for the health of his two children and for Else, the love of his life. How had his world gone from one catastrophe to another? He knew now that he and Else had to leave Vienna, and prayed for God's help to convince her to move to the safety of Dresden. He had had enough.

* * *

Else's Journal
DRESDEN – 25 NOVEMBER 1944

We arrived in Dresden about a week ago. We were lucky in that Viktor knew a banker here who had an available apartment in the central city. I am happy with it because it is close to shopping and the neighbors seem nice. But hopefully, we will not be here long.

I was not pleased to leave Vienna. It had been my home all my life. I hated leaving my friends, our apartment, and all my favorite places in the city. I was upset with Viktor when he first mentioned moving here. The thought of moving to a strange place, meeting new people, and finding my way around felt overwhelming. I was pretty awful to Viktor for some time. When the Allies began to bomb Vienna regularly, it took a real toll. Even when there were no raids, we expected one at any time. I fear Vienna is being bombed repeatedly now, experiencing the destruction the German cities have endured.

Viktor's banker friend is Ulrich Uhlmann. He and his wife live in a suburb not far from the central city. He and Viktor have spoken many times on the telephone but have never met. Ulrich has even suggested there may be an opening at his bank after the war is over. However, I am not sure I want to live in Germany. I am assuming there will be an Austria again.

Dresden is a lovely town, with a long history of cultural and artistic splendor. The city was known as the Jewel Box, because of its baroque and rococo city center. This is why many residents feel they have been spared the destruction the rest of Germany has experienced. We will see if this theory holds up, but we know Vienna is being bombed unmercifully.

I have written Fritz and Elke about our move. We had a nice long letter in return from Elke, fully supporting us, but have heard nothing from Fritz. I am worried about him, but Viktor says there is nothing to worry about. He is a general and has a lot of duties and little time.

Our next door neighbor is Eva Schiller. She has been very helpful but she talks so much it is hard to get away from her. My biggest concern is the inadequate coal supply, especially with winter coming. A few days ago, Eva took me to a place where

I could get some potatoes. These are wretched times. I hope we have made the right decision. God be with us!

*   *   *

Viktor was waiting at a restaurant in the central city for a lunch meeting with *Herr* Uhlmann. He was thinking of asking him about the possibilities of employment with the Dresden bank. They were both economists, but since Ulrich's bank was larger than Viktor's, it might have more opportunities for advancement than LänderBank. But with Christmas just a few days away and the temperature quite cold, Viktor was more interested in how to obtain more coal. The previous week he had made six trips lugging low-grade coal to his cellar, an effort that exhausted him. While waiting at the coal merchant he overheard the chatter of women who were fetching coal themselves because their men were in the army or the factories. One said she had heard the Russians had broken through at Lake Balaton. Viktor reasoned if that were true, Vienna was threatened.

His thoughts were interrupted by a joyful, "*Guten tag, Herr Baur!* I am very sorry we have not been able to get together more often, but I am buried at work." Ulrich was a tall man about Viktor's age. He had an outgoing personality and seemed to know everyone in town. He had lived in Dresden most of his life except for Naval service in the Great War. "With the Russians coming in from the East and bombers overhead, I have no time. But I am glad you seem to be settling in. Are you able to get what you need in a city short of coal and even shorter of food?"

"Else and I are making do, but I have never hauled so much coal before."

"I really think the war will be over soon and you and Else can go back to Vienna, unless I can convince you to stay here in Dresden."

"I am glad you mentioned that. We have lived all our lives in Vienna. I miss the people and the music, but Vienna has been bombed heavily. The economic opportunities will be tough for several years and my bank will have limited opportunities for some time."

"If I may interrupt you, Viktor. Dresden has not seen the destruction Austria and Germany have, so you think economic opportunities will be better for you here. I totally agree. Let us get this damn war over with, and then you and I will sit down and make plans."

"You have been very good to us and we are enjoying your city. But we may yet win the war. I have heard wild stories, that we are building turbines which can suck aircraft out of the sky and airplanes with no propellers that can fly at high speeds. I hope they're more than wild hysteria." Viktor said this to inject some humor in the conversation. Also, he was not sure Else would want to remain in Dresden.

Ulrich said, "I feel as you do; those are stories of hysteria. New weapons aside, I am afraid we are simply outmanned and outgunned. Things will slow down for me after Christmas, and my wife and I will have you to our place for dinner. How is Else handling the shortage of food? Although, it is probably the same in Vienna."

"*Ja,* the same shortages but with the chance of being killed."

The conversation continued for some time. Viktor found Ulrich's optimism and sense of humor refreshing. Ulrich really seemed to enjoy life, even under these circumstances.

It was beginning to get dark. Viktor knew Else was uneasy in a strange city at night. The men said their good-byes. Viktor felt cheered that Ulrich was a good person and would be of help when he could.

*   *   *

Else's Journal
DRESDEN – 1 JANUARY 1945

I face the future indifferently and with little hope. It is uncertain when the war will end. With the offensive in the

West at a standstill and Budapest lost, German prospects have sunk again. So far Dresden has been spared, but I am becoming reconciled to the thought of death. It is a matter of maintaining one's dignity until the end. Everybody's nerves are on edge. Today, the talkative Eva and I queued for a half a ration of coal. A woman in front of us got a whole ration. A woman behind me yelled, "She gets a whole ration, why don't I?" The woman with the whole ration became agitated. Almost weeping, she said: "I would happily change places with you. I lost my family in Berlin. I have no strength left. Then I am told I am complaining."

Everyone is afraid. What's more, a conversation like this could lead to punishment from the authorities.

Else's Journal
DRESDEN – 25 JANUARY 1945

The weather has turned mild, almost 44 degrees, a welcome respite from the recent bitter cold. The women I talk to are scared, expecting the Russians to march in, perhaps within a few days. The stories are flying fast and furious. Even stories no one believes, such as the Germans killed one and a half million Jews at Auschwitz and ground down the bones for fertilizer. What a story! The reality is the restaurants have no food, and gas for cooking and heating is almost completely depleted, even when it is supposed to be available. One can hardly boil water. Potatoes cannot be cooked at all. My neighbor, Eva, had a fainting fit yesterday because she is worn out and poorly fed. I cannot help her, and I am very depressed. I dream of having enough to eat.

*   *   *

To: Elke Baur
From: Ulrich Uhlmann
Date: February 16, 1945

Dear *Fräulein* Baur:

It is with a heavy heart that I write this letter. Your parents had given me your address in case anything should happen to them. As you undoubtedly know, on the night of 13 February, British and American warplanes dropped firebombs that incinerated the central city of Dresden, including the area of my apartment where your parents were living. This morning we were finally allowed access to that area. I am sad to tell you everything was destroyed; nothing could have survived the hellish fire. I combed through what was left of the apartment. I found one thing that belonged to your parents, a metal box, burned badly, that contained your mother's diary. I will be sending it to you in the next few days.

I will describe the attack so you will understand that sadly, your parents had no chance of escape; the entire central city was ablaze. Dresden had become a magnet for refugees from all over Germany. Two days after the attack, terrified strangers wandered unfamiliar streets of a city still burning. Initial estimates are that two hundred and fifty thousand died, but I think this is too high.

We had dinner with your parents a few times over Christmas and found them to be wonderful people who loved you and Fritz very much. They were so proud of both of you. We all thought Dresden would be spared, both because we are a cultural center, and because we hoped Dresden would become the capital of the new Germany. Our hopes were dashed.

My wife and I live in a suburb outside the central city, yet the bombs made the night as bright as day. The first attack sounded like a huge conveyer belt rolling over us, punctuated with detonations and tremors. It lasted for about twenty-five minutes. After it gradually ceased there was absolute quiet. I went outside after that attack. The night sky was illuminated pink and red. The houses were black silhouettes, and a red cloud of smoke hovered over everything. I saw people distraught, smeared with ash, and with wet blankets wrapped around their heads. And the voices! "Everything's gone, everything is on fire."

Many people gathered in our courtyard, which was still intact. Everyone talked at once until someone yelled, "They're coming back, they're coming back!" It was sheer panic, for myself and my wife as well. We thought it wasn't possible that the Allies would drop more bombs on a city that was already an inferno. Afterward, although there were no windows and the entire roof had been torn off, our home was still standing, a true miracle.

The fact that we have survived this attack gives me no joy. Yet the loss of our apartment brings me no sorrow. I weep with you in recognizing this war has not only destroyed ancient buildings and countless treasures but the lives of good people. Who was ultimately responsible for this? The simple answer is Adolph Hitler. We followed him blindly as he exploited the accumulated Jew-hatred of two thousand years. Voltaire once said: 'History never repeats itself, man always does.'

Please let me know if there is anything I can do.

Yours truly,
Ulrich Uhlmann

23

Elke Baur

1948

Once again, to quote Daniel Goldhagen: "Germany during the Nazi period was a country in which government policies, public acts of other sorts, and the public conversation were thoroughly, almost obsessively antisemitic. Even a cursory glance at this society would suggest to the unsophisticated observer, to anyone who takes the evidence of his senses to be real, that the society was rife with antisemitism. Essentially, in Germany during the Nazi period, antisemitism was shouted from the rooftops: 'The Jews are our misfortune we must rid ourselves of them' . . . That the Jews were fundamentally different and maleficent, was at the time an axiom of German and of most of Christian culture. This evaluation of Jews was shared alike by elites and, more importantly by the common people."

L ife had gotten no easier for Elke during 1948. The war had been over for three years, and she had been back home in Vienna for over a year. She had a job in a hospital, mostly cleaning bed pans, but it didn't last long. She then had a job with a small Vienna newspaper, but that, too, ended quickly, because she was continually at odds with fellow employees.

She didn't need to work, because once her parents had been confirmed dead in the bombing of Dresden, she became their sole living heir. The government had declared her brother Fritz missing in action after five years—with no knowledge of his whereabouts. She had inherited a substantial investment account. Viktor had invested wisely. When Germany attacked Russia in 1941, he had been concerned things would not go well for Germany. From clients, he knew that wealthy Jews were getting their money out of Germany and to the bank of Warburg & Company, in Amsterdam. He decided to follow them and got lucky. After the German conquest of Holland, the Nazis were at pains to prove they had no plans to formally annex Holland as they had Austria. They demanded and received a large bribe to not bother the Warburg Bank, and to allow Jewish members of the bank to emigrate to America.

Elke had no interest in living a lavish lifestyle on her father's investments. She had reoccurring dark thoughts. The passage of time had not healed the disintegration of her world in 1945. She still could not understand how Germany had lost the war. She told herself that England, Russia, and America had "ganged up" on her Germany that wanted only to live peacefully by itself once the subhuman Jews had been eliminated from the Fatherland.

Vienna was beginning to put itself back together. Funds were being raised to rebuild the beautiful roof of St. Stephen's Cathedral, and monies were now available to restore the beloved Opera House. The Prater was once again becoming a place families could enjoy on a warm spring day.

It was on just such a day that Elke intended to watch the children playing in the Prater. She hoped it would lift her spirits, but for some reason she changed her mind and went to Stadtpark instead. She hadn't been there since her school days when she spent happy hours there with Kurt Hoffmann.

The park was not quite what she remembered, but the monument of Johann Strauss, the composer known as the "waltz king," was still standing. Elke spent an hour walking through the lovely park with its many flowers and ponds, and peacocks strutting about among squealing children.

Elke knew she needed to get herself together. If she spent wisely, her father's money should last her lifetime. She had a persistent cough that would not go away, but the hospitals were filled with patients with much more serious ailments. Reluctantly, she boarded the tram back to Daringergasse. After walking the three flights to her apartment she saw a note stuck in the door. She began to read: *I am just back from Russia. Lots to tell if you want to see me. I would love to see you! I am staying at the Sacher for a few days. You can reach me there. Kurt Hoffmann.*

She hadn't seen Kurt since the night in Krakow when she ran from him in tears after what she had told herself were lies about a few Jew killings in Poland. These were nothing but rumors, he could not possibly have seen such things firsthand, she thought. He had had no business passing on those lies. She had worked in Poland throughout the war, helping Germans set up homes there. She shook off a gnawing feeling of discomfort that came over her when she thought of Kurt's account. Poland was a backward land in which Poles and Jews were living as if in the Dark Ages. They needed to give up the land so the more advanced German people could better utilize the area.

In a fit of anger, she tore up the note.

*   *   *

Kurt stayed at the Sacher Hotel for only a few days. It was an extravagance he couldn't afford for long. When he didn't hear from Elke, he rented an apartment near the university, hoping to get a feel for student life, since he was considering enrolling. He managed to meet and befriend several students at nearby coffee houses. Kurt's new friends from the university were fascinated by his stories of how he had survived a Russian prison camp near Stalingrad in 1943, especially since so few of his fellow prisoners ever saw freedom.

But on beautiful spring days, Kurt preferred the outdoors of Stadtpark. It soon became a favorite for him. It was one of the few places in Vienna that had retained its charm during the eight years of his absence. Most of the coffee houses in Vienna had either been destroyed in the bombings or had been owned by Jews and were now either shuttered or owned by people who seemed to have lost the easy comfort of the former owners.

Kurt ran into Elke at the cafe at Stadtpark. He was disappointed when he received no reply to the note he'd left at her apartment. Often, during a break from his studies he went to the park, hoping she would be there. On this day in May the stars aligned; she walked into the café as he was enjoying a coffee.

The eight years since they had seen each other seemed to have passed in a heartbeat. She looked as lovely as ever, if tired. She saw Kurt as she entered the café. Their greeting was friendly but awkward. Her memories of him during their school days were pleasant, but their last night in Krakow overwhelmed the good memories. However, Elke decided to take a chance and speak with him.

He told her the story of his onerous time in the Russian prison camp.

"My luck changed when I was selected to be a waiter for the regional commander, Gen. Andrei Voroshilov, who was having a party at his villa near Rostov. It was pure chance that the general was an expert on Leo Tolstoy and was interested in me because I was well read on the author.

"During the party I had a brief conversation with the general and mentioned I hoped to visit Tolstoy's home in Yasnaya Polyanna. The general's eyes lit up with obvious pride. He said his permanent home was at Polyanna. There is no doubt my knowledge of Tolstoy saved my life, because the general had me transferred to his command. At the war's end I was sent to his palatial villa in Yasnaya Polyanna. This was a dream come true. I was at Tolstoy's hometown, and if I did what I was told, I just might see Vienna again.

"However, it was not going to be as easy as I first believed. I found myself with other young soldiers of various nations who were doing odd jobs around the villa. Some were cooks, others were gardeners, others were mechanics for the general's many automobiles. It slowly became evident that many, if not all, were there for the sexual satisfaction of the general. I knew almost nothing of homosexuality and was at a loss of how to handle this information. The general made no outward suggestions or advances to me, but as time went on he relaxed during our Tolstoy discussions over a bottle of excellent wine. Occasionally, the general would allow his hand to touch mine and linger a little longer than necessary."

"Did you ever submit?" asked Elke, not sure she wanted the answer.

"*Nein,* I came close near the end of my stay because I felt if I didn't I would be back at the gulag and probably end my life there. Then one day the general came to me with a train ticket to Vienna, some money, actually quite a lot of money, and my release papers. While waiting at the train station to get home, I read in a newspaper that the general had committed suicide."

"So what now?" Elke said, with an air of condescension. "Will you use the money to get a job or stay in school?"

"Gen. Voroshilov encouraged me to study Shakespeare at university. He had several of Shakespeare's plays. I found them challenging but I really think I could teach Shakespeare."

"Do you have the money for that? How would you live while going to school?"

"I can't live forever on what the general gave me, but it is enough for a degree. I believe this was his intention for the gift of the money. He thought teaching would be a good career for me after the war."

Kurt put his coffee down and looked into Elke's eyes. "That is my plan. What are you going to do? You have been here for over a year. Do you have enough money to not work?"

"I have enough for my short future." Elke said this with indifference, which concerned Kurt.

"What do you mean? You are only thirty years old and a very smart, attractive lady. The economy will get better. Europe has to rebuild and there will be jobs. A new Europe will emerge from this war. Wait and see."

"That will take years and I don't have a lot of time." More coolness on her part.

"For God's sake, you are still young! Then attend university with me."

Elke's eyes were unfocused, her thoughts were far away. She finally said, "My future died with the Third Reich. I am not sure I want to live under the Russians."

"Look, I want to be in charge of cheering you up. Can I see you again? How about dinner tomorrow night at the Sacher? I found an apartment in the American Zone and will be moving into it as soon as it is ready. This would be a nice way to celebrate."

Finally, a smile on her lovely face. It felt like a breakthrough for Kurt when she got up to leave and said, "See you tomorrow at six."

*   *   *

On 1 July, the American Marshall Plan began. It was designed to rebuild war-torn regions, remove trade barriers, and modernize industry, but its main goal was to stem the tide of Communism in Europe. Seventy million dollars was slated for Austria, which had big problems. In 1948, its cases of tuberculosis had increased by six thousand over the previous year. Also, there remained almost half a million displaced persons in Austria who needed to be cared for, of which one hundred and ninety seven thousand were war widows. Additionally, a million prisoners of war in Austria were waiting to return home.

*   *   *

As Christmas neared, along with the end of Kurt's first semester at the university, his life was slowly improving. School was going well. He had met some interesting people, among them his instructors, who had opened his mind to many great authors. He was taking several literature classes and enjoying them all. Even his relationship with Elke was improving. Their dinner at the Sacher had gone well. Since then, they had gotten together a number of times. She seemed to enjoy his company and was developing a better outlook on life. Kurt was thinking of asking her to marry him.

One morning, taking a break from reading, Kurt needed a cup of coffee to revive his flagging attention. Scanning the student coffee shop for an empty chair, he discovered all but one was taken. Kurt approached the table where an older gentleman was reading and sipping coffee, and asked if he could take the empty seat. The man graciously gestured to the chair and continued reading. Kurt assumed he was a professor because of his age, his unkept head of white hair, small white goatee, and rumpled tweed jacket. Not sure what to do next, Kurt was irritated with himself for not bringing something to read. Lord knows he had plenty. Kurt was not even sure the professor, engrossed in his book, noticed him.

"*Danke mein heir!* I don't mean to bother, but do you teach here?"

The professor looked up from his book, startled. "Oh, *wie bitte*? When I am reading I am oblivious to everything around me. My wife tells me this all the time. I am Dr. Alfred Altschul, and I am assuming you are a student at the university."

"I am Kurt Hoffmann. And *ja*, I started classes in September."

"What are you studying, *Herr* Hoffmann?"

"My main interest is literature: Shakespeare, Tolstoy, Dickens. Wait a minute . . . I have heard of you and of your book, *The Austria of Yesterday*. I am sorry to say I have not read it yet."

"Oh, do not worry. I am not in the same class of the authors you mentioned. I do find myself fortunate to be here and meet young students, many of whom were in the war. How about you, *Herr* Hoffmann?"

"I am afraid my war fighting experience was rather limited. I joined in 1940, but was captured by the Russians in 1943."

"You survived the fighting and a Russian prison camp. You are fortunate we can even have this conversation," said the professor.

Kurt explained how a love of Tolstoy had led to his protection by the Russian general who assigned Kurt to his villa in Yasnaya Polana.

"Ah! Tolstoy's home!" The author's interest in his new tablemate increased.

"That is quite a story, young man! So now you are at the University of Vienna and, I assume, preparing to teach someday. Is that correct?"

"*Ja,* I have thought of it."

"Are you married, *Herr* Hoffmann?"

"*Nein.* I have a lady I love, but she has struggled with the war. She had a high position in the BdM. Hitler and Nazism were her life. She still clings to Hitler's dogma. Also, she lost her parents in the bombing of Dresden. I am afraid she is still finding her way."

"She still believes in Hitler; does she have a conscience?"

The question took Kurt by surprise.

"A conscience? I am not sure. She is mostly in denial about our atrocities toward the Jews, but a conscience, I don't know. She loved her parents very much but had few friends in school . . . wait, what do you mean?" He was struggling with the question.

"A person's conscience is the need to behave consistently with recognized ethical principles. Behavior contrary to conscience leads to feelings of guilt. Conscience, ethical values, a capacity for empathy, and the ability to love must be developed and nurtured in a child. The capacity to love and empathize comes with development and maturation. Fear hinders empathy."

"How did we get into this mess, Professor Altschul?"

"We must understand, Hitler spoke of a desire to improve things. He promised something for nothing. All Germans blame the Nazis for losing the war, and proclaim ignorance of Nazi crimes. But some of the worst killers who sent thousands to their death were members of police units or those who operated the trains which took Jews to the death camps. The list is endless. A perpetrator is anyone who knowingly contributed in some way to the mass slaughter of Jews, even those who 'only' helped to bring about their deaths. Those who cordoned off areas where their compatriots shot Jews were perpetrators. Also guilty were railroad engineers and administrators who knew they were transporting Jews to the camps. And church officials who identified Jews as non-Christians, again leading to their deaths. And don't forget the "desk-murders," mostly women, whose paperwork lubricated the wheels of destruction.

"The gas chambers in the death camps have been the focus of scholarly attention. But this 'assembly-line' killing has siphoned attention away from one-on-one killings. These went on for years before it was decided a better process was needed to reach the goal of a *Judenrein* Europe. The result is that the people who worked in the less notorious institutions of killing have largely fallen from view. These people will never be punished."

"Professor, Austria claims to be the first victim of Hitler. Is there any truth to that?"

"*Nein!* First victim, my ass! What a lie. When Hitler and his Wehrmacht marched into Austria in 1938, Austrians overwhelmed him with flowers and adoration. Believe me, Poland and France did not give him that same glorious welcome. Austrians like to change the story when it suits them. They seem to forget it was Austrian police who rounded up the Jews, took them from their homes and businesses, and escorted them to the rail cars. They claim they didn't know what was happening to the Jews. What did they think was happening? Their Jewish shopkeeper, from whom they bought sausages for years, is suddenly gone. Their neighbors are gone. Their doctors are gone. They all suspected, they just didn't want to know. Germans and Austrians claim they are innocent, but that is a lie. They all have blood on their hands, and it will not wash off as long as they live."

At the mention of blood, Kurt thought of Fritz, and his rank. "Professor, Elke has a brother who was in the SS. She has heard nothing from him since 1943," he said. "The state declared him dead, but she would like to know more. Can you be of any help? His name was Gen. Fritz Baur and he was in Poland."

The professor raised an eyebrow but said nothing as he wrote the name in his notebook. "*Ja,* if he is a general in the SS, I will be able to find him easily. I will get back to you soon. By the way, shortly after the war ended, I had an interview with a young American lieutenant. He was a Jewish boy from New York, I don't remember his name, but I was impressed with him. He and two other officers, whom I didn't meet, were exploring the Germans' reason for this hatred of Jews. I believed they were trying to understand an Austrian woman who was high up in the BdM. As I remember, she was unrepentant. They were trying to determine where this hatred came from. She may have been your girl."

*   *   *

At Christmas in 1948, Vienna still suffered from a shortage of almost everything, from food to coal. The war had ended three and a half years earlier, and people were beginning to get on with their lives as best they could. Snow now covered the trees and the ground, making everything look prettier than it actually was.

Kurt was thinking of asking Elke to marry him; Christmas seemed a logical time. Looking up from studying Shakespeare's *The Merchant of Venice,* he glanced at his watch and noticed it was 3:15 p.m., the time the mail arrived. He walked to the mailboxes, where several students greeted him with a joyful "Merry Christmas!" There was only one letter in his box. He smiled with anticipation when he saw that the sender was Dr. Altschul. It had been several weeks since their talk. Kurt was surprised it had taken the professor this long to find information about Fritz. He hurried from the noisy mailroom to a quieter place, tore open the envelope and began to read:

My Dear *Herr* Hoffmann:

First, let me apologize for this long delay in getting the information on Gen. Baur I promised several weeks ago. It was quite difficult to uncover the true facts about your friend's brother. For reasons you will soon understand, the Nazis kept his death secret. He was assassinated by Polish conspirators on 27 May 1943 as he was being driven to the airfield near the Polish town of Lviv with the top down on his convertible. One of the conspirators threw a hand grenade into the car, but Baur did not die right away. Because of the secrecy I cannot be sure exactly what day he died. He had a reputation as one of the most brutal killers in all of Poland. He oversaw four units of the Order Police, the people most intimately involved with the genocidal killings.

In fact, Herr *Baur was the commander of the Police Battalion that torched the Polish town of Bialystok in June 1941. Unfortunately, this is but one example of his cruelty. A year later, it reached new heights in the small Polish town of Józefów, south of Lublin. The evening before his Order Police entered the town, they were issued whips made of ox hide that were to be used to drive the Jews out of their homes. Baur told his men they were embarking on a momentous undertaking. They received explicit orders to shoot the most helpless Jews—the old, the young, the sick, the women and children—but not men capable of work. The soldiers went door to door to bring the Jews to the assembly place, Józefów's market square. Anyone of the designated group who put up resistance were to be shot on the spot. During this evacuation, all patients of a Jewish hospital were shot in their beds. These soldiers walked into a house of healing and shot the sick. One imagines they must have been terrified, cowering and begging for mercy. They killed babies whose tiny corpses were dropped like so much trash and left to rot.*

The Germans then applied themselves to uncovering the concealed places in the town. They left no wall untapped. The soldiers were thorough; they even brought in the battalion doctor to explain the best way to kill. Obviously, he did not think his Hippocratic oath applied to Jews.

There are many other incidents. I can share them with you if you so desire. There are even rumors (unproven) that Baur and his men staged a fake Polish attack on a German radio station, which was Hitler's pretense to start the invasion of Poland.

He was one of many such soldiers, and no one in Europe escaped Germany's viciousness. The war mobilized virtual children for the front. It made women the prizes of victory. It demanded the annihilation of entire peoples. It generated realities worse than any nightmare. Chaos seemed natural and it brought about twelve years of rule by bestiality and ignorance. It was the way things had always been, the way things would always be and destroyed two thousand years of German civilization. But the Allied bomber offensive was a major mistake. The bombing of German cities caused millions of men conscripted into the Wehrmacht to see themselves fighting, not for the Third Reich, but for their families and their homeland.

I am afraid your friend's brother played a major role in all this. Gen. Baur was a brutal killer from his early days in the SS. He did his job without rules or mercy. This brutality assumed a life of its own, and apparently, he thought his unmitigated cruelty could go on forever. But no one is innocent. All Germanic people bear responsibility for the atrocities of the war. I am sorry to bring this news and I don't know if you want to pass it on to his sister.

Let me know if I can be of further help and good luck in your studies.

Yours truly,
Dr. Alfred Altschul

This news nauseated Kurt. *This letter will devastate Elke, but should I even tell her?* If he didn't tell her and she heard it from someone else her reaction could be even worse. At least she would learn the news from someone who loved her. He needed time to think how best to handle the situation. He decided to go to his favorite bar near the university. At mid-day, it was unlikely his fellow students would be there. He needed quiet and a scotch whisky. Unfortunately, he found a group of friends who wanted to drink beer and talk politics.

"*Hereingekommen, Hoffmann!*" yelled his friend Horst Krones, a large man with closely cropped dark hair. "Help us to straighten this idiot out," he said, pointing to Otto Steinhoff. "He still thinks Austria was only a victim of Hitler."

"Poor Otto, he has been reading too much Austrian propaganda. Did you tell them about your Jewish grandmother you loved so much?" This from the lighthearted Werner Beck generated laughter all around.

Otto was not one bit intimidated by this beer-fueled group. "Quite funny gentlemen," he said, looking over his glasses, "but I believe we had Hitler forced upon us. You have forgotten that Hitler did not come to power because of anti-Semitism. He was carried to power on a wave of nationalism and the miserable economic situation in Austria."

Now the usually reserved blond-haired Ulrich Herz spoke up. "Most Austrians don't want to know about guilt or the past. They don't care about the judgement of history; all we want is for the suffering to cease."

More men now joined the conversation, including Johann Kumm, an instructor at the university. "Otto, I don't agree with you about anti-Semitism. Many think Austria was even more anti-Semitic than Germany. But today the only thing most Viennese are interested in is: When will we be rid of the Russians? The room exploded with cries of "*Ja!*" "When will the new tram lines be finally ready? When will we have coal and wood for heating?" "*Ja Johann!*" "When will there be glass for the windowpanes?" The men around the table broke into applause.

Ulrich said, "I have little sympathy for most Austrian Nazis. They say they were forced to join the Party and they had been compelled to torture hundreds of thousands of people, to gas them and kill them in other ways. I have no patience when I see these, now innocent, lambs." He reflected for a moment. "And yet, only he who has lived twelve years under Nazi terror can judge how enormous the pressure was and how much heroism was required to resist it."

The party began to concentrate on drinking beer and talking about women. Kurt felt better, drinking beer with his friends. In fact, he decided to call Elke and invite her to dinner at his apartment. Perhaps she would even spend the night with him.

*   *   *

Elke finally believed she might have a future. She felt better about herself and maybe, just maybe, Kurt had played a part in this change. After she received his dinner invitation, she walked to a small neighborhood dress shop, hoping they still had a dress she had seen in the window. It was a bitter cold day; she had to be careful not to slip and fall on the ice-covered sidewalks. To her delight, the dress, of a soft floral fabric, was still there and she tried it on. It had half-sleeves, a narrow belt at the waist, and a full skirt that came just below the knees and swished when she walked. She asked for it to be wrapped. As she reached into her handbag for the schillings needed to pay for the dress, she realized she had not spent this much money on anything for herself in months, maybe longer.

Back in her apartment, she spent more time putting on makeup and getting ready than she had in years. When she was satisfied, she stood in front of her mother's full-length mirror, one of the few pieces of her parents' furniture left. She smiled, admiring her figure in the dress, she grabbed her coat and went out into the cold night air to hail a taxi. For the first time in a long time she felt feminine.

Kurt's wide grin when he opened the door reflected his happiness at seeing Elke. He was dressed in a tweed jacket. Like a university student, she thought, perhaps emulating one of his professors. His hair looked as if it had not been cut in several weeks. He looked like an absent-minded professor, too engulfed with his studies to care about a trifle like a haircut.

"I am so glad to see you," he said, giving her a quick kiss on the cheek. But he noticed she looked tired, which led him to wonder about her health.

"I like your apartment!" She said this even though the disarray with books and papers everywhere, gave the same impression as his disheveled hair—that his studies were more important than his living quarters' physical appearance. His small living room contained an overstuffed chair and a sofa.

Kurt poured two glasses of wine and motioned for Elke to sit on the sofa while he, ever the gentleman, sat in the chair. She glanced around the apartment to the small kitchen, which surprisingly was clean and orderly. This indicated to Elke that Kurt ate out often.

"I have a pork roast cooking in the oven; it should be just about done. Just don't ask me how I got it," he said with a playful grin.

"Kurt, did this furniture come with the apartment?"

"Ja, I have no time for shopping. School is overwhelming. Surprisingly, I am enjoying Shakespeare."

"I read some in school, but I didn't like it because I didn't understand it," said Elke.

"I am reading *The Merchant of Venice*. I have had to read it several times, but I am learning how to read Shakespeare."

"It is a play about Jews, isn't it?"

"A Jewish moneylender named Shylock,"

"Was Shakespeare a Jew-hater also?" This question confirmed to Kurt that she hadn't changed.

Kurt answered, "I doubt if he ever knew any Jews. They were deported from England by royal decree during the Middle Ages." Then, to change the subject, he said with concern, "Are you getting along all right, Elke?"

"I would like to have a good friend, maybe even more than a friend, someone I can rely on to talk about things," she said wistfully.

"What kinds of things would you like to talk about? Elke, I would love to be that kind of friend to you. You know I've had feelings for you since we were young," he said, leaning forward in his chair. "I am busy with my studies, but I promise I will always have time for talks with you."

"I don't know how to talk about this, but it feels as if my whole world has been torn away from me."

"Everyone does! It was the war. It was Hitler and our armies who attacked Poland and later, Russia. You can't blame yourself for something you didn't do. In fact, you were helping German families get resettled in Poland. You had nothing to do with forcing the Poles and the Jews out of their homeland so Germans could move in." Kurt felt that talking about the good she had done during the war would help lift Elke out of her dark mood. She was too smart to go through life with such depression.

"Poland attacked us first. We just retaliated."

As she said this, Kurt could see some of the old hatred well up on her face.

"That is certainly not true." He said this and suddenly stopped, remembering the letter from Dr. Altschul. He desperately did not want Elke to see the letter. He was relieved to remember that it was stuck under some papers.

"I think the roast is done. Would you pour some more wine and I will get the dinner ready?"

The dinner went well; the pork roast turned out better than he had expected. With another glass of wine, Elke began to open up about her life. "I still really enjoy Stadtpark. I like to read there and watch children at play while I drink a coffee."

Kurt asked, "Do you wish you had children?"

"I don't know. I would hate to think of a child growing up with a depressed mother like myself."

He said, "Maybe a child would be just what you need to relieve this depression. Elke, the war is over. Austria will become a new and better country. You can be part of that. You would make a terrific mother and if motherhood doesn't interest you, maybe consider teaching."

"Are you volunteering to be the father?" she said with a cheerful smile that took him by surprise.

"I don't think either of us are ready to be parents. But I hope someday, if you still like me, we can consider it. You would be a wonderful mother. I am not so sure about me a father, however. But you give me hope for the future."

Elke suddenly said, "Let me hear a little bit of Shakespeare."

Kurt had been hoping she would be open to this. "I would like to practice some reading out loud which helps me better understand. *The Merchant of Venice* has taught me a lot about the mess we got ourselves into with our hatred and treatment of the Jews. During the Middle Ages, much of Europe expelled non-Christians; they were intolerant of people who were "different." But Shakespeare points out that Venice, a successful merchant city, was full of foreigners: Turks, Jews, Arabs, Africans, and Christians of various nationalities. This open-mindedness was linked to the wealth of the city. To keep the markets running smoothly, the rules of the marketplace must have little to do with religion or nationality."

"All right, I will listen, but don't expect me to agree with you," Elke said.

"Let me give you a bit of background first. Shakespeare puts together, side by side, the social relation of Christian and Jews based on economic self-interest. The Christian gentlemen comprise a community with a common ethnicity and value system. They are aware of what they have in common and are liberal lenders to each other.

"Unfortunately, it becomes obvious the Christian generosity has a racist tinge. Shylock, the Jewish moneylender, relies on contractually enforceable promises. This shows he doesn't think about money the way the Christians do. He tends not to spend but to conserve, not to expand but to defend, not to seek risk, but to minimize it. Shylock's Judaism teaches him that contracts should be rigorously enforced.

"The Christians are more complicated than they appear. Human values are supposed to transcend marketplace values and Christians are commanded to love not only their neighbors, but even their enemies. To Shylock this exposes Christian hypocrisy. He points out the Christian practice of slavery, which sets a monetary value on human beings. Christian creed mandates universal love, but they fail to behave in accord with their precepts. Does this sound familiar, Elke, with what we have experienced during the Nazi period?"

Elke sat quietly, intently listening but not sure what to say.

"Christians can love some people, disregard others, and treat another group as non-human. My favorite part of the play is Shylock's response to two Christians who ridicule him. He responds as follows. If you will allow me, madam."

Kurt stood in the kitchen area and proceeded as if he was performing at Stratford on Avon: "I am a Jew. Hath not a Jew eyes? Hath not a Jew hands, organs, dimensions, senses, affections, passions; fed with the same food, hurt with the same weapons, subject to the same diseases, healed by the same means, warmed and cooled by the same winter and summer as a Christian is? If you prick us do we not bleed? If you tickle us do we not laugh? If you poison us do we not die? And if you wrong us shall we not revenge? If we are like you in the rest, we will resemble you in that. If a Jew wrong a Christian, what is his humility? Revenge. If a Christian wrong a Jew, what should his sufferance be by Christian example? Why revenge. The villainy you teach me I will execute, and it shall go hard but I will better the instruction."

Elke walked over to him, took away his wine glas, and kissed him passionately.

*   *   *

Dawn was beginning to break when Elke awoke. Glancing out the window as she snuggled next to Kurt, she saw that it had snowed during the night. Neither of them had noticed anything except each other. Elke had had sex before, but she had never experienced such intense intimacy. She looked over at the sleeping Kurt and smiled. She thought back to their lovemaking. He had been strong, yet tender. Afterward they had held each other and talked into the wee hours. She had never had such a profound conversation with anyone. Maybe it was the warmth and strength of his body that had relaxed her.

Elke wanted to do something for him. She glanced around his apartment, which looked like a male's apartment with no female input. It wasn't dirty, but it was cluttered. There were books and papers in odd places. Perhaps they had been moved to make room for her to sit.

She rose from the bed slowly so she wouldn't disturb Kurt. She quietly slipped on her clothes and her coat, since the apartment was cold. She looked back at the warm bed and the warm male body lying there and asked herself, why had she left that comfort? She wanted to do something for the man who had made her feel like a woman. Doing the dishes would probably wake him. The next best thing, she decided, would be to straighten the clutter a bit. Books and papers were strewn everywhere. She began to place them in neat piles.

Under a messy stacking of documents, she noticed a letter. She started to put it with the research papers—until she saw her brother's name. She began to read the professor's letter. Shock turned to intense anger. This couldn't be the Fritz she knew. She remembered him as a youth, playing dazzling Mozart pieces at the piano. She had looked up to him as an officer in the elite corps, the SS.

She thought of Kurt performing the play in his kitchen. Were Jews really just like her, with eyes, hands, senses, passions? Could it be that what she had believed for so long, right to her very bones, was wrong? How could she not see the brutality that had gone on around her for so long? She didn't have blood on her hands. How could she? She didn't kill anyone!

She stormed into the bedroom and screamed at Kurt. "Bastard! Hypocrite! Fake!" Her voice grew louder with each word. "You believe these accusations against my brother. I hate you! I hate you! I hate you!" Her whole body shook. She threw the letter at him, grabbed her things and ran from the apartment.

Still bleary-eyed from sleep, Kurt was unable to respond as Elke slammed the door behind her.

Elke kept running with no thought of where she was going. She wanted to get away from Kurt's apartment, perhaps from life itself. Soon, exhausted, she fell onto her knees in the snow. Almost hysterical from crying, she looked down at her hands. They seemed to be dripping with blood. "No, no, no!" she screamed. Still on her knees, she looked ahead and saw what seemed to be a graveyard, unlike any she had ever seen. Three rows of twisted old sticks surrounded her. There was no uniformity to the sticks. Poking out of the snow they somehow resembled headstones. The sky was dark with clouds, the snow was dirty, but these gnarled sticks in the snow, in no particular order, frightened her. That seemed to go off into the distance—forever. Was this the graveyard of the Jews? A graveyard the victims of the Holocaust would never have. A graveyard for those who left behind no heirs to tell their story because entire families had perished—grandparents, parents, and children. The sight of the cemetery pierced her soul and she looked again at her hands. More blood seemed to be dripping into the dirty snow. She continued to stare at her hands and moan. Then she passed out, falling face first onto the snow.

1962

Conclusion

Professor Grant Edwards had been looking forward to this trip for a long time. Today he would leave New York on the Italian liner Cristoforo Colombo for Naples, Italy. It would be his first trip to Europe since his army days. After his release from the army, he enrolled at his alma mater, the University of California, to further his studies in European history. While studying for his Master's degree, he met his wife, Ann. Life was good for the couple. Grant got his doctorate and started teaching, while she seemed to enjoy her job as a secretary in the Business department. California was a growing state and their future looked bright.

Unfortunately, after five years, the marriage soured. Ann grew restless with bridge clubs, her job, and shopping. A fling with another professor became something more, and their marriage ended. Grant blamed himself. He should have realized Ann was unhappy and felt alone because he was always reading Austrian history or writing about it. Their friends were all Cal fellows. At dinners, the men discussed European politics while the women talked endlessly about shopping or their children, neither of which interested Ann in the least. She was the daughter of a wealthy executive who worked for Standard Oil. Her family had substantially more money than Grant made as a history professor.

Grant's interest in European history came from the two years he had spent in Munich, Germany during World War II. His studies in European history led him to question where the Germans' unconscionable hatred of the Jews had come from. The stories of the atrocities committed against other German/Austrian people because they followed another religion, made no sense to him. Grant had no interest in the gas chambers. He wanted to know how a German soldier could walk up to a four-year-old Jewish girl, shoot her in the head, then go home to his family. How could a mature human being do that and live with himself? Recently, he had earned his sabbatical from Cal and was determined to write a book trying to illuminate these questions . . . if he could. It wasn't going to be easy.

His mind kept going back to Elke Baur, in the prison camp near Munich. She was a tough young woman and might make a good model for his book. Grant had talked with her several times before she was released by the army and returned to Vienna. The second, third, and fourth interviews went no better than the first. She would not budge in her view that Hitler was right for trying to rid the world, or at least Europe, of its Jews.

As time went on and Grant dove more deeply into the subject, he found Vienna had been a hotbed of anti-Semitism. He read somewhere that while the Germans were great Nazis, they were lousy anti-Semites. The Austrians, conversely, were lousy Nazis but great anti-Semites. Grant felt he needed to go to Vienna for his research—even if the question of how the profound hatred of Jews had come about turned out to be unanswerable.

One of the first things he wanted to do was try to find Elke. After all these years, he was still upset that the army had treated her with an almost cavalier attitude, assuming she would be able to put her life back together. Grant remembered his concern and his hope that her parents' apartment would still be standing. He had never been able to get her out of his mind. He planned to make a contact at the University of Vienna and use their resources to either find Elke or determine her fate.

On St. Valentine's Day, Grant boarded the Cristoforo Colombo in New York for the eight-day trip to Naples. Unfortunately, his trip began during a major snowstorm that only grew worse as the ship navigated the Atlantic Ocean. Grant celebrated the beginning of his adventure with a scotch on the rocks. By the next morning, walking to the dining room was impossible without the assistance of large ropes strung in the middle of the passageways. After a quick breakfast, his stomach felt unsettled. He decided to spend the rest of the day in his bunk, hoping the next day would be better. By day three, he could at least hold down food. Soon, he discovered his sea legs and adjusted to the rolling of the large swells. He found he had another advantage. With most of the passengers sick in their rooms, he had easy access to the ship's bar and there was no one to disturb his reading in the lounge.

One evening, while Grant was sipping a drink in the lounge before dinner, a tall, gray-haired man approached him. The man introduced himself as Michael Case, a professor of modern French history at the University of Michigan. Could he join Grant for dinner? Grant described his own teaching credentials and said he would be delighted.

Over a dinner of filets of mackerel and sautéed white cabbage they discussed their respective jobs and destinations. Grant mentioned that he hoped to spend a few days in Pompeii and Rome before heading to Vienna.

"Vienna would be a good location to get a feel for threats from the Reds," Case said.

"Are you interested in the Communists? It's hard for Americans to get into Communist Europe."

"Yes, I'm concerned about the threat Russia poses to the West. I'm also convinced that Europe is going to have to form a common market—countries that could become a united states of Europe, as it were, to avoid another war. Churchill said this years ago, and I agree."

"Good luck! It probably would help avoid another conflict, but I'm afraid two thousand years of hatred between European countries is too much of a barrier for it to work."

They concentrated on the meal in silence for a few minutes.

Chase looked up from his dinner. "Okay, so why Vienna?"

"I'm on sabbatical. I was in the army in Munich the first few years after the war. I've never understood hating others because of religion, skin color, or country of origin. In Munich I was assigned to interview German prisoners involved with the genocide of the Jews. None were actually killers, but most expressed a profound hatred of Jews. Although few knew any Jewish people other than through business dealings, they gave the impression they did. On questioning, I could tell what these people thought they knew was from hearsay or articles from the Nazi press.

When the news of the Holocaust came out, all, without exception, claimed innocence; they had absolutely no knowledge of the camps or the killings. I was struck by the fact all used the same term, they had 'no blood on their hands.' A young woman I interviewed intrigued me. She was appealing, in her 20s, from a good home in Vienna. Her father was a banker, so she didn't fit the profile of a typical Nazi who came from the lower class, out of work, and not well educated. She loved Austria and firmly believed Hitler would make Germany and Austria great. I had the feeling she hated the Jews because she thought they were holding down the potential greatness of the Austrian homeland."

"What happened to her?" asked Mike.

"I don't know. The army released her in 1947, sent her back to Vienna with some money, and washed its hands of her. I questioned her only four or five times, but still think about her. She seemed very bright, attractive, and with a potentially good future. But she remained consumed with hatred—not only of Jews but of every country involved in Germany's defeat.

"Let me change the subject and ask you this: "Is it possible Austria can remain neutral considering today's threat from Russia?"

Case said, "Well first, Austria's deep militant Catholicism in itself would keep her from being neutral. I think Austria's only qualification for a neutral role is her habit of compromise, her traditional policy."

"How can such a small country preach tolerance to a continent of angry giants?"

"Oh, I think she must. Remember, throughout history Austria had a triple role in the military defense of the West against the East, holding the political balance between Teuton and Slav, and the consolidation of the Danube Basin under Christian culture. She is too weak to play any role in military defense, but she still has a part to play in holding the political balance between Teuton and Slav. She can only do this if she becomes the chief non-Communist unifying force in a divided Central Europe. Can she do it? I don't know if the Austrian people have the interest.

"My good man, I am tired of all this political talk. Do you like jazz? The seas have eased a little and I understand there will be a small American band playing at 9:00 p.m. I could use a scotch."

*   *   *

The Atlantic crossing took six days. After reaching the relative calm of the Mediterranean, it was two more days until the ship arrived in Naples harbor. The lure of Rome and Pompeii beckoned. Grant spent a day in Pompeii. Although the weather was cold and rainy, he enjoyed the day thoroughly. The idea of an entire city where life was snuffed out by a volcanic eruption fascinated him. But after four days in Rome, he was anxious to leave a city where it had rained every day of his visit.

After changing to a sleeper train in Florence, Grant was on the final leg of his long journey to Vienna. The cold rain of Italy had turned to cold snow in Austria, but the train car was warm and he was in awe watching the Austrian scenery. He began to consider his reasons for coming to Vienna. It sounded good to the lords of the History Department at Cal that he would study the pre-war anti-Semitism of Austria. However, other than an appreciation of Viennese pastry and the music of Mozart and Beethoven, Grant knew little about the place where he would spend the next six months. In his heart, he knew the real reason for this trip was to learn what had happened to Elke. He felt this added a bit of romance to his quest. He didn't mean romance with Elke, although when he'd last seen her fifteen years ago she had been a beautiful woman; he was thinking more about the challenge of trying to find her.

Grant initially stayed in a hotel, but soon found an apartment in a building from the nineteenth century—Vienna's golden age. The structure had certainly seen better days, but it was conveniently located just off the Ringstrasse, a short walk to the Hofburg and the university. Perhaps it was his imagination, but Grant found the nineteenth century still alive in this neighborhood.

In the early '60s, Vienna was just beginning to distance itself from the post-war era. Grant found it to be a city of one color only—gray; various shades of it, to be sure, but still gray, the result of decades of accumulated dirt and soot. The winter weather contributed to his depression; the skies were often overcast and he feared the city's bone-chilling dampness would not lift until the arrival of spring.

Adding to the coldness of the weather was the coldness of the family from whom he had rented the apartment. They made the weather seem balmy. The dreary weather, the grayness of the buildings, and the aloof landlord's family aside, Grant was excited. He soon discovered a relaxing afternoon could be enjoyed at a place like Demel's where he could relax over a coffee and a taste of whipped cream, chocolate or marzipan. The Viennese tradition of fine baking and confection had lost none of its vitality.

*　　*　　*

It was a cold and cloudy day with two or three inches of snow on the ground when Grant got off the Strassenbahn and began the two-block walk to the old apartment building on Daringergasse, a nondescript gray structure of three stories. Inside, Grant walked up the three flights noticing how well the interior was maintained. There was no name on the door. With some trepidation, he rang the bell. When a young man opened the door, Grant realized his lack of fluent German could be a problem.

"*Guten Tag! Sprechen se English?*"

The young man nodded. "*Ja*, a little."

Grant nervously replied, "I am looking for a woman who once lived here. Her name is Elke Baur. Would you know where I might find her?"

The young man was in his early twenties, well dressed in a white shirt and a dark tie. His slight smile indicated to Grant he would help if he could.

"*Nein*, I only live here about *sechs* months. Everyone in building has been here only short time." He seemed sincere.

With a sad *danke!* Grant nodded and walked back to the tram stop. He was disappointed that his first effort to find Elke had been a failure. Since he had plenty of time, he decided to explore the area where she had grown up. The city hadn't changed much since the last century, but what were the suburbs like? He saw many women talking in groups. They wore head scarfs and long, heavy coats. He passed one of the many parks and was surprised to see six older gentlemen wearing white shirts, jackets, ties, and business-like hats, playing cards. However, turning the corner he came upon two young women walking along, looking in shop windows, their hair piled high in American-style bouffants. A bit further he came upon three teenagers, smoking, wearing black leather jackets with their hair combed back in the American "duck tail" style. To set the picture perfectly, the boys were standing in front of a poster of Marlon Brando in a black leather jacket. Perhaps Grant wasn't as far into the nineteenth century as he had thought!

By the next morning, more snow had fallen. He was already struggling with the damp cold of early March in Vienna. The university was close by. On the walk over, he cursed himself for not doing more preliminary work. He had no idea whom he should see; he doubted Elke had gone to university—she hadn't seemed like the scholar type. There was an attractive young woman at the Information Desk. He gathered his thoughts before approaching the counter.

"*Guten Tag! Sprechen se Englisch?*" he said.

"Yes, and I am happy to use it. How can I help you, sir?"

She had put Grant at ease with her excellent, German-accented English.

Grant introduced himself as a visiting Austrian history professor from California, and explained that he was researching Austrian history during the first few years after World War II. Would he be able to meet someone who could help him find an individual from those years?

"Well, professor, we have several. I am thinking Professor Hoffmann may be able to help. He is quite knowledgeable about those years. Unfortunately, he is on holiday and will not be back for two weeks. Why don't I give him your contact information when he gets back and the name of the individual you would like to find? I am sure he will want to talk with you."

"*Danke, Fräulein!* I am looking for an Austrian woman, Elke Baur, who was a prisoner of the American Army after the war. She would be in her mid-forties. She used to live on Daringergasse in the 19th District."

"And what is your reason for wanting to find this woman?"

"I was an officer in the American army at the close of the war and *Fräulein* Baur was a prisoner I interviewed. She was an impressive young woman and I would just like to know if things worked out for her."

"Let us hope Professor Hoffmann can be of help to you."

Professor Edwards faced the damp cold of Vienna with renewed enthusiasm. He walked to the Staatsoper and bought a ticket for the evening's performance of Verdi's *Aida*. He was no fan of opera, but this was Vienna, a city of great opera, and he now had something to celebrate, however small.

*   *   *

Two weeks later, Grant was relieved when the same young lady was at the Information Desk and remembered him. "Good morning, Professor Edwards," she said. "*Herr* Hoffmann is expecting you. How are you enjoying your stay in our city? Don't give up on our weather, spring is not far away."

"Thank you for your kindness. I am enjoying Vienna. Although I'm not fond of the dampness, I do enjoy the snow."

She smiled and said, "*Herr* Hoffmann is up the stairs to the right, room number four."

Grant became more anxious the closer he got to room number four. He entered and shook hands with a well-dressed man in his mid-forties. Hoffmann was of medium height, with dark black hair and a stern demeanor. "Please sit down, *Herr* Edwards. Can I get you some coffee?

"Yes, that would be great! Vienna's coffee is quite wonderful," Grant said.

"Have you kept busy since you have been here?" Hoffmann seemed distracted, as though he were looking for something. It was a normal question, but Grant felt it was asked with a lack of emotion. He was not sure Hoffmann wanted an answer.

"I have seen most of the tourist sites; they make me want to study Austrian history in more depth. I'm a jazz fan, so I saw Ella Fitzgerald and Oscar Peterson the other night. Oh! I also went to the opera and enjoyed it."

"I'm glad to hear it," Hoffman said, then got down to the business at hand. "What is your interest in this Austrian woman you are looking for?"

Grant explained that Elke was considered pro-Nazi, and the U.S. Army was detaining and questioning Nazi supporters. "When I interviewed *Fräulein* Baur (he refused to use the word interrogate) she had so much hatred for Jews and everyone who was against National Socialism. I couldn't understand why. I'm researching a book about the pre-war anti-Semitism of Austria and would like to know how life turned out for her."

"Well, *Herr* Edwards, not everyone recovered from the war. Many succumbed to death or have spent their days in mental institutions. Some have walked a fine line between the two. Why are you interested in this particular woman? You must have interviewed hundreds of former Nazis. What makes this woman so special, unless you have special feelings for her?"

"That's absurd, professor!" he protested. "There are people in this world who genuinely care for those who suffered during the Hitler years. Some, perhaps even Elke Baur, were caught up in the Nazi bullshit, succumbed to it, and later regretted their participation." Grant needed to pause for breath. "Actually, I have asked myself the same question and don't have an answer. She is someone I once knew and have thought about and I'd just like to know if she is all right. But I see I am wasting my time." Grant rose from his chair.

"*Pardon, mein Herr!* You have not waisted your time. I have possibly been unfair to you. Please, let me buy you lunch so I can explain some things."

Grant realized this quick turnaround by Hoffmann indicated he knew more than he'd said. They left the building and Hoffmann hailed a taxi, instructing the driver to take them to the Belvedere Palace. A friendlier Kurt began to talk. "Professor Edwards, please call me Kurt. I have a long story to tell you. I know Elke Baur very well. We have been close friends since we were young. And to let you know up front, yes, she is alive and doing well. She has gone through some very difficult times because of the war, as have many people. I was unsure for a long time that she would survive. I wasn't sure I should tell you this story, but you seem sincere, so I will. She and I would deeply appreciate that this story go no further, especially since you plan to write a book."

"You have my word. My writing is strictly historic. I understand, you didn't know me or my reason for asking about Miss Baur. You had to be careful."

"I believe you are one more person caught in the web of this interesting, complicated woman. You need to hear the entire story. Have you seen the art collection at the Belvedere? It is one of the finest in all Europe. This is where our story of the current Elke Baur will begin," Kurt said. They got out of the taxi. Kurt opened his arms to emphasize the beauty of the spectacular gardens in front of them. Grant decided to wait and see where this was going.

After a short tour of the art in the gallery, where Grant was overwhelmed by the paintings of Gustaf Klimt, the two chose seats in a quiet corner of the Belvedere Café. As the waiter approached, Kurt said, "I hope you don't mind if I order for you, but I know this place well."

"I don't mind at all. I realize I'm having lunch in the home of Prince Eugène of Savoy. If I remember correctly, he was a French general who offered his services to Louis XIV. But Louis, in his great wisdom, turned him down—because he was too short and too ugly to be in the service of such a great monarch. So, the Prince offered his services to the Duke of Marlborough, John Churchill, and the two of them literally dominated Louis' army."

Kurt smiled. "Yes, one of the great 'bad decisions' of all times."

The two settled comfortably into the café's soft chairs. Kurt began: "This doesn't get a lot of attention, but one of the great heists of all time was the Nazi confiscation of the great art of Europe, not only famous art in museums but art in private collections. The Nazis called it 'Degenerate Art.' A German law allowed the Nazis to confiscate anything which was remotely art. The second great heist is now being perpetrated by the Austrian government, which is refusing to return the art to its rightful owners. I am not talking just about famous pieces by Klimt, Picasso, or Cézanne, but also the work of unknown artists. Their heirs feel the art rightfully belongs to them."

Grant didn't know what this had to do with Elke, but he did know Kurt was telling him this for a reason.

"As I said, I have known Elke since our gymnasium days. Even then, she was overcome with the Hitler phenomenon, and had a hatred of Jews. I don't know where this came from. Her father was a banker and an anti-Semitic, like most bankers in those days. Her mother was a sweetheart, but the stress of the hyper-inflation caused her to fall into a depression and she bought into the propaganda that the financial crisis was caused by Jews. Elke joined the BdM early. I believe she was caught up in the comradeship and the marches which attracted so many of the young."

"What about yourself during this time? Surely you were caught up in this also?"

"From early on I despised the Nazis. I have always loved literature, art, and music, and much of this great talent is Jewish. That is all I cared about; one's race or religion meant nothing to me. However, I wanted to stay alive and to do that one had to go along. I joined the Wehrmacht but spent two years in a Russian prison camp."

Kurt summarized his experience with the Russian general who loved Tolstoy. "When I got back to Vienna I was anxious to see Elke again," he continued. "But the Elke I found was not the one I had left. She had turned inward upon herself; I don't know another way to describe it. Of course, there were reasons for this. Her parents were killed in the bombing of Dresden and she was distressed at being unable to learn how her brother, an SS commander, had died. She had no interest in or need to work because her father had invested wisely. She avoided seeing me, had no social life. She developed a persistent cough but refused to see a doctor."

Grant knew this would not end well for Elke. He leaned forward, intent on the story.

The waiter appeared with coffee on a silver tray, glasses of cold water, and an attractive bowl piled high with sugar cubes.

Sipping his coffee, Kurt continued, "I went for weeks without seeing her. I tried, but she almost never returned my calls or letters. Occasionally I would get a short reply, a thank you for calling or something similar. At Christmastime in 1948, I noticed a bit of softening. She would meet me for coffee, or even a glass of wine. I felt I had made a breakthrough and I made a bold move; I invited her to my apartment for dinner.

"Things went well. We had a wonderful evening together. Unfortunately, my timing was terrible. Some weeks earlier, I had met a professor who had done research on the SS. I asked if he could find information on Elke's brother, Fritz. The professor's report showed what I had suspected: Her brother was one of the worst of the SS killers. In my excitement at seeing Elke, I forgot that the letter was in the apartment. Of course, she came across it by accident. It sent her over the edge. She screamed at me and ran out of the apartment.

"When I followed minutes later, she was gone, as if into thin air. I found her later in a nearby park. She was talking to herself, more mumbling than talking, really. She claimed she was in the middle of a Jewish cemetery, with haphazard sticks as headstones in rows that stretched to the horizon. She was staring at her hands, claiming they were covered in blood and no matter how hard she tried to clean it off with the snow on the ground, it wouldn't wash off. I picked her up, carried her back to my apartment and called for an ambulance. The men said she should be institutionalized. I didn't know what else to do."

"That's quite a story."

"Well, fortunately, it does not end there," Kurt said. "At first, the Vienna General Hospital kept her well-guarded. I might add that Vienna General is probably the best hospital for psychiatric care in Vienna, and the home of Sigmund Freud. But to continue. Perhaps they thought she was a danger to herself. I wasn't allowed to see her for months. When they lifted the restriction, I could see her only briefly and always with an aide beside her.

"But being there was good for Elke. With some persistence, the institution allowed us to have more time together. I have always felt she is a woman of ferocious courage and inner strength. I wanted to convince her she had the ability to change her life for the better. One day, she allowed me to put my arm around her and I whispered, 'You are a terrific woman; you can do anything you want.'

"Grant, I don't want you to think I was totally responsible for her recovery, the institution is forward-thinking and was the biggest element in her healing; they encouraged me to continue. I have my work, and saw her perhaps once a month, but felt we were making progress.

"One day the administrator suggested I begin exposing Elke to art and music. I tried music, but she seemed indifferent. However, the idea of art made sense. I made arrangements to bring her here, to the Belvedere Palace. The first time we visited it was a bright spring day, and Elke had taken care to wear a new red-and-white dress and do her hair. She was obviously looking forward to coming here. She asked if there would be pictures of ladies in beautiful dresses. I replied yes, but art doesn't have to be pretty and sometimes can be about things that are not pretty. Or, it can be a tonic for even the saddest of days. Everyone is sad sometimes and art is a wonderful remedy when we are sad. I thought I saw a light in her eyes. I told her I believed art still spoke to her and she didn't have to say anything in reply.

"I thought the bright colors of the artwork would appeal to her and they seemed to. She motioned to a painting of green grass waving in the wind, with green clouds against a deep blue sky and a bright orange patch of wheat in the distance. She asked, 'Why are the clouds green?' I answered: 'Because that is what the artist saw. The artist is free to paint the picture as he or she sees their subject.' I wanted to bring her to the Belvedere to expose her to a variety of art.

"And that is why I wanted to bring you here, because the museum helped Elke tremendously on her road to recovery. It has been a long process. The scene I just described happened fifteen years ago. I believe art awakened a new Elke Baur. Slowly she started on a new path, one which currently has her involved in a movement to help Jews retrieve art stolen from their families during the war. You are lucky, Grant. Elke will be hosting a seminar here in a couple of weeks about that art and how difficult it will be to get it back from the Austrian government. If you are still available, I would be honored for you to come as my guest."

"I wouldn't miss it."

"Good, I will introduce you to Elke, but only as a history professor from California. She may or may not recognize you. She is busy at these things, so you won't get a lot of time."

It had been quite a day for Grant; he was anxious to get back to his apartment and put his thoughts together.

*   *   *

The Belvedere Gardens are special at any time of year, but on a cloudless day in early spring they are breathtaking. These beautifully kept gardens are bookended by the Lower and Upper Belvedere Palaces. The scene seems out of a costume drama film set, with sculpted hedges, graceful fountains, and cherubic statues. But this wasn't a film set. It was a meeting place for a group of concerned Austrians trying to convince the government to release to the heirs, the art stolen by the Nazis during the 1930s and 1940s.

Kurt approached Grant holding two glasses of wine. "Well, are you impressed with Vienna enough to leave California and move here for better weather?" he asked.

"I must say I've enjoyed my time here. I plan to leave in July, which will give me enough time to get settled prior to the fall semester. My stay in Vienna has been an absolute pleasure, but I don't think I can go through another winter."

"Have you been treated well during your stay?"

"My landlord has an air of arrogance, but we have little contact other than the monthly rent check. Yes! People seem very friendly, possibly because I am an American. They all think I know President Kennedy and Jackie. Tell me, Kurt, how is the government able to keep the art from the previous owners or the heirs of the previous owners?"

"Various cases have gone through the courts, but every decision has been in the government's favor. There are a few art objects, not just paintings, the government *is* giving back to the families, but they are generally of a lesser value. Even so, in order for them to be returned, families must sign over their higher quality artworks to the government. In exchange, the heirs acknowledge they have no further claim to the better pieces."

"That makes no sense at all," said Grant, with a look of disgust.

"This isn't America, Grant! Austrians seem to have learned to accept all this, but I am glad some Viennese are fighting it. Here is one now." As Kurt looked up from his wine with a smile, a stunningly beautiful, well-dressed woman, whom Grant assumed was Elke, joined them.

"Elke, good to see you!" Kurt exclaimed, giving her a kiss on the cheek. "Elke, I would like you to meet Professor Grant Edwards. He teaches German and Austrian history at the University of California. Grant, this is Elke Baur, a long-time friend who is organizing this small revolt against the Austrian government. It is probably no surprise that it is mostly Jewish families for whom she is trying to retrieve the art. You began this quest about ten years ago—is that about right, Elke?"

"Pleased to meet you Professor Edwards," Elke said, extending her hand.

As they shook hands, Grant looked closely at Elke's eyes for any hint of recognition, but he saw none.

"Yes," Elke continued. "It has been a long time and I am disappointed with our progress. Gustaf Klimt's paintings of women get most of the publicity, but there are literally thousands of art works, not all museum quality to be sure, but what difference should that make? A stolen painting, good or bad, if the rightful owner wants it back, they should get it back. It has been twenty-four years since the Germans invaded Austria in the *Anschluss*. We are only now beginning to understand the vastness of the Nazi thievery. Austrian officials are only tentatively beginning to open this chapter on our nation's history."

"Are you an artist, Ms. Baur?" asked Grant.

"Oh heavens, no! In fact, I owe this gentleman all the credit. I was quite depressed after the war and Kurt introduced me to great art here at the Belvedere. I soon discovered all art is great art, if you enjoy it. I suppose this is why I am concentrating on helping people get back art, whether or not the art critics think it is beautiful. I have learned, Professor Edwards, if you are lucky, life teaches you how to survive."

Elke inclined her head. "And with that, gentlemen, I must move on. Professor Edwards, it has been a pleasure to meet you, and I am sorry this must be so brief. However, please enjoy the rest of your stay in Vienna."

She began to walk away, then paused momentarily. "I have a strange feeling we have met before, but I know that would be impossible."

"I only wish we had, *Fräulein* Baur. I only wish we had."

Grant put down his empty glass, thanked Kurt for the introduction, and went out front to hail a taxi.

* * *

Grant decided that rather than take the ship back to the U.S., his time would be better spent in Berkeley, preparing for his classes. He booked a flight from Vienna to London and then on to New York. On the day of departure, he boarded an old, World War II Douglas DC 3 at Aspern Airport. He hoped this wasn't the same airplane he had been flown to Paris in during 1946.

While the plane was idling on the tarmac, his thoughts turned to Elke Baur and Austria. He could not help the feeling that in some way, Elke *was* Austria. The millions of Austrians who stood by and let the Nazis murder millions of Jews, gypsies, and others, would always carry a legacy of guilt.

But what could they have done? It is easy to say, "I didn't kill anyone, I don't have blood on my hands." They do have blood on their hands, and for future generations the blood will remain, because their ancestors allowed the Jews to go to their deaths. *How could a woman as Elke Baur with such beauty, be filled with such evil? After seeing her again her beauty had still remained, but the evil had been erased. When will the world learn that all people are alike beneath the skin?* Grant thought. *All we can do is hope for a better future.*

The old DC 3 picked up speed down the runway and gradually lifted Grant into the air. Thus ended his quest for Elke Baur . . . or did it?

Also by Larry Hilton

Europe: Chained by History: What Force Can Break The Chain?

CPSIA information can be obtained
at www.ICGtesting.com
Printed in the USA
BVHW040354181021
619116BV00005B/3